ADAPTIVE PLAY
for
SPECIAL NEEDS CHILDREN

ADAPTIVE PLAY
for
SPECIAL NEEDS CHILDREN

STRATEGIES TO ENHANCE
COMMUNICATION AND LEARNING

Caroline Ramsey Musselwhite, Ed.D.
Communication Disorders Specialist

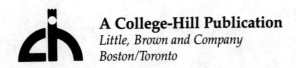

A College-Hill Publication
Little, Brown and Company
Boston/Toronto

College-Hill Press
A Division of
Little, Brown and Company (Inc.)
34 Beacon Street
Boston, Massachusetts 02108

Library of Congress Cataloging in Publication Data
Main entry under title:

Musselwhite, Caroline Ramsey.
   Adaptive play for special needs children.

   Bibliography; p. 237
   Includes index.
   1. Play. 2. Handicapped children. 3. Play therapy. 4. Handicapped
children — Education. I. Title.
HQ782.M87 1985   371.9′043   85-11323

ISBN 0-316-59213-7

Printed in the United States of America

This book is dedicated to families everywhere who are giving women the support they need to attempt their goals, but especially to my family.

CONTENTS

PREFACE

The title of this book, especially the term "adaptive play," may call up different images for various readers. In this context, adaptive play refers to play that has been altered in form, complexity, or intent to serve the needs of children with disabilities. This can range from developing new play materials or altering the form of traditional play materials for children with severe physical disabilities to modifying the rules of play or setting up situations to promote play opportunities for children who are cognitively impaired.

This book is intended for professionals, paraprofessionals, and parents of children with a variety of disabilities. It should be used as a textbook for professionals including speech-language pathologists, physical and occupational therapists, and special educators. It is also intended for inclusion in the personal libraries of professionals or paraprofessionals currently serving children with special needs. Finally, it is hoped that the specific examples will make this book applicable to parents and other caregivers of children with disabilities.

This book evolved from a need to make information on adaptive play strategies available in a comprehensive format. There is a need for a single book that summarizes recent advances in using play as a learning tool, developing adaptive play materials, teaching specific skills through play, and supporting the use of play in all settings. The first section of this book presents an overview of adaptive play, including a rationale, a description of the functions, and general strategies for introducing adaptive play. The second section covers strategies for selecting, adapting, and making play materials for children with special needs. In the third section, both general and specific strategies are presented for teaching selected communicative goals. This includes goals for skills that may be considered preliminary to communication, such as activation and object interaction. Both oral and augmentative communication skills are considered. The final section covers a variety of support systems for adaptive play. The topics are diverse, including the development of a toy lending library to promote adaptive play in all settings, the use of adaptive play to promote interaction between disabled and nondisabled children, and the incorporation of adaptive play into arts programming. Appendices provide annotated references as well as listings of supportive organizations and manufacturers.

ACKNOWLEDGMENTS

Many people have provided support to allow this book to — finally — reach completion. My immediate family has been extremely helpful. My husband, Robert, took over extra responsibilities and made many forays to pick up and drop off materials. My children, Matthew and Kathryn, showed great self-reliance and have provided me with play ideas and a playful spirit throughout the last 10 years. My parents, Julia and Gene, have giving loving child care and moral support, and my extended family has shown great encouragement.

Friends and co-workers at the Irene Wortham Center have spent many hours providing direct and indirect support. The Director, Bruce Fitchett, and the lead teachers, Jo Edens and Jo Ownbey, have shown consistent support for my efforts in and out of the center. Several teachers and therapists helped review chapters or provided information: Susan Batchelor, Denise Golden, Shirley Guice, Carolyn McMahon, Gil Morissette, Ariane Piercy, Julie Roueche, and Kim Spivey. Debbie Banks and Lisa Pegg helped copy the manuscript and Jean Ann Williams helped by fielding phone calls and keeping me laughing. These and all other staff members have provided and tried out numerous ideas over the past several years. The IWC children and their parents have also provided inspiration and given great help and pleasure.

Several people have helped to locate obscure but important sources of information: Judyth Lessee of the Special Needs Service, Tucson Public Library; Yvonne Hardy of the Children's Room at Pack Library in Asheville, NC; Nancy Renfro of Nancy Renfro Studios; Jim Jenkins of Highland Hospital Music Therapy Department; and Michael Smith, head of the Communication Disorders Program, Western Carolina University. Marcelle LeBlanc and Stacy Small have provided much-needed pony express services between Western Carolina and Asheville.

Many professionals have reviewed chapters and given helpful suggestions that were incorporated into the book: Dennice Ward, Kathy Fox, and Pam Gilbert of the South Metropolitan Association in Illinois; Margo Haynes, Joy Rowe, and Carol Houston of the Newton-Conover Public School System; Sally deVincentis of the USA Toy Library Association and the Lekotek of Evanston; Sandie Barrie-Blackley of Tri-County Speech-Language Services; and Barbara Armstrong, South Carolina Department of Mental Retardation, Coastal Region.

Friends have also provided the needed balance to manage this project. Notable among them are the entire cast of Asheville Community Theatre's *Brigadoon*, Carol Goossens', Susan Batchelor, and the Friday lunch group.

PART I
OVERVIEW OF ADAPTIVE PLAY

Chapter 1

Introduction: Play as a Childhood Occupation

WHAT IS PLAY?

Chance (1979) suggests that "Play is like love: everybody knows what it is but nobody can define it" (p. 1). A definition is elusive, as the entity known as "play" varies according to several factors, such as the setting, timing, participants, and perceived intentionality. For example, a child may put her head on the floor and close her eyes as if sleeping. Whether this is intended as play by the child or perceived as such by observers will depend on features such as the *time* (if close to bedtime, parents may assume that the child is merely sleepy and not enter the game); the *age* of the participant (an older child would be less likely to evoke a play routine from this strategy than would a toddler); and the apparent *intentionality* of the child (if the child smiles or produces a fake "snore," this may elicit more involvement by others). Thus, it may not be possible to write a definition of play that meets all possible combinations of factors.

Themes of Play

While an all-encompassing definition of play may not be useful, various themes of play can help to identify instances of play. Bronfenbrenner (1979) describes three themes of play, each of which may interact with the other two.

First, play can be seen as an *intrinsic activity,* or one that is done for its own sake, rather than as a means to achieving any specific end. This can be seen in the isolated play of an infant in his crib, amusing himself with his toes.

Second, Bronfenbrenner asserts that play is essentially *spontaneous and voluntary,* undertaken by choice rather than by compulsion. Preschool teachers will agree that most children do not need to be coerced to participate in some way during free play time, although some may not readily play with others.

Third, play includes an element of *enjoyment*, something that is done for fun. Thus, Singer and Singer argue that "Play may be the main 'business' of childhood, but if it's not fun, it's not really play" (1977, p. 14).

These three play themes can be readily observed in the play of nondisabled children as well as of most children with disabilities. However, when adults choose to utilize play as a medium for learning, the three elements may be distorted. It is extremely important to remember these three themes and to support them as closely as possible when teaching skills through adaptive play. For example, allowing children to "discover" play materials that have been placed in reach or hidden can encourage spontaneity, as opposed to continually directing children regarding play materials to be used. Likewise, an adult who focuses on the theme of enjoyment will observe when the activity begins to be less pleasurable, and can make modifications (increasing animation, introducing new play materials, changing tasks).

Types of Play

Chance (1979) identifies four kinds of play. These four categories are not developmental but can all be found at varying age levels, although of course the complexity of tasks will vary. In addition, they are not mutually exclusive; thus, games can involve physical, manipulative, or symbolic play, or all three.

Physical Play. The emphasis in physical, or sensorimotor, play is on action. Typically, this type of play is social, boisterous, and often competitive. Examples are tickling, wrestling, and playing games such as tag, hide and seek, and tug-of-war. For ideas on adapting physical play for children with disabilities, see Chapter 17.

Manipulative Play. The focus in manipulative play is on an attempt to manipulate, to gain control over, or to master the environment. Sample play opportunities are provided by toys such as rattles, puzzles, shape-sorters, and cause-effect toys (e.g., wind-ups). Chance (1979) notes that this includes social manipulation as well as object manipulation. Chapter 9 provides ideas for adapting manipulative play opportunities.

Symbolic Play. This type of play involves the manipulation of reality. It includes pretend or fantasy play and nonsense rhymes and other forms of speech play. Typically, this involves a deliberate misrepresentation of reality, as in pretending to eat a nonexistent cookie or using a block as if it were a truck. Chapter 10 presents strategies for assessing and promoting symbolic play in children with special needs.

Games. This refers to play that is governed by rules or conventions. Samples would be hide-and-seek, card games, and board games, such as Parcheesi. Very early games may be referred to as "routines." The section on *Early Peer Interaction* in Chapter 8 presents simple routines that can be used by children with various disabilities.

Wehman (1979a) suggested that, for purposes of play intervention, two further categories be delineated. He identifies free play as "any action or combination of actions which the child engages in for the apparent purpose of fun," whereas structured recreation is defined as "the goal-oriented and purposeful acquisition of a selected leisure skill, such as riding a tricycle" (p. 70).

ROLES OF ADULTS IN ADAPTIVE PLAY

Several authors (Cherry, 1976; Manolson, 1984; Singer and Singer, 1977) describe various roles that adults may take with respect to play. These roles may assume even greater importance when play is used therapeutically and adults are serving as intervention agents.

The four roles described by Manolson (1984) are especially clear and useful. Each of these roles is described in Table 1–1, along with the goals, the tactics used by the adult, and the implications of that role. All four roles have a place in play interaction. However, too often an adult becomes locked into one role, to the exclusion of others. Ideally, adults should emphasize the role of the conversationalist, as that role teaches the child the balance of power in interaction, including skills such as initiating, responding, and turntaking.

In adaptive play, the importance of using a diversity of roles may be even greater, as adults tend to be more directive when working with children who have special needs. In addition, children with disabilities may take longer to respond, make less ob-

Table 1-1. Roles of Adults in Making Play Work

Role	Goals	Tactics	Implications
The Entertainer	To get and keep child's attention	Jump up and down, be animated, put on a show	Child is not encouraged to participate in play
The Director	To teach the child specific skills	Demonstrate and instruct, provide endless commands	Adult totally dominates the interaction
The Observer	To determine the situation	Sit back and watch, or give a play-by-play commentary of the action	Adult avoids entering into the play
The Conversationalist	To be an equal partner	Initiate, respond, and encourage the child to take his or her turn	Turntaking is enhanced and neither partner dominates the interaction

Adapted from Manolson, A. (1984). *It takes two to talk: A Hanen early language parent guide book.* Toronto: Hanen Early Language Resource Centre. Used with permission.

vious responses, or initiate less frequently, thus allowing adults to overemphasize the entertainer and director roles at the expense of the observer and, especially, the conversationalist roles. Thus, these four roles need to be made explicit to all adults working and playing with a child with special needs.

STAGES OF PLAY

A number of researchers have investigated the development of play skills in nondisabled children (Barnes, 1971; Lowe, 1975; Nicholich, 1977; Parten, 1932). For the purposes of this book, the general developmental sequence of toy play skills presented by Wehman (1979c) is used. This sequence is an adaptation of the work by Barnes (1971) and Parten (1932). Although the norms included observational categories such as "unoccupied," this sequence presents only stages that can be considered targets for intervention. The following section provides a brief description of each stage, and Table 1–2 presents samples of traditional and adapted play behaviors at each stage, to offer a preview into the types of intervention possible through adaptive play.

Exploratory Play. Wehman (1979b) subdivides exploratory play into four basic stages of development: (1) orientational responses, responding to gross stimulus changes (typically unfamiliar and unusual stimuli) in the environment; (2) locomotor exploration, moving about the environment and receiving sensory and affective feedback; (3) investigatory exploration, testing the object and investigating the outcomes of interactions; and (4) searching behavior, looking for new stimuli or situations as the individual tires of the old.

Independent Play. Also termed "isolate play," this refers to appropriate play actions on objects. Examples would be playing musical instruments and working puzzles.

Parallel Play. At this level, a child still plays independently with objects, but now will be in close physical proximity to peers. For example, two children might swing next to each other.

Associative Play. At this stage, the child must demonstrate a limited number of approach responses to peers, making brief physical contact or regular eye contact, or both, with peers during play.

Table 1-2. Stages of Play: Traditional and Adapted Activities

Stage	Traditional Activities	Adaptive Play Activities*
Exploratory Play	Grasping, squeezing, mouthing toys Throwing, mouthing toys	Batting toys suspended from an Activity Frame (4) Grasping toys using Velcro mitt (9)
Independent Play	Using playground equipment Manipulating toys (blocks, puzzles, stacking toys, books, tops)	Using hammock or adapted tire swing (16) Activating toys through switches (5), working adapted puzzles, playboards (4)
Parallel Play	Swing, build block tower, color next to peer	Sit under Activity Frame next to peer (8) Sit at wall of toys next to peer (8)
Associative Play	Approach peer with toy Brief physical contact with peer	Bat toy toward peer Touch peer while sharing playboard during sidelying (8)
Cooperative Play	Ball-rolling or block-building with peer Pulling peer in wagon Taking turns hitting Bop Bag	Sending battery toy to peer via switch (8) Pushing adaptive vehicle for peer Taking turns at computer game
Symbolic Play	Domestic make-believe with dolls, cars, house, dress-ups, and so forth	Make-believe using Velcro mitt (10), mitt with metal washers on magnetized surface to access toys (10)
	Puppetry, paper dolls	Puppetry with puppet bracelets, and so forth (15)

*The adaptive play ideas presented in this table are described further in the chapters indicated in parentheses.

Cooperative Play. Also known as social play, at this stage the child regularly approaches and responds to peers and adults, with mutual participation seen in their activities. Examples would be operating a seesaw jointly or playing catch with a partner.

Symbolic Play. As indicated previously, this level includes a deliberate misrepresentation of reality, as seen through make-believe with real, miniature, or imaginary props.

For some children with severe disabilities, the ability to move through these various stages of play development will depend to a great extent on the adaptations that can be made in positioning, materials, and required responses. The remainder of this book will present a rationale for the use of adaptive play, and will describe strategies for using adaptive play to enhance both life and learning for children with special needs.

Chapter **2**

Functions of Adaptive Play

The importance of play has been well documented by the developmental psychologist Jean Piaget (1962). He has demonstrated that observation of play can yield rich information on the cognitive and social functioning of children from infancy through adolescence. Not surprisingly, most early research on the development of play considered only children without disabilities (e.g., Parten, 1932). Increasingly, the actual and potential usefulness of play for children with disabilities has come under investigation.

It is important to consider the philosophical perspective from which play has traditionally been considered. As Bronfenbrenner (1979) notes, "For a culture built, as ours is, on the Protestant ethic of work and achievement, play presents a problem" (p. xv). Thus, play is seen as something done in any "spare time" that might exist. With regard to the integration of play into therapy (with the exception of treating emotional disorders), the behavioral approach that dominated treatment of children with disabilities throughout the 1960s and early 1970s downgraded the importance of such activities. However, a relatively recent growth of studies and "how to" resources attests to the burgeoning area of adaptive play as one tool for use in intervention with a variety of disabilities.

WHY PLAY? RATIONALE FOR USING ADAPTIVE PLAY

This section presents reasons for using play as a goal or a therapeutic tool, and suggests that play is an excellent resource for parents and intervention agents. Initially, it is important to examine the role of play in children without disabilities.

11

General Goals for Play Program

Numerous writers have observed that play is the primary occupation of childhood. Cherry (1976) notes that, regardless of
the purpose and structure of a preschool program, the main
goal of the children is to play. Therefore, many programs for
nondisabled children have adopted the "don't fight them — join
them" attitude in using play as a framework for learning. Play
can be used as a vehicle for learning typical skills that may be
deemed worthwhile in a preschool environment, such as: social
skills (sharing, taking turns); preacademic skills (colors, numbers, vocabulary concepts); and creativity (role-playing, dramat-
ics, art). Thus, there is a strong background for using play,
rather than more didactic methods, in working with children
with disabilities.

Play as a Goal or a Treatment Tool for Children with Disabilities

It is important to distinguish between the use of adaptive
play as a goal and its use as a treatment tool. Thus, some children with disabilities will actually need to be taught to "play," as
a goal in and of itself, whereas others will be taught other skills
through the use of adaptive play strategies. Of course, often
these needs will overlap in a single child. Numerous goals of
adaptive play have been stated in the literature or cited in anecdotal accounts. These goals typically fall into four general
categories.

Integration of the Child into the Mainstream

The integration of the child into the mainstream is the primary goal of Lekotek organizations throughout the world (see
Appendix B). Play can be a very powerful means of enhancing
normalization and helping the child develop within the family,
the classroom, and the community. For example, adequate toy
play skills and athletic skills were cited as factors that predicted
higher sociometric standing for preschoolers with severe disabilities (Strain, 1985). Wehman (1979c) suggests that adequate, independent interaction with play materials may reduce
the need for institutionalization, as the children will require less
supervision and "entertaining." Taken together, these research
findings and observations suggest that intervention through
play can help children fit into the mainstream of society.

Development of Enjoyable Leisure Pursuits

The literature on people with developmental disabilities includes numerous references to an abundance of leisure time (Bender, Brannan, and Verhoven, 1984; Gozali and Charney, 1972; Stanfield, 1973; Wehman, 1977a, 1979c). This is also true for others with severe disabilities, such as physical limitations. This sometimes excessive leisure time is seen in the evenings, on weekends and holidays when the child is at home, and during the summer months (Wehman, 1979c). Development of leisure skills should not be viewed merely as a way to "fill up" this time; instead, it should be a time to establish enjoyable pursuits that will enhance the quality of life. Thus, adaptive play strategies can be used directly in training appropriate and enjoyable leisure skills. For example, Rast (1984) suggests that occupational therapists, who traditionally use meaningful occupation for intervention, consider play to be a child's primary occupation and select it as a direct treatment goal. Numerous studies have documented positive change in appropriate play following intervention, primarily with people who are mentally retarded (Hopper and Wambold, 1978; Wambold and Bailey, 1979; Wehman and Marchant, 1977). At issue is the assumption that play is so integral to childhood that a child who does not have opportunities to play is cut off from a major portion of childhood. Children who cannot participate in such basic experiences would also be at risk for development of "learned helplessness," in which the child does not develop an awareness of his or her ability to control the environment.

Facilitation of Specific Areas of Development

Sufficient evidence now exists to assert that adaptive play intervention can assist in promoting skills other than toy play. The following section provides a brief overview of the potential in several major domains of development.

Gross Motor Skills. Locomotion skills such as walking, running, and climbing can be promoted through playground play, games such as tag and hide-and-seek, and more formal sports such as ball play, although modified rules or equipment, or both, may be necessary. General improvement has been documented in gross motor development following a play program (Newcomer and Morrison, 1974), as has learning of specific skills, such as tricycle-riding, ball-throwing, and sliding (Peterson and McIntosh, 1973; Wehman and Marchant, 1977).

Fine Motor Skills. Toy play has been found to enhance fine motor development (Friedlander, Kamin, and Hesse, 1974; Newcomer and Morrison, 1974). This is not surprising in view of the multitude of opportunities provided by interaction with play materials, including practice in reaching, grasping (palmer, pincer, radial), manipulating (push, pull, rotate), and releasing (to a partner, into a container, onto a surface) (Musselwhite and Thompson, 1979).

Social Skills. Play is an ideal medium for training social skills such as turntaking, initiating interactions, and sharing. A variety of studies have documented success on training various aspects of social competence through play (Knapczyk and Yoppi, 1975; Morris and Dolker, 1974; Newcomer and Morrison, 1974; Strain, 1975; Wehman, 1977b).

Self-Help Skills. Play activities can be used to practice a variety of self-help goals, such as feeding (tea parties), dressing (dress-ups), and personal hygiene (doll play). This can be a nonthreatening approach, with the emphasis on play rather than on perfection.

Cognitive Skills. The direct results of play activities on the development of cognitive skills is not clear, although numerous curricula advocate practicing early sensorimotor skills (object permanence, means ends) through play. Several researchers also recommend using play tasks in assessing cognitive status of children with disabilities (Chappell and Johnson, 1976; Uzgaris and Hunt, 1975; Westby, 1980).

Communication Skills. Play offers an ideal framework for modeling and teaching receptive and expressive communication skills. For example, research studies have shown success in teaching instruction-following through ball play (Kazdin and Erickson, 1975) and training verbal labeling by means of a table game (Bates, 1976). Adaptive play can also promote nonspeech communication, either unaided (e.g., using sign language) or aided (e.g., using pictorial symbols).

Reduction of Undesirable Behaviors

Play activities have also been found to reduce undesirable behaviors, including stereotypies such as head-banging or rocking (Flavell, 1973; Kissel and Whitman, 1977; Wehman, 1977b). Thus, an adaptive play program can simultaneously increase desirable behaviors and decrease undesirable ones. Presumably, the reduction in stereotypies will also increase opportunities for further learning.

WHY PLAY HELPS: THEORIES AND ASSUMPTIONS

The usefulness of play strategies in intervention can be attributed to a number of factors. These factors are not carefully researched but are primarily drawn from observation and anecdotal reports.

One primary reason why play can support intervention programs is *motivation.* As Rast (1984) notes, play can be used as a tool to enlist a child's cooperation. For example, a child can be encouraged to shift her weight and extend her trunk in order to reach a toy that is held out to her. However, Rast asserts that in using activities that can be partially rewarding and partially frustrating, the adult must be alert to the child's level of tolerance. Thus, instead of tantalizing a child with a toy, which is then removed so a child can reach for it yet again, she recommends using stimuli that are more rewarding when touched than when held. Examples are bubbles that can be popped, toys that be set in motion by a push, or adaptive switches that can be activated as the child shifts his or her weight and reaches, touches, or pushes the stimulus item. The key concern is that, when using play as a motivator, the needs of the child must be kept in mind. In short, "if it isn't fun, it isn't play."

A second feature that makes play attractive for intervention is its *potential for carryover.* Play materials can be readily available across a variety of times, settings, and people to help promote generalization. In addition, the enjoyment value of play can increase the likelihood that tasks based on play will be carried out by adults, including staff members, parents, and other caregivers. That is, adults may directly enjoy engaging in play interactions and also may be reinforced by the pleasure of the child. The enjoyment level may also encourage children to engage independently in play tasks that can afford practice of skills, such as those involved in fine motor development.

Manolson (1984) suggests that another factor contributing to the usefulness of play in intervention is the *potential for repe-*

tition. Engaging in the same games or interactions repeatedly is a key element of play for nondisabled children. Thus, repetition within a play context is highly normative, offering numerous opportunities for practice.

Play allows *integration of the senses,* as observed by Manolson (1984). Thus, the child can see, hear, and touch a toy simultaneously, fostering additional learning opportunities.

To summarize, although the reasons for successful integration of play as a therapeutic tool have not been documented, several potential factors can be suggested. Each of these factors can be further highlighted to increase the potential for success.

WHO CAN USE ADAPTIVE PLAY?

Children with Disabilities

Adaptive play strategies can be used with all groups with disabilities. As discussed previously, a primary goal will be to teach appropriate, enjoyable play skills. Research indicates that children in a variety of disability groups fall behind their nondisabled peers in development of play skills; this includes children who are cognitively delayed or autistic (Tilton and Ottinger, 1964; Weiner, Ottinger, and Tilton, 1969; Weiner and Weiner, 1974; Wing, Gould, Yeates, and Brierley, 1977) or language disordered (Kahmi, 1981; Terrell, Schwartz, Prelock, and Messick, 1984). Children with visual impairments will have special needs relating to toy play (Guthrie, 1979), and youths with physical disabilities will require intervention in the form of motor training or adaptation of play materials, or both.

Children having various disabilities can also benefit from use of adaptive play in intervening in other areas, such as facilitating skill development or decreasing undesirable behaviors. The extent of this intervention will of course depend on the nature and severity of the disability.

Intervention Agents for Adaptive Play Strategies

The adaptive play strategies described in this book can be used by a variety of intervention agents. Primary users of this technology are the following groups.

Parents (and other caregivers). Since a major goal will be to help integrate the child into his or her family, parents will be key agents of intervention. Adaptive play can be a highly pleasurable, nonthreatening framework for interaction between child and parent, with the added benefit of enhanced skill learning.

Special Educators. Adaptive play can be used to introduce or practice a variety of skills in the areas listed previously, as well as in preacademic and academic areas. It is well suited to group intervention, which will be required in many classrooms.

Speech-Language Pathologists. The use of play as an intervention tool is increasingly viewed as one appropriate medium for communication specialists (Faulk, 1984; Terrell et al., 1984; Westby, 1980). As Terrell and colleagues suggest, "in clinical intervention with some impaired children it may be appropriate to direct primary attention to verbal expression of the meanings and relations already evidenced in play" (1984, p. 428). Play can also be used as one tool for assessing language potential (Chappell and Johnson, 1976; Lowe, 1975; Lowe and Costello, 1976; Westby, 1980).

Physical Therapists. A variety of movement skills can be taught or practiced through adaptive play. In addition, many leisure skills, such as ball play, tricycle riding, and sliding, directly involve both movement and play. Play can also be used as a motivator for engaging in activities that may be uncomfortable if the adult is cautious to maintain the fun in the play component.

Occupational Therapists. As Miller (1984) and Rast (1984) note, play can be used in assessment and intervention for children with motor disabilities. Rast makes a strong case for teaching play directly, as it can be considered the occupation of childhood. Play also affords extensive opportunities for working on fine motor development and self-help skills.

Siblings. Although not traditionally considered intervention agents, recent research and reports focus on siblings of children with disabilities (see Appendix B, *People to People*, 1985, 6(4) and Siblings Understanding Needs for reference to current readings and other resources). Including siblings as play partners of children with special needs can further enhance integration of the child into the family unit. In addition, since children are naturals at playing, siblings may provide excellent models with minimal training. Siblings may also have more time and inclination to play than their parents.

In summary, although it certainly is not a panacea, adaptive play can offer a tool and a framework for intervention with a variety of disabilities by a number of professional disciplines. The following sections present general and specific strategies for assessing and intervening via adaptive play.

Chapter 3

General Training Strategies for Adaptive Play

Although adaptive play training can yield excellent results in specific skill areas, such as visual tracking, use of general training strategies can also promote general goals. Several desirable outcomes can be expected following generalized training strategies.

One desirable and crucial outcome is the generalization of classroom skills. This refers to generalization across various task features, such as time of day (behavior not restricted to Circle Time), people (child makes eye contact with persons other than mother), cues to respond (behavior not under limited control of verbal cue, such as "Put in, Gary"), and places (child performs task at home, in classroom, on playground). Williams and Fox (1977) refer to this extensive generalization of a skill as mastery.

Use of the general training strategies described in this chapter can also promote normalization, as learning trials will be conducted in a variety of settings, with a range of trainers, and will follow more normalized teacher-student and peer interactions.

Opportunities for increased interaction will be extended through incorporating the general strategies described in this chapter, as they do not rely on traditional one-to-one, stimulus-response learning situations.

Finally, because they do not focus on isolated training, the general strategies presented are conducive to teaching functional skills rather than splinter skills. For example, the skill of putting objects into a container will be taught across a variety of tasks, such as putting toys back into a toy box after completing a play session rather than being restricted to training tasks, such as dropping a 1 inch cube into a plastic container.

The general strategies described in this chapter are not limited only to teaching adaptive play but are appropriate for training many types of skills. These strategies have been drawn from research studies and clinical experience.

GOAL SETTING: MAKING THE MOST OF ADAPTIVE PLAY

Adaptive play lends itself well to training across all activity domains (social, cognitive, self-help, and so forth). Many disabled children have a large number and variety of training needs scattered across activity domains. It is important that teachers select goals that will make a difference in the child's life (rather than merely being simple to implement and record) and can be integrated with other goals, so that the child is not learning a series of splinter skills. The following strategies for goal-setting are intended to assist in selecting integrated, meaningful goals.

Emphasize Generic Training Goals

McLean, Snyder-McLean, Jacobs, and Rowland (1981) distinguish between process, or generic skills, and product, or setting-specific skills. Generic skills are those very basic human skills "that are generic to all ages, that all of us need, whether we be infants or octogenarians" (p. 7). These skills are important in all activity domains and have the major advantage of assisting children in "learning to learn." Examples are establishing joint focus, using primitive tools, imitating motion, and locating visually hidden objects. Setting-specific skills, on the other hand, may be important, but they are highly context-based; they are less likely to cross activity domains. Pulling pants down, copying a vertical line, and screwing bolts onto nuts are all examples of setting-specific skills. Bruder (1984) notes that more generalized skills, which she terms critical behaviors, have several important advantages for severely disabled learners:

They can be used across a variety of skills in different domains. For example, bringing hands to midline, pincer grasp, and wrist rotation are crucial elements of varied tasks, such as fully independent eating (self-help), assembling wooden cars (pre-vocational), and card playing (social).

These behaviors are necessary components for building more complex skills. For example, motor imitation can lead to sign acquisition, and simple turntaking routines facilitate later verbal communication interchanges.

These behaviors can facilitate stimulus generalization. For example, learning verbal labeling as a general behavior across many tasks increases the likelihood of its use with new stimuli.

Table 3–1 presents sample generic training goals, along with sample training activities using adaptive play strategies. It should be noted that some generic skills, such as fine motor skills, are often taught as isolated skills, perhaps because they are included as such on assessment tools. For example, if object release is introduced only through the traditional goal of "Child will take a 1 inch cube and drop it into a container," opportunities for the generalized use of the skill will be limited. Thus, selecting generic skills for training will not be sufficient to promote functional use of those skills, unless the general training strategies such as those described in the following section are also implemented.

Telescope Goals and Activities

This strategy refers to the practice of working on several goals simultaneously, rather than one by one. Although there may be one primary goal for which data are being recorded, other goals can be introduced simultaneously or carried over. A major advantage of this strategy is the increased efficiency of training, as separate training sessions will not be required for each individual skill. In addition, telescoping goals shows the child that individual skills do not occur in isolation. McCormick, Cooper, and Goldman (1979) applied this concept to integrating instruction with caretaking, demonstrating that the amount of instructional time by teachers can be increased. Sample telescoped activities are working on turntaking with vocalization during positioning; providing practice on object grasping while diapering; and increasing joint attention during feeding. Kaczmarek (1982) suggests a number of specific opportunities for teaching communication skills in the context of motor activities. Several factors should be considered to use this strategy most efficiently and effectively.

Select One Goal to Be the Primary Goal. If logistics limit data-keeping, this represents the one goal for which careful data

Table 3-1.   Sample Generic Training Goals

Goal	Description	Sample Adaptive Play Activities
Functional Object Use	Manipulation of familiar objects according to conventional use (comb hair, eat with spoon)	Gather objects from daily living (brush, hat, washcloth, spoon, doll) into a colorful Fun Box; remove one item at a time and use it in an animated fashion, taking turns
Direction Following	Showing that commands given gesturally or verbally (or both) are followed	Generalized direction-following, through games such as "Simon says," and by noun + verb direction-following in a matrix form (push car/train/baby; kiss baby/dog/cat); see Striefel, Wetherby, and Karlan (1976)
Turntaking	A basic building block for communication and many social skills	Set up games that are conducive to input from two or more; Example: set object-in-the-can switch so it will not activate the toy until several objects have been dropped in, and let each child drop in one item

For additional generic training goals, see McLean et al. (1981).

should be kept. Focus should be on this main goal, with additional goals introduced or practiced as they occur naturally.

Combine Goals That Are Naturally Related. Consider the main goal, and determine what skills accompany it; for example, skills that naturally accompany adaptive switch play include turntaking, commenting on action of toy, and visual tracking of moving toy. This is related to the activity sequence, as described by McLean and colleagues (1981). They define an activity sequence as a sequence of steps (or operations) required to complete an activity or task. Thus, a student can learn a variety of skills within the same general task format.

Consider the Principle of Partial Participation for Secondary Goals. This principle states that "severely handicapped individuals, regardless of their limited independence or level of functioning, should be permitted to participate at least partially in chronologically age-appropriate environments and activities" (Liberty, Haring, and Martin, 1981; Wehman, 1984). This may require one or more of the following techniques (Wehman, 1984): (1) modify the environment (e.g., suspend toys from Activity Frames); (2) modify the skill sequence of a task (e.g., "throw" a ball by placing it on the child's hand, in the lap, and lifting the arm so the ball is propelled); (3) adapt materials (e.g., place a puppet on a wrist bracelet); or (4) provide personal assistance (e.g., set up the switch and tape recorder so the child can activate it independently). Partial participation is especially useful when telescoping goals, because the goals, although functionally related, may not be of equal difficulty for the child. With partial participation, the child can be introduced to related goals that otherwise would be ignored.

If the previously mentioned factors are controlled, the practice of telescoping goals and activities can lead to the development of integrated rather than splinter skills. Table 3–2 presents several examples of telescoped goals.

Plan Ahead: Consider High-Risk Areas

This area is particularly pertinent with regard to development of communication skills. Many infants with disabilities may be considered at high risk for normal speech or language development (McDonald, 1980). For these children, working on goals that would facilitate rapid development of augmentative communication skills, if that becomes necessary, can provide a major advantage. This certainly does not mean that oral speech should be rejected in the young infant, but that preliminary skills to augmentative communication be considered, so that if the decision is made to elect an augmentative mode, rapid progress will be enhanced. It is generally recommended that a decision regarding election of a nonspeech communication system be deferred until the child is at least 18 months mental age and has attained Stage V sensorimotor intelligence (Shane and Bashir, 1980). However, numerous factors, taken together, can predict a poor prognosis for oral speech development. Both McDonald (1980) and Shane and Bashir (1980) suggest areas of concern that can help identify children at risk for speech development (e.g., those with persistent oral reflexes, neuromuscular involvement, praxic disturbance, excessive drooling). Children thus identified can be introduced to preliminary skills, such as visual tracking and scanning or motor imitation, that will enhance later learning of augmentative communication systems. As Musselwhite and St. Louis (1982) note, "This seems to be a safe approach which in no way rules out the eventual development of vocal language" (p. 14). Table 3–3 provides specific examples of skill areas that are preliminary to augmentative communication.

Table 3-2. Telescoping Goals: Sample Clustered Activities

Primary Goal	Secondary Goals	Telescoped Activities
Body Part Identification	Visual tracking Requesting *more* Turntaking	Use puppet, mouse-covered vibrator, or similar object as a "tickler"; have child visually track it as it moves playfully; have object say "I'm going to get your *nose* — Where's your *nose?*"; after tickling, ask if the child wants *more* (elicit nod, vocalization, gesture, or sign, as appropriate)
Sound Production	Sign or verbal labeling Functional object use Peer interaction	Place objects representing sounds in a box or colorful bag; draw objects out with fanfare, or let students choose objects, encouraging labeling through words or signs; sing a song for sound of object (e.g., cup = "guh-guh"), then have child use object or give it to a peer
Differential Object Use	Decision-making Object release Attending to task	Hold up two objects and ask which one child wants (accept eye gaze, pointing, or vocalization); help child use object differentially (example: shake or bang rattle), then have him or her release object into a container or the adult's hand

GENERAL TRAINING STRATEGIES

Use a Variety of Training Arrangements

There appears to be a general assumption that severely disabled children learn best (or only?) through individual instruction settings. Favell, Favell, and McGimsey (1978) reviewed literature over 2 years in journals dealing with severely retarded individuals and found that, in approximately 9 of 10 articles, training was carried out on a one-to-one basis. This may not be a

Table 3-3. Planning Ahead: Preliminary Skills for Future Goals

Future Goal	Preliminary Skill	Sample Learning Task
Future Symbol Use	Visual tracking	Watch moving toys such as Playful Penguins
	Visual scanning	Play "Which-cup-is-it-under"
	Decision-making	Allow child to choose snack, shirt, toy, and so forth
	Head control	Use mercury head switch to activate toy
	Interface switch use	Use adaptive switches with battery toys; have child start and stop toy on command in races
	Symbol recognition	Affix symbols (Example: Picsyms) to early books and to objects or places in the environment
Future Sign Use	Handshapes	Example: Index finger isolation = use finger as paintbrush, beep noses, use finger puppet
	Sign locations	Example: Chest = play "Tarzan"
	Sign movements	Example: Circular = dial toy telephone, trace adult patterns through Plexiglas
Later Peer Interaction	Close proximity to peers during play	Place two children face to face under an Activity Frame
	Independent peer play	Set large box on side, place two toddlers in, and put toys in a communal box between them
	Early peer-peer play	Introduce games such as "Pair-up-patty-cake" and "Tug-of-war" (with scarf, rope), giving adult assistance only as needed

realistic method of service delivery for many settings, such as institutions or schools, in which teaching personnel is limited. In addition, restricting students to individual training limits opportunities for peer interaction and does not follow the principles of normalization.

Brown, Nietupski, and Hamre-Nietupski (1976) suggest considering a variety of instructional arrangements for a portion of each day, in addition to the traditional one-trainer, one-student arrangement:

- *Small-group instruction:* Training is provided simultaneously for all students. Example: Teach, or help students practice, activities using the five primary handshapes for ASL signs (play drum to practice fisted handshape).
- *Clustered individualized instruction:* A group of three to five students watches while the teacher engages in individualized interactions with each student in turn. Example: Assist students in activating a penny pincer switch, to make a robot carry messages around the group.
- *Adaptive student interactions:* Students engage in appropriate interchanges without direct teacher involvement, although teachers may set up situations to enhance the probability of interactions, suggest interactions, and so forth. Example: Give one child a puzzle frame and another child the puzzle pieces, so that they have a reason for working cooperatively.

Studies indicate that small-group instruction can be as effective as individual training sessions, while employing staff time more efficiently, promoting generalization, and allowing students increased opportunities for interaction. Storm and Willis (1978) demonstrated success in an imitative training program with profoundly retarded men, whereas Favell and colleagues (1978) documented learning on a word-recognition task with retarded individuals ranging from 9 to 25 years of age. Generalization also may be greater for skills taught in group sessions. Oliver and Scott (1981) reported significantly greater generalizations to exemplars of adjective concepts taught to severely handicapped individuals (aged 19 to 21 years) in group versus individual sessions. Clustered individualized sessions can also enhance generalization. In a study by Kohl, Wilcox, and Karlan (1978), all of the moderately handicapped students were taught the same signs in the individual speech therapy sessions, whereas each student was assigned different signs for training in small group classroom sessions (clustered individualized training). The group condition promoted incidental learning of other students' signs as well as better generalization of signs acquired. Use of small group instructional strategies has also been found productive for developmentally disabled preschoolers. Fink and Sandall (1980) noted similar acquisition and retention rates for verbal labeling in group and individual sessions; however, individual training required more than twice as much time for instructional sessions. Clearly, factors such as the task to be taught, the behaviors of the students, and the physical setting will need to be considered in deciding when to use small-group sessions.

Use Naturally Structured Training Strategies

Musselwhite and St. Louis (1982) distinguish between naturally structured techniques focusing on events that are, or at least appear to be, naturally occurring, and artificially structured techniques using rote instruction apart from context. It is hoped that naturally structured training events will have the added advantages of context and intention. An obvious example would be to teach undressing skills at the swimming pool, so that the child has the context of other people undressing, clothes hanging from wall hooks, and the sight of the swimsuits, in addition to the intention of undressing in order to put on a swimsuit and be allowed to enter the water. Although there will be some training goals or settings that are most conducive to artificially structured strategies, it is advisable to consider ways to alter the situation slightly to allow naturally structured activities. Table 3–4 presents several examples of tasks that have been modified from artificially to naturally structured.

Create a Communicative Environment

To create an environment that fosters communication, it may be necessary to engage in some environmental engineering. The major goal is to avoid "show speech" and encourage real communication. The trainer should first ask "Does the child have a reason to communicate in this situation?" If not, the objects, events, or actions of people in the setting may need to be altered to achieve a reason for communicating. Constable (1983) provides an excellent summary of potential methods for manipulating the environment to elicit specific language functions. The following methods include sample training activities for each goal.

Requesting. Withhold objects, such as snacks, or turns, such as tickles, "accidentally."

Commenting on Objects. Present objects that are unexpected (e.g., hair dryer), or have them appear from concealed or unexpected place (e.g., comb in purse, spider descending from string on ceiling).

Commenting on Actions. Present unexpected actions (e.g., wind-up toy walks off table).

Protesting or Denying. Violate routine events (give child entire milk bottle instead of cup), or violate object function or manipulation (comb hair with spoon, put shoe on hand).

Table 3 - 4.   Adapting Tasks from Artificially to Naturally Structured

Goal	Artificially Structured	Naturally Structured
Motor Imitation	Instruct child to do what you do; have child perform *x* number of trials of same behavior	Train actions in context (Example: help child wave as staff members or peers leave the child's view)
Verbal Labeling	Show 50 pictures and ask child "What's this?" for each one	Hide objects in various places (in drawers, boxes) and encourage labeling as each is "discovered"
Object Placement	Have child put 10 pegs in a pegboard following the verbal directions "Put in"	Have child put 10 toy people in a toy bus, then take them for a ride
Visual Tracking	Present 10 trials, with the trainer moving objects in the child's vision according to predetermined paths	Select wind-up toys that offer appropriate speeds, paths, and distances

Describing Objects or Actions. Use barrier tasks; for example, one child has a set of pictures and the partner, on the opposite side of a screen, describes one of the pictures (see Chapter 11 and Table 11-5 for discussion and examples).

The foregoing examples summarize general methods that can be used to elicit language functions. The prompts that adults provide to students can also have an impact on encouraging communication. Olswang, Kriegsmann, and Mastergeorge (1982) suggest several adult behaviors designed to elicit requests in pragmatically impaired persons. Although two of these techniques — direct models ("Tell me, 'I want juice' " or "Say, 'Jump me' ") and direct questions ("What do you want?" or "What should we do?) — typically are overused with pragmatically impaired children, the other three techniques may be extremely productive in many settings. Halle, Alpert, and Anderson (1984) review three natural environment language training procedures that can be applied wherever the child is, by the child's natural caregivers. In some cases, this will require slight rearrangement of routine events to allow opportunities for environmental intervention. All six of these interactive training or prompting strategies are described in Table 3-5, with examples provided for each. Whether verbal or nonverbal, these tactics require more from the child than do direct questions or direct

Table 3-5.   Interactive Training or Prompting Strategies

Strategy	Description and Sample
Indirect Model	Provide a verbal model of a request, command, or similar mand, but do not ask the child to imitate. Instead give a choice ("Do you want to sing or play house"), provide a model plus an elicitation request ("If you need help, let me know"), ask the child to share the content of the indirect model with a peer, doll, or puppet ("Tell Molly to give you one").
Obstacle Presentation	Also known as "sabotage" or "creative stupidity," this involves giving a command but providing an obstacle to elicit speech. This may take the form of a barrier ("Make robot go" but batteries are missing), or missing objects ("Get the ball" but ball is not in usual place).
General Statement	This involves a verbal comment that gives a general idea of what can be requested but provides no model ("Something in my pocket!" "This book looks funny"). Nonlinguistic cues can also be used, such as holding up a box, shaking it, and looking expectant.
Mand-Model Procedure	This promotes natural environment generalization of trained language or direct language training. Targets should focus on child's interests. As child approaches material, the adult mands (verbally instructs) the child to describe the material ("Tell me what this is"). Appropriate responses yield specific praise ("Oh, you want the red hat") plus the natural consequence (child gets the red hat). Note that this procedure often violates the rule of avoiding "show speech."
Time Delay Procedure	The adult sets up a situation in which a particular behavior is appropriate (e.g., show closed jar with raisins inside to elicit sign "Open," "Want"). The adult delays for a predetermined length of time (e.g., 15 seconds) while looking at the child expectantly, then praises and immediately provides the natural consequence if the child completes the behavior. Failure to produce the behavior yields predetermined prompts from the adult (e.g., verbal, gestural, physical).
Incidental Teaching Procedure	This strategy facilitates elaborated language and improves conversational skills. The environment is first arranged to encourage child verbalization (as described previously), then the adult repeats the child's verbalization in an expanded manner ("You want the doggie? He's a big doggie. Woof-woof!").

Adapted from Olswang et al. (1982) and Halle et al. (1984).

models. In addition, unlike direct questions or models, these prompts can be presented unobtrusively and may therefore be less threatening to some children. Finally, interaction-oriented prompts and natural environment tactics allow the child to develop more control over communication and to be less dependent on direct intervention from adults.

TEACHING OTHERS TO USE GENERAL TRAINING STRATEGIES

These general training strategies will be most effective if all adults working and playing with a child learn to use them. Thus, parents, paraprofessionals, and professionals (including physical and occupational therapists, special educators, and speech-language pathologists) who interact with disabled children should be introduced to general training strategies. It is important to note that all the groups just listed use many of these strategies naturally. However, they are not used frequently enough, or in a sufficiently organized manner to yield effective results. For example, a teacher may occasionally provide general statements ("I have a little piano!"), but not often enough, or with sufficient models from peers, to produce desired results. Similarly, a therapist may inconsistently use time delay prior to facilitating a movement (independent scooping with a spoon), without setting up a schedule of delay time (15 seconds) and predetermining prompts (verbal prompt, "Scoop, Brian") in case the child does not produce the desired behavior. Thus, these general training strategies cannot be applied in a haphazard manner; their use should be consistent and planned in advance. Two primary teaching methods can be combined to teach effective use of general training strategies.

Model General Training Strategies in the Natural Environment

Since the training strategies focus on use of the child's natural environment and on functional training goals and tasks, they can best be taught in the natural environment. The optimum process is to describe the target strategy briefly, demonstrate its use, discuss what just occurred, and then provide opportunity for practice by the adult(s) learning the strategy. Some adults may feel more comfortable practicing the strategy first with another adult, then with the child. Following is a sample training sequence for use of the time delay procedure.

Describe. Note that this procedure has been used successfully to teach a variety of skills (verbal requesting, sign use, dressing). First, explain the typical process: (1) set up a situation in which a desired behavior is appropriate (hook up toy, place switch within reach); (2) delay for a predetermined length of time (30 seconds) while looking expectantly at the child; (3) provide natural consequence if child performs behavior (if child activates switch, natural consequence will occur); (4) provide predetermined prompt if child does not perform expected behavior (tap switch to focus child's attention).

Demonstrate. Go through the process presented in the description phase, mimicking the steps as closely as possible.

Discuss. Review the target training strategy (time delay procedure) and discuss its use in the demonstrated situation, with that specific child ("Did you notice that, on the second trial, she pulled the switch after 20 seconds of delay?). Also consider problems and possible solutions ("I had to turn her head in addition to tapping the switch in order to provide focus").

Practice. Encourage the adult to try out the new strategy, first on you, then on the student; ideally, the adult can first repeat the demonstrated trial, then modify it in a new trial presentation (e.g., use a 15 second time delay to encourage a child to imitate sounds produced by the adult during play).

Hold Brainstorming Sessions to Consider Applications for Strategies

A problem noted previously is insufficient use of a strategy that could be highly effective if employed more consistently. One way to overcome this problem is to help potential trainers see the wide variety of applications of each general training strategy. Brainstorming sessions can help to meet this goal because they encourage input from a number of people with different perspectives; in addition, people are all more likely to carry through on ideas that they have helped develop. The following section presents sample brainstorming topics for selected general training strategies.

Telescoping Goals. Parents and professionals from several disciplines can share major goals to determine activities that incorporate several goals. For example, the occupational therapy goal of undressing (removing pants), the physical therapy goal of weight-shifting while standing, the educational goal of following two-part commands, and the communication goal of requesting assistance could all be combined into a dress-up game, with the child dressing up in response to the lyrics of a song "Get the pants and put them on" (two-part command). It could be expected that the child could pull the pants off by himself or herself but would need to request help putting them on.

Selecting Generic Goals. Setting-specific or task-specific goals can be identified (signing "Eat" at mealtime, playing patty-cake), and team members can be challenged to retain the purpose while making the goal more generic (requesting through signing, interacting with peers by means of games). This can put the focus on the intent of the goals, so that intervention is goal-oriented, rather than activity-oriented.

Developing Naturally Structured Tasks. Teams can be asked to identify five artificially structured tasks that they have used and determine at least one way to make each more naturally structured, by attempting to introduce context and intent.

SUMMARY

Several of these strategies are based heavily on common sense. However, it is all too easy to enter into a teaching "mode," focusing on tasks that are relatively unimportant in terms of life skills, and using training strategies that promote performance (e.g., show speech) more than productive learning.

PART II

SELECTING, ADAPTING, AND MAKING PLAY MATERIALS

Chapter 4

Toy Selection and Adaptation

THE NATURE OF THE PROBLEM

It is becoming increasingly clear that selection of play materials can enhance or hinder success in a program. This chapter will present strategies to assist parents and professionals in choosing play materials that will yield optimal results for the disabled children who use them. Toys must be selected to match both child and system needs, as outlined in the following paragraphs.

Motor Needs. Children with motor disabilities require toys that can be manipulated using the motor skills they can manage; for example, toys that require considerable pressure or fine motor manipulation for activation will not be usable for many moderately or severely physically disabled children.

Sensory Needs. Children with various disabilities of vision, hearing, or touch need access to toys that provide input to their intact sensory features; for example, blind or visually impaired infants may interact especially well with toys designed to foster touch.

Developmental Needs. Cognitively disabled children should be allowed to interact with play materials at an appropriate level for their cognitive development; for example, a 6 year old girl functioning at the 18 month level will not be ready to take advantage of the fantasy element inherent in many toys intended for her chronological age.

Normalization Needs. This relates to the need for age-appropriate play materials, even though the child may be at an earlier developmental stage. Thus the 6 year old functioning at the 18 month level should not be relegated to playing with infant toys, such as rattles. This may be the most difficult need to meet on a consistent basis.

Program Needs. The goals, setting, and budget of the child's environment will also influence toy selection. For example, the skills to be facilitated through toy use, the space considerations of the setting, and the money available for toys must all be taken into consideration in choosing optimal toys.

TOY SELECTION CRITERIA

Williams, Briggs, and Williams (1979) present a comprehensive list of 11 areas of consideration in selecting toys, such as purchase information and user's capabilities and limitations. Each general area includes 10 to 50 questions for in-depth consideration of that feature (e.g., design features, operation or use subcategory: "minimum touch, grasp, pressure? easy to do? useful for self-instruction? provides feedback? self-correcting? low frustration level?", p. 23). They point out that once teachers become aware of the questions, they will be able to abbreviate or exclude those considerations not relevant to their population or environment. The extensive list of considerations would be especially helpful for persons involved in large acquisition or development projects, such as buyers for toy lending libraries or large institutions or developers of play materials for disabled children. A condensed listing of criteria for toy selection is presented in the following paragraphs.

Features Inherent in the Toy

General features of toys should first be considered. Although there are scores of toy-related features that could be discussed, this presentation is limited to several features that have been found through research or clinical experience to be important with regard to toy use by disabled children.

A primary consideration for any child is *safety*. This can be of even greater concern for disabled children, who may have behaviors (e.g., banging, throwing) or problems (e.g., drop seizures) that increase the likelihood of injury. Jeffrey (1981b) suggests six safety considerations: overall strength; materials used in making the toy (nontoxic? washable?); size of toy and its parts (likely to be swallowed?); dangers resulting from fall (protruding parts?); risks from misuse (danger from throwing, using as a hammer?); and risks from use in different settings (safe for unsupervised play?).

Toy *durability* is another feature that is important in any setting. Again, it may be a more substantial problem when working with children with special needs, as older children may use toys designed for younger, less physically strong children. In addition, stereotyped toy use, such as flapping, or destructive play patterns, such as banging, can cause greater stress on a toy than was anticipated by the manufacturers.

The degree of *realism* should also be considered when matching toys to specific children or groups of children. A toy can range from a faithful replica in miniature of the item it represents to a highly stylized version of that item. Chance (1979) summarizes research with nondisabled children, and reports that for very young children (under 2 years of age), highly realistic toys are more desirable; however, as children grow older, less realistic toys may encourage imaginative play. Clearly, these findings have implications for developmental as well as chronological age levels.

Chance (1979) reports similar findings with regard to the degree of *structure* of a toy. Structured toys, such as trucks and tea cups, may limit the way the toy is used, whereas play materials such as clay and blocks may enhance imaginative play. Again, there may be a relationship to developmental age, with older children benefiting most from less structured play materials.

Another feature that can aid in toy selection is the *reactive*, or *responsive*, nature of toys. A recent study (Bambara, Spiegel-McGill, Shores, and Fox, 1984) investigated the effects of reactive and nonreactive toys, using identical toy pairs, except that reactive toys were capable of producing sound or sustaining motion, or both, as a consequence of manipulation. They found that severely cognitively impaired subjects engaged in manipulative activity for a significantly greater amount of time with reactive than with nonreactive toys. Lewis (quoted in Chance, 1979) notes that the control over the environment allowed by reactive toys "can be extremely important not only in teaching the child causal relationships, but in giving the child a sense of competence, a sense of power" (p. 48). Switch-operated battery toys would fall into this category.

Jeffrey (1981b) identifies the general feature of *motivational value* and *attractiveness*. This can be related to features such as realism and reactiveness; such child preferences may be highly individual. Williams and colleagues suggest numerous additional design features, such as simplicity or complexity and malleability, as well as a variety of sensory stimulus characteristics regarding the possibilities for visual, tactile, vestibular, olfactory, and auditory stimulation. These features would be especially helpful in selecting play materials for students with multiple sensory impairments, such as deaf-blind students.

Age Appropriateness

The issue of age appropriateness is closely related to the concept of normalization. It is extremely difficult for adults to interact with an adolescent in an appropriate manner if that student is typically observed playing with infant toys. Selection of age-appropriate materials will follow different rules depending on whether the person has delayed toy play skills because of primarily motor or cognitive impairments.

Wehman (1976) addresses this concern in relation to adolescents or adults who are physically mature but developmentally young. He suggests that play for this population be centered on gross motor activities, using play materials such as old tires, mats, trampolines, stationary exercise cycles, and open-ended barrels. These materials meet the durability requirements and can be adapted readily for various exploratory play, social play, and group game play activities for severely cognitively disabled people.

Although considerable energy and fund-raising may be required, advanced technology has yielded a variety of age-appropriate play materials for severely physically disabled children with normal cognitive skills. These play materials range from battery-operated devices (toys, tape recorders) activated by adaptive switches, to adapted electronic games, to highly interactive computer games, art, and music programs. In addition, severely physically disabled children should be encouraged to direct activities (e.g., dressing and manipulating a doll, operating a robot) through speech or alternative communication modes such as symbol boards; in this way, a peer can help to carry out those actions that the disabled child cannot perform.

The playboards designed by Carlson (1982) can be adapted to meet the needs of moderately to severely physically or cognitively disabled children. These playboards can be fitted with normative toys (e.g., miniature vehicles and people) that are attached to a play frame or fixed over a slot so they can readily be moved with a minimum of physical effort. For older disabled children, playboards can be outfitted with more age-appropriate materials, such as a wig stand and wig, with various hair care items attached to the playboard; a train set affixed to the playboard, with accessories loosely attached (some ideas from van Tatenhove, personal communication).

Another approach to age-appropriate play materials for physically or cognitively disabled older children is to encourage the use of collections. Although an adult playing with a locomotive would be viewed as rather strange, having a "collection" of toy trains is viewed as perfectly acceptable. Table 4–1 presents an overview of the use of collections for older cognitively delayed students. This simple strategy can help "normalize" a cognitively disabled child's continued interest in items such as dolls and balls after he or she has passed the chronological age for which they are appropriate. Traditional collections (stamp, rock, coin) can also be useful, especially for higher-functioning adolescents (Bender et al., 1984).

Wehman (1976) emphasizes that persons engaged in selecting play materials be sure to consider the usefulness of everyday surroundings in promoting play and leisure skill development. This would include general outdoor play activities, such as hiking, as well as seasonal opportunities, such as playing in the snow and building a snowman, piling up and jumping in autumn leaves, and splashing or wading in a stream. Wehman observes that these activities can promote normalization and integration with nondisabled peers. In addition, each of the activities suggested previously is appropriate for an unlimited age range.

Therapeutic Value of Toy Use

A major issue in toy selection is a determination of the purposes for which the toys will be used. This can include development of specific skills or training independent play and use of leisure time. As discussed in earlier chapters, toys can enhance development of skills in all basic areas. This can include general skills, such as facilitating communication through talking about toys, or specific skill development, such as fostering production of target sounds through pairing them with toys ("z-z-z" for bee) or actions on toys ("shhhh" as doll sleeps). Similarly, fine motor development can be promoted by providing the child

Table 4-1.   Collections as Age-Appropriate Play Materials

Rationale	Items within a collection are deemed acceptable across age ranges; often the same items (matchbox cars, puppets) would be considered inappropriate if used out of the context of an organized collection
Sample Items	Adolescent, cognitively delayed students could collect play materials such as matchbox cars, toy trains, hats, key chains, jewelry, puppets, transforming toys, battery-operated vehicles, balls, and stuffed animals
	Adolescents with physical disabilities but higher cognitive skills may enjoy traditional collectibles, such as stamps, coins, cans, patches, and campaign-type buttons
Storing and Displaying	Collections can be housed in a variety of ways, including bulletin boards, pegboards, tackle boxes, display cases, shoe boxes, and shelves; the method of storage should be adapted to the motor and cognitive skills of the individual
Advantages	Unusual interests can be normalized by turning them into collections. The collector has something to look forward to when shopping or traveling, possibly enhancing motivation to engage in both. The objects provide a topic of conversational interest to the collector. Collections can be a joint activity for the collector and others with similar interests in the home, classroom, or community. They suggest appropriate categories for gift-buying
Resources	For further information, see Lear (1977) and Bender and colleagues (1984).

Adapted from Wendy Ashcroft, Memphis State University (personal communication, October 1984).

with a number of developmentally appropriate toys requiring a variety of fine motor patterns, and encouraging the child to manipulate them. If training is required on a specific fine motor skill, such as pincer grasp, toys can be chosen to increase the likelihood of using that skill (e.g., Lite Brite, pick-up-sticks). Thus, this selection feature can be used as a generic criterion, allowing choice of materials that provide a range of opportunities within a skill area, or a specific criterion, suggesting selection of play materials intended to enhance particular skills. Jeffrey (1981a) suggests several assessment questions to determine the activities encouraged by a particular toy for a specific child or group of children (e.g., "Will the child notice that the toy can be used in the ways intended or desired by the therapist?", p. 3–5).

Several published toy lists (Beesley and Preston, 1981; *Good Toy Guide, 1983;* Riddick, 1982; Sinker, 1983; Webb, 1978) relate specific toys to the therapeutic goals that they may be expected to facilitate. For example, Beesley and Preston (1981) present a poster-format chart listing 10 major skill areas (e.g., visual, tactile, perceptual), and indicate toys that enhance skill development in subcategories (e.g., visual skills: visual activity, eye tracking, visual stimulation). These toy lists can be an excellent resource if used properly. However, they may become outdated rapidly; for example, a list more than five years old is likely to include many toys that are no longer available for purchase. In addition, geographic variations may cause problems, as a list published in one country may describe toys that are not readily available in another country.

Cost-Effectiveness

The factor of cost-effectiveness requires the toy selector to rate the actual cost of the toy against such issues as the number of students who will be able to use the toy; the potential replacement cost for parts such a batteries; the variety of skills that can be taught using the toy; and the importance, in terms of priority ratings, of skills taught through the toy. Thus, a toy that might be judged too costly for one facility could be justified in terms of potential benefits for another site.

Use of Toy Selection Criteria

The preceding list of considerations for toy selection is far from exhaustive. A number of other features may also be important, such as the attractiveness of the toy to peers and family members: This follows the premise that they will be more likely to interact with the child if provided with enticing play materials. However, if a list of considerations is too unwieldy it may not be used in making toy choices. The aforementioned factors have been condensed into a checklist for choosing or purchasing toys for specific groups, children, or goals (Table 4–2). This checklist may be used when evaluating a specific toy in relation to the children who will use it, or when attempting to locate a toy for an individual child.

ASSISTING PARENTS IN SELECTING TOYS

Selecting toys for severely disabled children can be an extremely frustrating experience for parents and other family members. This is a special concern at gift-giving times, as toys chosen for disabled children are often inappropriate and the toys are then not used. Discussing toy selection issues with parents can provide an excellent background for considering general child needs, such as use of leisure time and specific skill development. It can also provide an opportunity for two-way sharing of information about a child in a very nonthreatening context. This section presents several strategies that have been used successfully to assist parents in choosing appropriate, stimulating toys for their children.

Parent-to-Parent Sharing. This involves requesting parents to identify specific toys that their children enjoy and learn from; information can be shared in written form, or, preferably, by bringing special toys to a sharing session, such as a PTA meeting.

General Toy Selection Worksheets. Checklists, such as the one presented in Table 4–2, can be given to parents to assist them in choosing toys. This can serve as a springboard for discussing specific issues of toy selection, and explaining why each factor is important.

Sample Toy Worksheets. Worksheets would present specific toy names in the left column, with additional information provided for each toy, such as brief description, cost, local source, skill areas facilitated (e.g., communication, social), and room for additional comments; this strategy would require less effort from the parents than use of a general worksheet, but it would not be as helpful in fostering parent understanding of the overall rationale for toy selection.

Toy Display. Exemplary toys can be gathered and placed on display, with a card describing characteristics such as cost, source, description, sill areas facilitated, and special features (e.g., appropriate for many ages); toys can be taken from those used at the facility, with additional toys borrowed from local toy stores in exchange for positive public relations (e.g., a notice informing parents that the store loaned the toys, and a media release describing the project).

Ideally, several of these strategies will be used in combination. For example, an entire PTA program can be devoted to toy

Table 4-2.   Sample Toy Selection Checklist

Toy	Toy Features						Child Needs				Program Needs	
	SAF	DUR	REAL	STRUC	RESP	ATT	MOT	SENS	DEV		THER	COST

Code:
SAF = safety; *DUR* = durability; *REAL* = realism; *STRUC* = structure;
RESP = responsiveness; *ATT* = attractiveness/motivational value;
MOT = motor needs; *SENS* = sensory needs; *DEV* = developmental needs;
THER = therapeutic value; *COST* = cost effectiveness

Sample Rating Scale:
+ = toy meets criteria
+ + = toy exceeds criteria
− = toy fails criteria
− − = serious problem

selection. Parents can bring in special toys and staff members can choose or borrow additional toys for a large toy display. A presentation can cover general considerations for selecting toys and general or specific toy worksheets can be provided to parents for making further decisions. Parents should be encouraged to share information and names of specific toys with other family members planning to purchase toys for their child. A comprehensive strategy such as this can have the added benefit of promoting parent interest in toy play and an awareness of the importance of play in their child's life.

TOY ADAPTATIONS

When considering toys that might be appropriate for a particular child, group, or goal, the selector often locates toys that would be perfect "if only . . . ." For example, a toy might be ideal for a situation if it were larger, more stable, less distracting, and so forth. This section presents ideas for adapting commercial toys or designing or making adaptive toys that suit the needs of children with disabilities.

Adapting Commercial Toys

Williams and colleagues (1979) present 10 basic suggestions for adapting materials, with several examples for each of these processes. Their ideas are especially suited to toy adaptations for mildly to moderately physically or cognitively disabled children. Table 4–3 summarizes those 10 categories, and examples are given for adapting specific toys. Two additional strategies that may be needed for severely physically disabled children are provision of physical access and provision for mechanical access.

Provide Physical Access. This modification may be necessary for children with limited control over voluntary movement; one procedure is to suspend toys so that they can be readily reached and manipulated. This can be accomplished by suspending toys from a bar for use by children in beds, in adaptive positions on the floor (e.g., seated in reclining chair, side-lying, in prone stander, over a wedge), or in adaptive wheelchairs. Figure 4–1 depicts a variety of "Activity Frames" for use in those various

Table 4-3.   Strategies For Adapting Play Materials

Strategy	Description	Example
Stabilize	Attach play material to steady surface	Affix play house to lap tray with C-clamp
Enlarge	Enlarge materials to enhance visual peception	Use large puzzle pieces
	Enlarge key parts to enhance toy manipulation	Affix large Plexiglas "button" over small Push 'n' Go button
Prosthetize	Affix parts to allow access for physically disabled	Use foam hair curlers (minus tubes) to add grip to brush handle
Reduce Required Response	Minimize: distance range of motion complexity of response	Place doll on elevated tray Use tray to keep cars within range Use plate switch rather than on-off
Make More Familiar	Relate to environment	Select symbols that reflect child's world
Make More Concrete	Reduce abstract quality	Demonstrate activity, toy play Add clues to graphic symbols
Remove Extraneous Cues	Consider goal and remove unrelated cues	If the task is shape recognition, do not simultaneously color-code items to be sorted
Remove Distracting Stimuli	Simplify "busy" backgrounds	Use dark background behind objects being visually tracked, or as a backdrop for puzzles
Add or Enhance Cues	Increase visual stimuli Increase tactile stimuli	Use bright, contrasting colors Affix fabrics to adaptive switches
Improve Safety and Durability	Avoid sharp objects Protect objects from drool Increase strength of toys	Round off or pad corners Laminate, add nontoxic sealant Replace cardboard with triwall Replace staples or nails with screws

Categories are from Williams, B., Briggs, N., and Williams, R. (1979). (Selecting, adapting, and understanding toys and recreation materials.) In P. Wehman (Ed.), *Recreation programming for developmentally disabled persons* (pp. 15–36). Baltimore: University Park Press. Reprinted with permission.

Materials
Two (2) 2' lengths of 2 × 4s (i.e., 2 × 2)
Two (2) 1 × 3s
Two (2) 3" L-braces
Six screw eyes
Dowel stick to fit screw eyes
Screws for attaching L-braces to wood
Contact paper (cover wood first)
Wood glue (glue before inserting screws)
Large rubber bands (to secure dowel)

Uses:
Child can be placed under frame in
    various positions or adaptive
    equipment (bean bag, side lying,
    Tumbleform chair, prone positioner)
Two children can be placed under one
    Activity Frame simultaneously
Promotes general activation, reaching,
    grasping, and so forth.

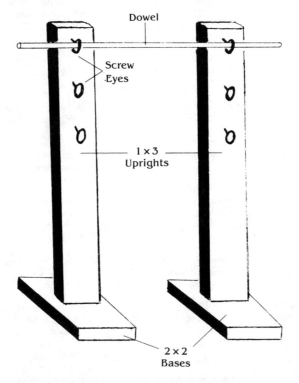

FLOOR BASED FRAME

Figure 4-1.   Providing toy access through activity frames.

EYE LEVEL FRAME

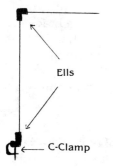

Ells

C-Clamp

Materials:
½" PVC tubing
One (1) C-clamp
Two (2) PVC "Ells"
Note: for highly active children, two (2) supports
may be needed

Uses:
Attach to desk, standing table, laptray
Promotes head control
Allows independent play in wheelchair

Materials:
½" PVC tubing
Two (2) PVC "Ells"
Two (2) PVC "Tees"
Two (2) metal hose clamps

Uses:
Attach to tubular frame of wheelchair
Promotes use of minimal hand movements
Allows independent play in wheelchair

LAP LEVEL FRAME

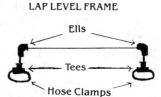

Ells

Tees

Hose Clamps

Note: Portaplay Toys markets a plastic portable frame for small
children (Order from Portaplay Toys, P.O. Box 12437, Toledo, OH
43606).

Figure 4-1   (continued)

settings. These activity frames also discourage mouthing and throwing of toys and allow access to several objects simultaneously. A very young child, or a child just learning volitional movement, can be helped to place one hand through a bracelet suspended from the activity frame; this can permit the needed stability to attain volitional movement. It may also help to pair a high-activity and a low-activity child, placing both under an activity frame simultaneously, as the high-activity child can provide stimulation for the partner.

Provide Mechanical Access. This strategy refers to allowing access to battery-operated, wind-up, or electrical play materials through use of adaptive switches. Chapter 5 in this book covers the rationale and procedures for developing mechanical access materials.

Determination of the most appropriate techniques for adapting commercial toys can follow from consideration of the child's needs, as described previously. Carlson (1983) suggests numerous simple adaptations for commercial toys or other play materials.

Developing Adaptive Toys

For some students or goals, even adaptations of commercial toys will not suffice. In this case, it may be necessary to develop entirely new adapted play materials. For example, Carlson's playboard (1982) can be built by affixing typical child toys (e.g., miniature vehicles, furniture, and people) to a play surface so that some are stationary while others can be moved along a track. Numerous ideas for adapting play materials are presented throughout this book, as they related to promoting specific skill areas.

Designing adaptive play materials is one area in which it is easy to "reinvent the wheel." When a need is identified for adaptive play equipment, it is wise to first check existing sources, such as small manufacturers, investigate plan books for building adaptive toys, and visit or consult with facilities serving children with similar needs. Charlebois-Marois (1985) used this approach in developing her book, which is a compendium of easily made adaptations (including adaptive play materials) collected from professionals working with augmentative communication users. A variety of sources are presented in the resources section that follows. If none of these sources yield needed materials or plans, it may be necessary to design equipment. Ideally, the design problem should be shared with a professional, such as an adaptive equipment designer; if this is not possible owing to lack of funds or logistical factors, the problem should be presented to a variety of people who work with the child, with possible assistance from appropriate volunteers such as Telephone Pioneers.

RESOURCES

A variety of resources are available to provide assistance in selecting and adapting play materials for disabled children:

Books or Articles (see Appendix A). Toy selection: *Good Toy Guide 1983;* Jeffrey (1981a); Sinker (1983); Webb (1978); Williams et al. (1979). Toy adaptation: Carlson (1982); Charlebois-Marois (1985); Howard (1979); Jeffree, McConkey, and Hewson (1977); Lear (1977); McConkey and Jeffree (1981); ten Horn (1981).

Organizations (see Appendix B). Canadian Association of Toy Libraries; Telephone Pioneers of America; Toy Libraries Association (Britain); and USA Toy Library Association.

Manufacturers (see Appendix C). Able Child; Brad's Toys; Toys for Special Children.

Chapter 5

Use of Adaptive Switches and Response-Contingent Devices in Adaptive Play

Reinforcing devices such as tape recorders and battery toys (e.g., fire truck, robot) are currently in wide use with children having severe physical disabilities. This chapter will explore the rationale for adaptive switch use, the types of children who might benefit from use of response-contingent devices, the specifics of choosing, buying, or making response-contingent devices, strategies for using them productively, and resources for further information.

ADAPTIVE SWITCHES AND RESPONSE-CONTINGENT DEVICES: A DESCRIPTION

An adaptive switch can provide an interface between a child and a reinforcing device, so that the child can activate the device independently, even though he or she does not have the fine motor skills necessary to activate the device in the usual manner (e.g., a small "on-off" switch). Wethered (1982) refers to these devices as "response-contingent materials," as they provide some type of response, such as music or movement, depending on the child's activation of an interface switch. Typically, a battery device such as a firefighter's hat is selected and a switch interrupter with a phone jack on the free end is inserted into the battery case to stop the power supply so that the toy will not be activated when it is turned on. Next, an adaptive switch can be purchased or built, with a phone plug on one end. The device is prepared by turning it on and inserting the plug into the jack. Now, operation of the switch by the child will activate the

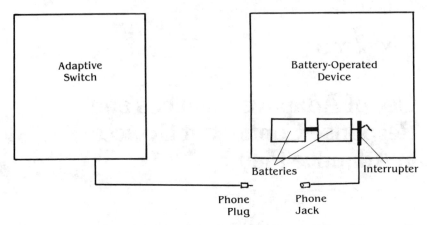

Figure 5–1. Schematic diagram of an adaptive switch arrangement. For use with electrical devices, adaptive switches must be interfaced to some type of control unit to ensure the child's safety (see Appendix C, Adaptive Aids, for a sample control unit).

device (see Figure 5–1). Sample response-contingent devices and adaptive switches are described in the following sections.

Sample Response-Contingent Devices

Response-contingent devices include materials that are powered by batteries, through a wind-up mechanism, or by electric current (*Note:* a special control unit must be used with electrical devices because of danger of electrocution). Battery-operated devices can be purchased commercially and adapted or made by hand. Commercial battery-run devices are most readily available at Christmas time and can be found in traditional toy stores, at airport gift shops, and through catalogue companies. Used battery-operated toys can often be located at flea markets or garage sales. Tape recorders are especially useful, as tapes can be changed as the novelty wears off. Many children especially enjoy listening to tapes made by favorite people (family members, friends) singing, telling stories, reciting nursery rhymes, or simply engaging in conversation. To accept an adaptive switch, the tape recorder must have an outlet for a remote microphone. Burkhart (1980, 1982) provides specific instructions for modifying a variety of types of battery-run toys, including standard AA, C, or D battery toys, 9-volt battery toys, and remote control toys. Some toys that are traditionally operated by winding a large knob (e.g., wind-up music boxes or record players) can also be adapted to accept adaptive switch input, although the process is slightly more complicated, as the working mechanism of the toy must be interrupted directly. Response-contingent and wind-up toys that have already been modified can be purchased from several sources (see Appendix C: The Able Child, Burkhart, and Toys for Special Children).

Response-contingent devices can be made by hand to reduce costs and to yield high-interest, appropriate learning material for children with special needs. Burkhart (1980) provides step-by-step instructions for making a variety of toys, including a lighted pegboard, electronic busy box, and happy face battery light. Wethered (1982) gives instructions for constructing a kaleidoscope and a rotary mobile that are battery-operated. When selecting response-contingent toys, careful consideration should be given to the goals that will be attempted. For example, if a major use of the toys will be to enhance visual tracking skills, toys that move in a variety of patterns will be desirable, such as the Radio Shack police car with an insert template to allow circles, figure-eight, hexagon, and so forth. If the primary goal is to teach the motor skill of head control, a stationary device with long-term interest would be preferable. Chapter 4 and Part 3 (Chapters 6 through 12) provide suggestions for types of response-contingent devices appropriate for facilitating particular goals.

Sample Adaptive Switches

Adaptive switches are also available commercially or can be constructed by hand. The cost of handmade switches can be considerably below that of commercially purchased switches, as free or inexpensive materials such as cardboard or film canisters can often be used. However, making switches is time-consuming, especially for the novice, and the results may not be as aesthetically attractive or durable as commercially purchased ones.

Interface to a battery device can be made by variety of actions and a number of body parts. Table 5–1 lists sample switches, potential body parts, types of activation, and sources to indicate the possibilities of switch interface. Clearly, switch activation to operate a response-contingent toy can be a preliminary activity to learning switch use for further environmental control, such as operating a wheelchair, electronic communication device, or bedside lamp.

Table 5-1.   Sample Adaptive Switches

Sample Switch	Potential Body Parts	Type of Activation	Source*
Treadle Switch	Hand, foot, elbow	Touch switch surface	TASH
Large Surface	Hand, arm, elbow	Touch (light pressure)	BTC
Leaf Switch	Cheek, chin, limbs	Deflect leaf by touch	ZYGO
Pressure Switch	Arms, upper body	Touch or pressure on large surface	BURK
Squeeze Switch	Hand	Squeezing motion	AA
L.T. Switch	Cheek, chin, limbs	Light pressure	DE
Wobble Switch	Head, hand, foot, shoulder	Minimum deflection in any direction	BTC
Wrist, Arm, or Leg Switch	Wrist, arm, leg	Mercury-type switch, activated by positional changes	AA
Pneumatic Switch	Mouth (sip and puff)	Breath control	ZYGO
Rocking Lever	Hand, arm, elbow	Light pressure	PRC

*These are merely sample sources; many of these switches can be purchased from numerous other distributors. Addresses for sources are provided in Appendix C. Source codes are as follows: AA, Adaptive Aids; BTC, Basic Telecommunications Corporation; BURK, Linda Burkhart; DE, Developmental Equipment; PRC, Prentke-Romich Company; TASH, Technical Aids and Systems for the Handicapped, Inc.; ZYGO, Zygo Industries, Inc.

Further information on switch use, including assessment for selecting an appropriate switch and suggestions for mounting switches so that the user can access them independently, are provided in *Guide to Controls* (1982). Several companies listed in Appendix C provide consultative service regarding fitting, mounting, or custom-making switches (e.g., Prentke-Romich, Zygo). Illustrated, step-by-step instructions are presented in the following books annotated in Appendix A: Burkhart (1980, 1982); Higgins (1982). The chapter by Wethered (1982) also provides brief instructions for constructing several switches.

RATIONALE: WHY USE RESPONSE-CONTINGENT DEVICES?

The appropriate use of response-contingent devices can yield a number of positive results for severely disabled children. Perhaps the most important result is that of *control*. For many severely physically disabled students, activation of a response-contingent device through use of an adaptive switch may be the first successful, independent effort to directly control the environment. This can have an extremely positive effect on the child's self-esteem, and can help to reduce the "learned helplessness" that is often seen in children who are unable to manipulate their environments (Zuromski, Smith, and Brown, 1977). In addition, this ability to exercise control over the environment can positively influence the perceptions of others (parents, teachers, peers) regarding the child's capabilities.

A second reason for using response-contingent devices is to *teach or facilitate specific skills* through adaptive switch use. A wide variety of skills can be introduced or practiced in this manner, including gross motor, fine motor, oral-motor, cognitive, communication, social, self-help, preacademic, and prevocational skills (Burkhart, 1982). Specific examples of potential for skill training in each area are presented in Table 5–2.

These response-contingent devices also present a *clear training format* for students, as they provide continuous training, immediate performance-based feedback, and objective evaluation of student performance (Arroyo, 1976). This consistent pattern of outcome helps device users understand cause-and-effect relationships (e.g., "If I hold my head up, I can hear the music."

A final reason to use response-contingent devices involves the issue of *logistics.* Because of poor staff-student ratios in many training settings and the need for one-to-one intervention for activities such as feeding, dressing, and toileting, there is typically considerable "down time" in a classroom for severely physically disabled children. This clearly has detrimental effects on learning for children with severe disabilities, as documented in a study by Fredericks and colleagues (1978). These investigators found that the number of minutes of instruction per day accounted for 65 percent of the variance between teachers whose students made high gains and those whose students made low gains. Adaptive switches can provide students with an opportunity to continue active participation and learning even if no staff members are available for direct contact. Campbell, Green, and Carlson (1977) stress that static positioning must not be an end goal, but should be accompanied by other goals, such as cognitive or language training. Adaptive switch use is one appropriate activity for students who must remain in a specific position, such as sidelying, for a predetermined length of time.

Table 5-2. Sample Skills Enhanced Through Use of Adaptive Switches and Response-Contingent Devices *

Skill	Switch†	Device†	Activity†
Gross Motor: body part dissociation	Wrist switch	Roll-over car	Activate switch by lifting arm with switch attached, without lifting other arm
Communication: acquisition of signs *On/Go, More/Music*	Plate switch	Musical train	Use signs to request action or recurrence, comment on action, label, and so forth
Cognitive: visual tracking (vertical path)	Ring pull switch	Climbing fireman	Pull ring, then watch fireman climb up and down ladder
Fine Motor: object placement	Ring stack	Buzzer	Children take turns stacking rings on post, until last ring is on and buzzer sounds
Self-Help: toilet training	Potty training switch	Tape recorder	When child urinates into the potty, the music will start
Preacademic: horizontal line "drawing"	Prewriting switch	Walking robot	Child traces a path on a metal cookie sheet using a metal bolt as a writing tool

*For additional applications of adaptive switches and battery-operated devices, see Burkhart (1982).

†Note: These are merely samples; typically a variety of adaptive switches, battery-operated devices, and activities could be used to accomplish the specified goals.

TARGET POPULATION

Traditionally, activation of response-contingent devices through use of adaptive switches has been reserved primarily for severely physically disabled children. Children with limited volitional motor control clearly are highly appropriate candidates for use of these materials, especially if they have difficulty manipulating other play materials. However, the wide variety of available adaptive switches and response-contingent devices provides opportunities for learning and enjoyment by children with less severe physical disabilities. For example, children who have low muscle tone (e.g., many with Down's syndrome) may benefit from using the devices and switches for working on skills as diverse as communication (commenting on action — "see man climb!"); fine motor development (pincer grasp — using penny pincher switch); cognitive development (means-end relationship); and oral-motor skills (blowing toys). The high level of reinforcement offered by many response-contingent devices can enhance motivation for many students. In assessing the appropriateness of switch or device use for a particular child, the adult should refer to the reasons listed in the section on Rationale to determine whether they meet the child's needs.

Because of the wide variety of skills that can be introduced or practiced through switch or device training, these materials may be helpful in a number of disciplines. The potential skills described in Table 5–2 include goals appropriate for teaching by special education teachers, speech-language pathologists, occupational and physical therapists, and parents and other caregivers.

SWITCH-MAKING: STRATEGIES TO ENHANCE EFFICIENCY

As noted previously, homemade adaptive switches and response-contingent devices may be less consistent and less durable than commercially purchased devices. In addition, they do not come with a warranty! Therefore, they must also be repaired at home rather than returning them to a factory. Thus, children who are likely to destroy a switch, through uncontrolled reflexes or behavior, will require either commercially purchased, warrantied switches or homemade switches modified for greater durability.

Homemade switches and devices have the primary advantage of low cost and can also be adapted to meet the needs of individual children. The low cost may enable a facility to produce duplicates of highly used switches so that they are readily available; clinical experience suggests that this will result in more frequent use. This section will present ideas for producing homemade switches and suggestions for making the switches more consistent and more durable.

Switch-Making Workshops

The most efficient and enjoyable method for constructing adaptive switches is to have a switch-making workshop. This allows a single trip for purchasing supplies and production of several copies of the same switch at one time. The strategies employed for organizing and leading the workshops are dependent on the background of the participants. For any group, the major goal will be to produce a number of working switches. However, additional goals may be desirable for certain groups, thus altering the manner in which the workshop is organized and conducted. It is recommended that a workshop leader be identified to plan, prepare, and lead each session. Three formats for switch-making workshops are presented in the following section.

Staff Workshop. The goals for this population will include getting a "feel" for switch-making to generate ideas for making and adapting future switches; understanding switch construction and function, so that minor repairs can be made at a later date, without consulting the workshop leader; learning all phases of switch construction (soldering, stripping, joining) so that the process can be repeated without help; and sharing information regarding switch use in the classroom. Thus, staff members should understand in advance how the switch functions and should be familiar with the instructions before beginning to construct the switch. Each staff member should also have a chance to try each phase of switch-making if future switch-making is intended. At some time, opportunity should be provided to share information and brainstorm regarding classroom use of adaptive switches and response-contingent devices.

Parent Workshop. Goals will be similar to those for the staff workshop, except that focus will be on individual rather than general applications of switch use. In addition, some parents may be intimidated by the process; therefore, it is advisable to allow ample time for participants to become familiar with the materials and procedures. A short presentation on switch or device use preceding or accompanying the workshop is recommended, as is having parents sign up for follow-up meetings to share information with staff on specific strategies for their child.

Volunteer Workshop. Goals for this group will be more limited, as participants are making materials that will be used by others and therefore do not need to understand all construction details. An assembly-line format is ideal as it enhances efficiency of use of both materials and personnel. Stations can be set up for accomplishing specific tasks, such as cutting, stripping, and twisting wires, soldering, preparing materials such as film cans, and so forth.

The preceding workshop suggestions assume that a workshop leader from the facility will plan and conduct the workshop. In some cases, it may be possible to provide switch-making instructions to a group and to have that group prepare the switches. One especially appropriate service organization for this project is the Telephone Pioneers of America (see Appendix B), a group that includes persons trained in electronics. Other appropriate groups include Scouts and adult civic organizations (see Chapter 14 for more suggestions).

Suggestions for Increasing Switch Reliability and Durability

Switch malfunction during training is frustrating to the teacher and confusing to the child. Since one major benefit of these materials is that they are "response-contingent," materials that do not respond to the child's appropriate input can impede rather than advance learning. Burkhart (1980, p. 40; 1982, p. 81) provides tips for trouble-shooting. These can aid in initial switch-making and repair of nonworking or malfunctioning switches. When testing new switches or repairing older switches, it is advisable to have a master switch and a master device that are extremely reliable. A questionable switch can then be plugged into a working device, and vice versa; this can help to isolate the source of the difficulty and identify whether it is in the adaptive switch or the response-contingent device. For a switch or device that will receive heavy use or will be used by a person with overly powerful responses, modifications may be made to enhance durability. For example, both glue and screws can be used to join parts, cardboard parts can be replaced by masonite, triwall, or hard plastic, pieces can be covered with plastic sealant to withstand moisture, and more durable components (e.g., microswitches) can be purchased. All switch-makers should be cautioned to attend to details during construction: for example, workers must solder joints carefully and avoid weakening connections by trimming off excess wires when stripping.

ADAPTIVE SWITCHES AND RESPONSE-CONTINGENT DEVICES: GENERAL USES

A critical issue in the application of adaptive switches and response-contingent devices is underutilization. Too often, these materials are used only for teaching cause-and-effect relationships or for entertainment of students. Although these are valuable goals, they are far from the only purposes for which the tools can be employed. This section will focus on general training strategies with switches and devices and specific goals that can be attempted.

General Training Strategies

A number of general intervention techniques can assist in efficient switch use. This section will describe three widely used strategies — shaping, response chaining, and response priming (Snell and Smith, 1978) — that are appropriate for teaching switch use.

Shaping consists of "the reinforcement of successive approximations or better and better 'attempts' of the target response" (Snell and Smith, 1978, p. 81). This can lead to the development of new behaviors and is appropriate for training skills that are not already in the child's repertoire. For example, a physical therapist might select a switch that the child can readily activate and hold it slightly to one side to facilitate lateral rotation while the child is seated. On successive trials, the switch could be moved more laterally, requiring a greater degree of rotation.

Response chaining is typically used to sequence together a series of related responses that are already in the child's repertoire. This strategy should be preceded by task analysis, in which the sequence of steps necessary to accomplish a task are determined. For example, the sequence for activating a drum-playing bear by pressing down on a Plexiglas plate switch (Higgins, 1982) would be (1) visually locate plate switch; (2) move hand to plate switch; (3) press down on plate switch; (4) visually locate activated bear; (5) release pressure on plate switch (optional). In *forward chaining,* "the individual is taught initially to perform the first unmastered step in the chain, as identified during baseline observation" (Snell and Smith, 1978, p. 82). Thus, the child would begin by visually locating the plate switch. It may be necessary to shape or cue this step. The child can then be physically guided through the remaining steps, with reinforcement for achieving the target step (e.g., "Hey! You found the switch — let's push it," plus assistance in activating the switch). Successive steps would be added as target steps until the entire process can be performed independently and correctly. For *backward chaining,* "teaching generally begins with the last step and progresses toward the beginning of the chain" (Snell and Smith, 1978, p. 82). In this example, the student would initially be guided through the first steps but would be encouraged (through shaping or cuing if necessary) to complete the final target step (releasing pressure on the plate switch) unassisted. When that step is mastered, preceding steps would be targets for direct training. Note that the "principle of participation," or the process of using the entire behavior in training, can be included in response chaining. Thus, although the programming may be directed toward the first step(s) only (forward chaining) or the last step(s) only (backward chaining), the child will be assisted in completing all steps (Liberty et al., 1981).

A third general strategy is *response priming.* Various types of assistance can be provided prior to the response, "which act to increase the likelihood that the desired behavior or a better approximation will be performed by the learner (Snell and Smith, 1978, p. 84). This assistance can take the form of directions ("Put it *in* the can, Jessie"), models (demonstrate placing objects in the can), cues (hold up the can, point to the object, tap the can), or physical prompts (guide the child in placing the object into the can and releasing it).

The intervention strategy chosen will depend on several factors. First, the goal will help determine appropriate strategies. For example, the goal may be successful switch use as a terminal object (e.g., leisure enjoyment), a motor movement made while activating a switch (e.g., palmar grasp), or observation of the response-contingent device as it is activated (e.g., visual tracking). An observation of the child's abilities can also assist in choosing strategies; if the target skills are not in the child's repertoire, response chaining would not be an appropriate strategy. Finally, it may be most productive to combine training strategies; for example, one child may learn best by means of forward chaining, with the first several steps achieved through the aid of response priming, and with shaping required for one difficult step.

Sample Ideas for Implementing Switches and Devices

In this section general and specific goals for use of adaptive switches and devices are suggested to help professionals and caregivers avoid the trap of minimal use of these potentially powerful materials. Three major goals have been alluded to previously, and these will now be delineated.

Adaptive Switch Use. Adaptive switch use refers to teaching the use of an adaptive switch for the direct benefit it can yield, such as leisure enjoyment (activation of tape recorder, television), mobility (wheelchair control), or access to communication (by means of an electronic communication device). Although these areas will require additional training, learning switch use is a major component.

Skill Learning Through Switch Use. Skill learning can be direct, such as learning to use pincer grasp by pinching together two pennies, or indirect, as in using a switch as a motivator for action, such as rolling to activate a pad switch.

Skill Learning Through Response-Contingent Device Use. Using response-contingent devices involves attending to some feature of the device activated, such as learning visual figure-ground discrimination by visually determining which of several toys is being activated.

Burkhart (1982) presents numerous specific activities for using switches and devices to teach a variety of skills. Each activity lists the materials needed, the rationale, and the training procedures. Most of these activities are appropriate for use by either professionals or other caregivers. Wethered (1982) presents additional general ideas for making the most of switch or device application. Ideas for using adaptive switches and response-contingent devices are presented throughout this book, where appropriate. Table 5–2 presents sample goals in a variety of domains, along with switches and devices that could be selected to work on those goals.

Several control units have been developed to increase efficiency and extend the capability of adaptive switches. For example, the Control Unit, manufactured by Adaptive Aids (see Appendix C), allows safe use of electrical devices such as televisions, radios, hair dryers, and lights by changing current from AC to DC. This unit also provides the following capabilities: (1) change switch from typically "off" to typically "on" (e.g., noise stays on until child activates switch); (2) vary length of input required (e.g., child wearing mercury head control switch must hold head up 10 seconds before tape recorder comes on); (3) vary length of output (e.g., child hits kitchen switch briefly and toy train is activated for 30 seconds); (4) vary number of inputs required (e.g., child must stack four rings to activate toy); and (5) record data (e.g., teacher can feed another child and keep track of number of times switch was activated in 15 minutes).

RESOURCES

Individual sections of this chapter cited numerous resources for further information on adaptive switches and response-contingent devices. A brief overview of primary sources as is follows:

Books, Chapters, Articles (see Appendix A and references). Burkhart (1980, 1982); Higgins (1982); Wethered (1982).

Organizations (see Appendix B). ISAAC *(Communication Outlook)*; Educational Technology Center, Inc.; Telephone Pioneers of America.

Manufacturers (see Appendix C). Able Child; Adaptive Aids; Developmental Equipment; Prentke-Romich Co.; Toys for Special Children; Zygo Industries, Inc.

PART III

ADAPTIVE PLAY STRATEGIES FOR COMMUNICATIVE GOALS

Chapter 6

Activation

RATIONALE AND DESCRIPTION

Some young disabled infants and severely cognitively delayed older children may show limited response to the environment. Thus, it may be necessary to work directly on activation, or the process of helping the child to act on the environment to produce desired outcomes. It is crucial to initiate this training as soon as possible after a child has been identified as nonresponsive to prevent the development of learned helplessness. In addition, this activation can serve as a base for future training. Adaptive play techniques can be further modified to provide training strategies for an activation program.

In a review of the literature, Granger and Wehman (1979) report that sensory stimulation has proved to have positive effects on extremely low functioning individuals, as it improves sensorimotor awareness. The literature also reveals interrelationships among sensory systems (e.g., auditory and tactile processes, auditory and gustatory stimulation), suggesting that a multisensory approach may be preferred. This section briefly reviews sensory activation, including visual and auditory attending, and the capability of accepting and responding to a variety of stimuli.

ASSESSMENT OF ACTIVATION LEVEL

Few standardized tools are available for in-depth assessment of these early behaviors, although many instruments include general items relating to skills, such as visual attending. Although visual and auditory skills such as acuity and discrimination should be evaluated by a trained professional (ophthalmologist for vision assessment, audiologist for hearing assessment), functional testing of these skills in the child's typical environments should also be done. It is important to gather specific information regarding how students use their skills in everyday settings. For example, although a formal vision evaluation may reveal intact sight, concomitant problems such as seizure activity and abnormal motor patterns can interfere with central or peripheral vision (Granger and Wehman, 1979). Two tools for functional vision assessment are *Guide for Functional Vision Assessment for Infants and Severely Handicapped Children* (Fieber, 1983), and *Functional Assessment of Visual Skills in Severely Handicapped Children* (Langley and DuBose, 1976). Suggested auditory assessment tools are *Hear-Kit System* (Downs, 1981); and *Auditory Assessment and Programming for Severely Handicapped Deaf-Blind Students* (Goetz, Utley, Gee, Baldwin, and Sailor, 1984). Each of these four assessment tools is described in Appendix A. A structured observation form standardized on a profoundly retarded population is the *Awareness, Manipulation, and Posture Scale* (AMP) developed by Webb (1971) and reprinted in part in Granger and Wehman (1979). The "awareness" portion investigates the level of avoidance (e.g., struggling when held tightly), approach (e.g., turning toward a hanging ball), and integrating memory with present stimuli (e.g., shifting attention from one toy to another). In addition to these tools, informal teacher observation forms can also be developed to examine specific behaviors of interest, such as visual attending or auditory attending.

INTERVENTION TO INCREASE ACTIVATION

Granger and Wehman (1979) stress that a preliminary goal must be *appropriate positioning* to allow the student the best possible interaction with the environment. This will be crucial for all of the following programs as well and will require input or direct assistance from occupational and physical therapists. For many severely disabled children, it may also be necessary to *decrease tactile sensitivity* before success is seen; however, this should be viewed as part of the adaptive play program, rather than as a separate prerequisite program. Granger and Wehman suggest that the backs of the hands and the forearms may be the least defensive areas, whereas the abdomen, chest, face, and feet are the most likely to evoke defensive reactions (turning away, grimacing, pushing stimulus away). The child's responses will indicate which stimuli and stimulus locations are offensive. Baker (1973) notes that touching oneself, either directly or indirectly, is a different neurological process from being touched by another. Therefore, the child may be helped to touch his or her own body as an early step in reducing tactile defensiveness. Including later tactile responses in the context of adaptive play, in which the child derives enjoyment from allowing touch sensation, will be helpful for students who are play- or socially oriented. For example, instead of the traditional approach of stroking the child with a variety of textures, puppets of various textures can be located or developed for interaction with the child, including stroking as one part of the interaction. Identifying parts of the body that are least defensive can also aid in programming. For example, tickling games are typically played at the abdomen, chest, or neck, all areas that may be highly offensive for many children; if this is so, less sensitive body parts can be tickled, or the child can be encouraged to "tickle" himself. Highly motivating methods may also help a tactily defensive child to initiate touching responses. An example would be to affix textured materials to a pressure switch so that the child is reinforced by a toy for touching various textures.

A number of traditional curricula include programs for visual and auditory attending. Chapter 9 presents ideas for making play materials both available and interesting, to promote visual attending and beginning motor responses. Introducing skills such as visual and auditory attending through adaptive play would mean that the enjoyment value is stressed, rather than a rote "look at me," followed by checking off 30 seconds on a stopwatch. For example, Ward (1979) suggests working on auditory attending and responding through music and play in the following manner:

- Move the sound in a *horizontal plane* at face level away from the child (in front, to side, behind, in curved or zig-zagged lines)
- Move the sound in a *vertical plane* in front of the child, gradually going from floor level to a very high level (by standing on a chair with arm raised)
- Change the *speed* at which the moving sound passes the child or moves in the directions indicated above
- Alter the *dynamic*, suddenly playing loud or soft, or making a gradual crescendo or diminuendo.

To introduce an element of play into this activity, Ward recommends including a commentary, describing what "he" (the musical instrument, such as a maraca) is doing ("He's coming to get you. Whoops — he's going away. He's going up. He's very quiet"). Alternatively, a puppet could manipulate the instruments, providing the commentary. Although the children will likely not understand the words, the tone and emotion of the language may be transmitted. It is also important to remember not to use a tone of voice that is immature with an older child. That is, although utterances should be short and simple, they should not be spoken as if talking to a baby, and babyish nicknames should be avoided.

The strategies suggested previously involve "passive stimulation," or "those things we do to the residents" (Active Stimulation Programming, 1984). Increasingly, intervention agents are exploring the possibilities of what Zuromski (Active Stimulation Programming, 1984) labels active stimulation programming. This involves the use of adaptive switches attached to reinforcers, such as battery-operated toys or tape recorders. This programming can involve in-depth assessment of the child's motor abilities and responses to various reinforcers (see Educational Technology Center, Inc., in Appendix B). Chapter 5 presents an overview of the use of switches in intervention, including activation.

Specific goals for an activation program may be pulled from one of the existing assessment tools or curricula that outline the initial steps in activating the child, including attending and responding to stimulation from all senses (e.g., Owens, 1982). The principles of adaptive play can be incorporated into the training objectives. Table 6–1 lists several factors to be considered in training visual activation, with suggestions for adaptive play applications. Following are additional ideas for incorporating adaptive play principles.

Focus on Interaction from the Beginning. Children with severe disabilities should be encouraged to focus on interaction with people (adults and peers) and objects even during this early activation training. For example, students should spend considerable time arranged in groupings that promote attending to each other, rather than being isolated in cribs or lined up in neat rows on mats. An awareness of objects must also be carefully programmed for children who have difficulty seeing, hearing, or touching objects as a result of sensory and motor impairments. Chapters 4 and 9 present numerous ideas for increasing access and stimulus strength of toys.

Table 6-1.   Considerations in Assessing and Training Visual Attending Skills

Stimulus: Developmentally, children respond first to light sources, and later to patterned stimuli such as faces	For high-risk children, begin in a dark area, using stimuli such as Christmas lights and blinking lights (e.g., pumpkin light); next use patterned stimuli such as puppets, focusing a light on the object if necessary; fade out focusing light and increase background lights
Distance: Both far-point and near-point visual attending should be taught	*Far point:* Play "I'm looking at . . .," focusing on a person across the room; when child locates target person, that person can call out, throw a kiss, make a similar response
	Near point: Use dangling toys with visually interesting patterns; place patterned stimuli within vision (e.g., paper plates with bright patterns)
Latency: Assess delay in looking, and reduce that delay if possible, as many real-life events are short-lasting	As the child's visual attending skills improve, make objects visible for increasingly shorter time periods (Ex: jack-in-the-box, toy peeks from behind barrier, then hides again)
Positioning: Conjugate gaze, with both eyes focused on the same point, is most likely if the head is well supported	Until the child develops conjugate gaze, provide head support and center head at midline; then work on developing visual attending in a variety of positions
Cue(s): These can be added:	
Vocal	Use intake of breath to cue child to look
Verbal	Use short cues (wow! look! Taylor!) with animation to prompt attending
Auditory	Begin with a noisy stimulus, then fade out
Gestural	Point to or shake stimulus
Physical	Position child's face so the stimulus is within vision

Replace Artificially Structured Tasks with Naturally Structured Tasks. For example, for visual attending, data can be taken while the subject is in the kitchen observing food preparation, rather than looking at the traditional set of three toys again and again. Auditory attending can be evaluated while the child has an opportunity to listen to something presumably interesting, such as other children on a playground, or environmental sounds tapes (if logistics prevent introducing actual children).

Telescope Goals. Allow opportunities for practice on reducing tactile defensiveness while performing routine care activities (diapering, feeding, changing clothes) using the materials appropriate to the task (clean paper, cloth diaper, bib or spoon, coat or socks) and rubbing them on target surfaces (forearm, hand), while describing what you are doing ("Time to eat. Here's your bib. Feel it?"). Another approach is to telescope activation goals with higher-level goals, using the "principle of partial participation." For example, the target activation goal of visual attending may be trained during an object exploration task, in which data are kept on the attending phase, and the child is helped to explore the object after each visual attending trial.

In summary, although activation is preliminary to other skills, training in other areas does not need to be postponed until the child reaches some arbitrary goal, such as maintaining eye contact with the trainer for 30 seconds following the command "look at me." Rather, activation can be seen as part of a total program, and can include both passive and active stimulation.

RESOURCES

Resources are increasingly becoming available for enhancing activation as treatment is expanded to help more severely impaired children. The following sources can provide additional information:

Books, Programs (see Appendix A). Bricker (1984); Downs (1981); Fieber (1983); Goetz et al. (1982); Granger and Wehman (1979); Langley and DuBose (1976); Owens (1982).

Organizations. Educational Technology Center, Inc.; The Association for Persons with Severe Handicaps.

Chapter 7

Tracking, Scanning, and Decision-Making

This chapter focuses primarily on strategies for assessing and training visual tracking and scanning skills. For children with severe visual impairments, the focus will need to be shifted to functional alternatives, such as auditory or tactile attending and scanning. The area of decision-making is also covered, as it relates to communicating needs and desires.

DESCRIPTION AND RATIONALE

The three areas of visual tracking, visual scanning, and decision-making are highly interrelated and have a major impact on the development of communication skills, as well as on skills in the domains of cognition, fine motor development, and social competence. Following is a brief description of each, with an explanation of its importance to normal development, and special concerns relative to children with disabilities.

Visual Tracking

This refers to the smooth visual pursuit of a moving object in a variety of paths. It can involve ocular pursuit (eyes follow object) or oculocephalic pursuit (head and eyes follow object). Visual tracking contributes to normal development by facilitating the acquisition of skills, such as object permanence (watching a rattle as it rolls behind a barrier, then into view) and social interaction (playing ball with a peer).

Children with disabilities may be at risk for developing good visual tracking skills as a result of motor or cognitive problems, or both. For example, a child with cerebral palsy may (1) be bound by abnormal reflexes that do not permit visual pursuit of moving objects; (2) have oculomotor problems such as strabismus (as in muscle imbalance); (3) demonstrate restricted head movements owing to poor head control; or (4) have reduced range of vision for tracking owing to interference from positioning (in a side-lying child) or equipment (head rests on an adaptive chair). However, visual tracking may be a more important skill for children with disabilities than for nondisabled children. For example, a child with limited movement skills, who spends a great portion of the day in static positions (prone standing, in a wheelchair, side-lying) will need to rely extensively on observation of the environment through visual and auditory tracking to gain stimulation. Promoting good visual tracking skills may enlarge the environment of children in such positions considerably.

VISUAL SCANNING

Visual scanning involves a visual search of parts of an object or the individual components of an array of objects (Scheuerman, Baumgart, Sipsma, and Brown, 1976). An early subskill to scanning is "shift of gaze," in which the individual shifts his or her eyes alternately between two items. Scanning is a preliminary skill to decision-making, as it allows the person to view each choice separately. It also contributes importantly to the development of such skills as differential object use (scanning an object for features that discriminate it and suggest possible uses); self-help skills (scanning the plate to see where food has been left); and social competence (scanning a partner's face to determine the response to a situation).

Fieber (1983) notes that children who do not scan without cuing will be "stimulus controlled." They will have difficulty in attending to stimuli that are relevant to a situation (form, size), and will be caught by salient stimuli, such as bright colors. In addition to its importance in normal development, visual scanning can be an extremely important skill for nonspeaking children, who can use it as a tool to access communication entries. For example, many electronic communication devices use visual scanning as a means to indicate messages. On a more simple level, the child who wants to send a message via a communication display (e.g., a word or picture board) must be able to scan the board visually to locate the target entry. Thus, children with severe physical disabilities may have a greater need than nondisabled children to develop good visual scanning skills.

Decision-Making

Decision-making refers to the ability to make choices, and to make those choices known in a method that is understandable to others, such as eye-gazing, reaching, pointing, vocalizing, or verbalizing. Clearly decision-making is a crucial skill in normal development, as it allows the child to assert independence and gain some control over the environment. The ability to make decisions and have them understood will cut across all areas of development, such as communication (requesting desired objects or events); social competence (deciding what game to play, developing rules); and fine motor development (choosing toys to play with).

Children with moderate to severe disabilities will typically be more dependent on adults for basic wants and needs. For example, they may be dressed, fed, and toileted with minimal input requested or allowed. Thus, learned helplessness may develop, in which the child learns to expect dependency and does not try to exert control over the environment. This is an especially serious problem for children who do not have the verbal skills to make their wants and needs known. Thus, decision-making skills may also be of greater importance for children with special needs than for their peers without disabilities.

ASSESSMENT ISSUES

Assessment tools for young children typically include one item for assessing each of these skills, although decision-making may often be omitted. The two functional vision assessment tools described in Chapter 6 can yield a more careful examination of a child's visual tracking and scanning skills. For example, the screening tool presented by Langley and DuBose (1976) includes procedures for evaluating a child's tracking and scanning of both lights and objects in a variety of paths of movement.

With regard to assessment of decision-making, a program by Porter and colleagues (1985) presents assessment questions and specific assessment procedures for skills leading to decision-making, with Step 5 examining the child's ability to use a signal to indicate a choice between two objects or events (see discussion on decision-making later in this chapter for all steps). Assessing each of these subareas can indicate where the child has difficulty in indicating choices and can determine the point at which intervention should begin.

INTERVENTION ISSUES AND IDEAS

This section is not an attempt to present a curriculum for development of visual tracking, scanning, and decision-making skills, as others have completed that task. Rather, ideas are presented for incorporating adaptive play into training on these areas.

Visual Tracking

Following a review of the literature, Musselwhite and St. Louis (1982) identified seven factors that should be considered during assessment and training of visual tracking skills. These seven areas are summarized in Table 7–1, with the addition of ideas for using play materials and adaptive play strategies in the assessment and intervention process. For optimal generalization, it is recommended that these factors be systematically manipulated during training.

Scheuerman and colleagues (1976) present a naturalized curriculum for teaching visual tracking, in which training takes place throughout the day across a variety of settings. This avoids the problem of presenting massed trials, with the likelihood that the child will become bored or overstimulated. The adaptive play ideas in Table 7–1 are also naturally structured, based on the assumption that enjoyable activities are more likely to create a desire to participate. Although it may be necessary to include some artificially structured training to offer sufficient trials, attempts should be made to normalize training, so that activities do not become rote. One way to do this is to telescope visual tracking trials into other tasks, such as the following.

Fine Motor Development. While working on the task of object placement, the adult can model placing a miniature person into a play vehicle, by marching the person to the vehicle, having the person "run" to the vehicle, and so forth. Thus, the focus is on

Table 7-1.   Considerations in Assessing and Teaching Visual Tracking Skills

Consideration	Sample Adaptive Play Applications
Stimulus: Size, color, pattern, and complexity (e.g., presence of moving parts) may affect learning	Use a wide variety of play materials rather than reusing a small set of toys Include two or more exemplars of each characteristic listed (e.g., color)
Location: Distance may be within reach or out of reach	Manipulate objects within reach, letting child play with each after tracking it After child watches event out of reach (children sliding), move child to event
The level relative to the child's eyes should be considered (above, below, and at eye level)	Provide opportunities for tracking at all levels: above (toy moving along string); at eye level (paper airplane flying); below (puppet marching across laptray)
Range: This can vary from a few degrees to 180 degrees Crossing midline is difficult for some students	The trainer may need to manipulate the extent of range directly When first crossing midline, choose slow-moving objects or events
Cue(s): Vocal Verbal Auditory Gestural	 Use rising pitch as toy goes up ("Oooo") Should be relevant or fun: "There it goes!" Use a noisemaker (maraca) as the stimulus Use nonlinguistic cues (point, open mouth)
Speed: A range is possible: Slow Medium Fast Supersonic	 Wind-up "walking feet" Battery-powered "attack" vehicle Push-n-Go vehicles Penny racers
Path: Potential paths include horizontal, vertical, diagonal, circular, and random	Some battery-powered vehicles (Radio Shack Police Car) come with template to alter path of movement
Barriers: Transparent Translucent Opaque	 Roll marbles in box with vinyl lid Walk animal behind filmy scarf "curtain" Roll ball into box with lid

Adapted from Musselwhite and St. Louis (1982); Robinson and Robinson (1978); and Scheuerman et al. (1976).

the movement toward the target vehicle, as well as on the act of putting the person in the vehicle.

Communication. While working on turntaking with objects, the adult can produce an action that involves movement (dumping a toy out of a dump truck into a box), while sitting next to the child and focusing attention on the movement.

Social Competence. Activities can focus on interactions that require visual tracking. For example, one child can blow a bubble and the partner can follow it, then pop it.

Visual tracking opportunities can also be built into routine caregiving events for children with severe disabilities. For example, when dressing a child, the adult can pause, direct the child's attention, and cue if necessary before assisting the child in pulling a zipper up or down. Similarly, before putting powder on an infant during diapering, the caregiver can build up expectation ("Here it comes!"), then can move the powder canister in an arc, ending with it upside down in position for pouring. As noted in Chapter 3 both telescoping goals and creating naturally structured activities should not be left to chance, but should be predetermined to that opportunities will not be missed.

Visual Scanning

Some children with special needs may need to be taught to shift gaze from one item to another and to scan component parts of an item, whereas others may also need to be taught scanning responses specific for augmentative communication. Although these skills are related, they differ greatly in complexity and function, so they will be discussed separately.

General Scanning Skills

During assessment, the trainer should note whether the child scans and shifts gaze spontaneously or if it is necessary for the adult to provide cues, such as (1) movement (wiggling each item in turn); (2) sound (noisemaker); (3) gesture (pointing to target item); (4) verbalization ("Look here"). The level of cuing should be recorded, and used as necessary in initial training. This cuing should be faded as soon as possible.

The program by Scheuerman and colleagues (1976) offers a naturalized approach to teaching children to scan for relevant features of items or events in the environment. Whenever possible, trials should appear natural and relevant to the situation. This skill can also be introduced and practiced in conjunction with other goals:

1. *Preacademic skills:* An early book can have all pages blank except one. The task will involve helping the child scan for the picture.

2. *Cognitive development:* In working on object permanence, allow a vehicle to roll behind a barrier then out, and encourage the child to scan the environment until it is located.
3. *Fine motor development:* Attach an adaptive switch to one of two battery toys. Have the child operate the switch and scan to see which of the toys is activated (Burkhart, 1982).
4. *Music:* Prepare a song strip with two symbols representing key words from a very simple, repetitive song (e.g., HELP me PUSH, HELP me PUSH, HELP me PUSH right now," with key words in capitals). Assist the child in scanning by indicating where to gaze or point.

Scanning in Augmentative Communication

In augmentative communication, scanning can be used as a process, referring to the individual's action in looking at all entries on a communication display to locate the target entry. This can be initiated through adaptive play, with the child helped to scan an array of objects presented in some manner, such as (1) on a choice board (a tilted board with up to four items displayed in vinyl bags; see Developmental Equipment, Appendix C); (2) on a playboard (a flat board with items bolted on; see Carlson, 1982, Appendix A); or (3) on an object-based communication board (adjoined "boxes" with objects placed on shelves or attached to hooks; see Porter et al., 1985, Appendix A). Figure 7–1 depicts those three arrangements. Initially, only one location will contain an item, with the child assisted to find the item (scanning for presence versus absence). As items are added, the child will be reinforced in some manner merely for scanning all items in the array. To achieve functional responses, it may be necessary to combine this training with decision-making, so that the child can receive the natural consequence of choosing.

Scanning can also be used as a technique for indicating desired message elements. In this context, scanning involves selecting message elements through signaling with a prearranged signal or switch. Adaptive play strategies for introducing or enhancing scanning as a means of indicating are presented in Chapter 11.

Decision-Making

Porter and colleagues (1985) have developed a program for assessing and training prerequisites to augmentative communi-

CHOICE BOARD

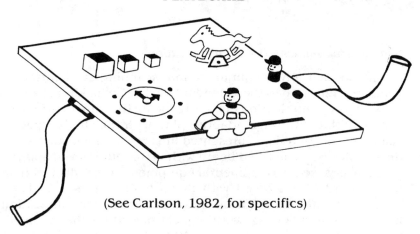

(Available from Developmental Equipment)

PLAYBOARD

(See Carlson, 1982, for specifics)

OBJECT-BASED COMMUNICATION BOARD

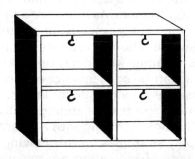

(See Porter et al., 1985, p. 27)

Figure 7-1. Sample arrangements for teaching visual scanning skills.

cation. The first five steps of that program teach the ultimate skill, decision-making: (1) the child must have preferences; (2) it must be possible to reinforce by objects or events that can be represented by objects or pictures, or both; (3) the child must have at least one signal or mode of indication; (4) the child must use a signal to indicate a desire for an object or event; and (5) the child must use a signal to indicate a choice between two objects or events. They stress the importance of proper positioning and suggest possible signals, such as looking, reaching for, or pointing at items. Specific training procedures and criteria are presented for each step, and the remaining three steps extend the decision-making to a choice between four objects, two pictures, and three pictures, respectively.

Once the child begins to make decisions, the primary concern is to increase the opportunities for making choices. In short, decision-making must be a normal part of everyday life. The intervention agent has the role of raising the consciousness of all persons who interact with a child regarding the need to provide suitable occasions for making choices. It should be stressed that, initially, the child may not make a definite choice; however, giving the child an item following an approximation of a response will allow the child to learn the natural consequences of decision-making. For example, looking at a puppet could result in a tickle (from the puppet), while looking at a wet washcloth could yield a cold face-washing. Follow-up may be increased by suggesting specific opportunities for decision-making during activities that occur frequently. Examples of such opportunities follow.

Dressing. As any parent knows, a typical nondisabled child past the age of 2 years will not allow the parent to make all clothing selections; children with disabilities should have the same opportunity to wear mismatched clothes! This can be accomplished by holding up two items (shirts, belts) and asking the child to choose one.

Feeding. The "five bite rule" can be used, meaning that at least five bites during a meal or a snack must be selected by the child. This can be a choice between a sip of drink and a bite of food, or a choice between two types of food, held in two separate spoons (see Williams and Fox, 1977, for further ideas).

Playing Independently. It is not uncommon for an adult to offer a child a toy for independent use; at such times, two toys should be presented, with the child given the one he or she indicates.

Outdoor Play. A child can be offered a choice of swings, play vehicles, or play activities (slide versus merry-go-round).

Therapy Activities. In some cases, activities can be symbolized, with the child selecting the first activity. For example, in physical therapy, a child might choose between exercises on a large ball or on a scooterboard.

In summary, all three of the skills described in this chapter can be integrated into the total program and telescoped with other goals. The key is to involve a wide range of settings and people. For example, each of the ideas for promoting decision making must be shared with all people who interact with the child; in this way, the child can learn that he or she can exert some control in many different situations, with a variety of people.

RESOURCES

Books and Articles (see Appendix A). *Assessment:* Fieber (1983); Langley and DuBose (1976); Porter et al. (1985); Scheuerman et al. (1976). *Intervention:* Porter et al. (1985); Scheuerman et al. (1976).

Chapter 8

Early Social and Communicative Interaction

A common concern regarding developmentally disabled individuals is that, although they acquire self-help, language, motor, and basic vocational skills, these are often not performed acceptably in vocational, home, or recreational settings due to inadequate social skills (Williams, Hamre-Nietupski, Pumpian, Marx, and Wheeler, 1978). In addition, recent research suggests that, although early childhood special education can yield durable progress in cognitive and motor skills, comparable progress may not be achieved in the social domain (Fredericks, Moore, and Baldwin, 1982). These failures typically involve both social interactions and engagement in appropriate isolative activities. For example, Niziol and DeBlassie (1972) reviewed research on the vocational adjustment of educable mentally retarded adolescents and noted that the majority of maladjustments in work were attributable to poor interpersonal skills. Foss and Peterson (1981) identified social-interpersonal behavior areas most relevant to job tenure for mentally retarded adults through a questionnaire sent to job placement personnel in sheltered workshops. They reported that three of the four areas rated most relevant directly concerned the supervisor-worker relationship (following supervisor instructions, responding appropriately to supervisor criticism or correction, and working independently of direct supervision). Although these findings refer primarily to the developmentally disabled, other individuals with special needs are also at risk for development of optimal early interactive skills. For example, physically disabled children may not have the movement skills to approach their peers, severely hearing impaired children may miss verbal requests to interact, and blind children will miss visual cues such as facial expressions.

SOCIAL COMPETENCE: GENERAL ISSUES

There is an extensive and growing body of information on the development, assessment, and training of social competence in children with disabilities. This chapter focuses only on strategies to promote early social and communicative interaction through adaptive play. A current model of social competence is presented by Bailey and Simeonsson (1985), and an approach to performance-based assessment of social competence is available in Odom and McConnell (1985). For a comprehensive textbook presenting recent findings on social development in children with special needs, the reader is referred to Schloss (1984).

Knowing the determinants of social competence in preschool children with special needs can also provide a framework for intervention. Strain (1985) reports on a naturalistic study of 72 severely disabled 2 to 5 year old children, half of whom were judged more highly rated sociometrically (by nondisabled peers) than the other half. Direct observation was made of social behavior, and ratings of nonsocial skills and attributes were determined. The higher sociometrically rated children engaged in more of these positive behaviors: (1) play organizer (e.g., "Let's play ball"); (2) sharing; (3) showing affection through patting, hugging, kissing, or hand-holding; (4) assistance (physically helping partner); and (5) responding to social initiations. they also showed fewer negative acts than their lower-rated peers: (1) motor-gestural acts such as hitting or pulling; and (2) vocal-verbal acts such as screaming or whining. The higher-rated children were also evaluated more positively by their teachers on measures of physical attractiveness, athletic skill, toy play skill, and level of disruption. Interestingly, these social skills and nonsocial attributes contributed equally to the prediction of higher sociometric status. Thus, social training alone cannot be expected to yield optimal results. However, note that, except for physical attractiveness, the nonsocial attributes (e.g., toy play skill) can be taught. While it has not been proved conclusively that the social skills and nonsocial attributes will enhance social competence, they are reasonable targets for both research and intervention and will be explored further in this chapter.

GENERAL STRATEGIES FOR PROMOTING INTERACTION

Research suggests that mere proximity of disabled and non-disabled children will not ensure interaction (Gresham, 1981;

Karnes and Lee, 1979). Teacher intervention in the form of structuring play situations may be necessary to enhance integration (Brophy and Stone-Zukowski, 1984; Devony, Guralnick, and Rubin, 1974). Williams and colleagues (1978) suggest that social activities involving extensive interaction (associative and cooperative activities) include at least five basic components:

1. *Recognizing the appropriate time and place for a social interaction.* For example, a developmentally disabled adolescent may attempt to begin a social interaction while the potential partner is busy working or talking to another. This student may need to learn to recognize when it is break-time, an appropriate time to initiate an interaction.

2. *Initiating an interaction.* Disabled children may not initiate interactions at all, or may need to be taught socially acceptable ways of beginning an interaction, such as vocalizing or gently patting the partner, rather than screaming or tugging.

3. *Receiving requests for interactions.* The recipient must first decide whether he or she wants to and is able to engage in the activity. Then he or she must accept or decline the invitation. For nonverbal individuals, this may consist of vocalizations of assent or head shaking.

4. *Sustaining interactions.* The student should be able to maintain participation for an acceptable amount of time, depending on the activity. For example, a simple turntaking game such as pushing blocks back and forth might last for several turns, whereas a structured card game is typically continued until it is completed.

5. *Terminating interactions.* The participants must determine that an activity is over (or that they want it to be over) and must indicate that it is finished and complete necessary tasks, such as putting away cards and acknowledging a closing ("Bye. See you later.").

The five areas listed are targets for disabled children to work toward. Adaptive play can provide a format for teaching these skills to children who are chronologically or cognitively young, as illustrated in Table 8–1. The following sections suggest early social interaction goals that can be trained through adaptive play activities.

Table 8-1. Ideas for Introducing Interaction Skills Through Adaptive Play

Social Skill	Adaptive Play Training Strategy
Recognizing Time and Place for Interaction	Role-play, using peers, puppets, or dolls who give signals (e.g., head down, engaged in task, versus smiling at child) to indicate appropriateness of interaction. Partner should also provide verbal feedback ("I'm busy now" or "Yes, I can play now")
Initiating an Interaction	Set up an inviting play situation (tea party, new set of blocks), encourage one child to approach the situation and help him or her to request a peer to join by modeling initiating behavior at appropriate level (looking, reaching, gesturing, vocalizing, verbalizing); prompt initiations if necessary
Receiving Requests	Teach peer to initiate request (e.g., point to adaptive switch, look at child, vocalize) and help child respond by accepting (head nod, vocalization, move to switch) or declining (head shake, pushing object or person away, vocalizing "no"); it may be necessary initially to interpret the situation ("Stacy has fireman! Wanna play? Tell her")
Sustaining Interaction	Offer play situations appropriate to the skill level and interests of both participants (e.g., computer game with two switches; dollhouse with weighted stand-up puppets attached to children's wrists)
Terminating Interaction	Model appropriate terminating behaviors via trained peer, puppet, or doll; for example, model closes door of play farm and says "bye-bye, animals," and wheels chair away; appropriate prompts can be used with target child as necessary

For ideas on adapting social skills using vocal and nonvocal means, see Williams et al. (1978, p. 284).

Joint Activity

Joint activity is one that is physically shared by two persons (typically the child and a significant other). As MacDonald and Gillette note, "communicative match requires a shared frame of reference, or joint action" (1984a, p. 1). They suggest several strategies to encourage a child to maintain a child's attention and engage him or her in a joint activity.

First, it is recommended that the adult *follow the child's lead.* In this way, learning interactions can be built on any child action. Clearly, a sense of balance must be maintained to require the child to enter the adult's world. One rule to ensure this balance is "Follow the child's lead until joint activity routines are developed, then begin to teach the child to follow your lead" (MacDonald and Gillette, 1984a, p. 3). An example of this strategy in an adaptive play context would be to suspend a toy from a string for a physically disabled child. The adult would follow the child's lead in batting, grasping, or otherwise interacting with the toy until both are engaged in the joint activity; then the adult would begin to teach the child to follow his or her lead (e.g., push and stop the toy).

A second recommendation is to *structure for give-and-take.* MacDonald and Gillette (1984a) note that "interaction" with disabled children often follows a "give, give" routine, in which the child is talked at and given to. Strategies that can promote the child's giving in order to get are (1) positioning for optimal eye contact — the adult should not be in a large chair while the child is seated in a small one; (2) holding the child for interaction — physical contact may encourage more give-and-take activities; and (3) selecting objects that yield to back-and-forth actions, such as balls. The delay procedure, presented in Chapter 3 (Table 3–5), can be extremely useful in encouraging give-and-take exchanges, with the adult looking expectant and allowing sufficient pause time for the child to interact.

A third suggestion is to *be animated.* Two cautions should be noted: the adult must change animation to maintain interest and must not overstimulate the child, causing him or her to move away or be startled. Animation can be added through methods such as smiling, exaggerated eye movements, touching the child in a variety of ways during interactions, adding sounds and noises (humming, imitating objects, and causing objects to produce sounds), altering body movements (snapping fingers or leaning forward), moving around, and miming the activities that are discussed.

The fourth strategy suggested by MacDonald and Gillette for enhancing joint activity is to *imitate,* or *be childlike.* The assumption is that a child is more likely to respond to familiar stimuli, such as his or her own actions. In addition, this imitation of the child may result in the child's imitation of the adult.

Each of the above-mentioned strategies can be used in adaptive play contexts with few modifications. Any toys used must be selected carefully to allow for motor, sensory, or cognitive disabilities. For example, a physically disabled child may be more successful if toys are placed on a tray so that they will not be knocked out of reach. Once joint activity routines have been established and child and adult are participating to the extent possible, the focus can be shifted to turntaking.

Turntaking with Actions and Communication

MacDonald and Gillette define a turn as "any behavior that is either directly responding to another person or is initiating contact with the person. It may or may not be communicative and it may take sensorimotor or linguistic form" (1984a, p. 7). Manolson (1984) and MacDonald and Gillette (1984a) offer excellent programs for teaching parents and other caregivers to facilitate turntaking with actions and objects. They note that turntaking is a crucial prerequisite for communicative interaction; without well-developed turntaking skills, children will become passive receivers. MacDonald and Gillette assert that "Parents may keep giving out of love, but the strangers the child needs to live and learn with may give him only to the extent that he gives back" (1984b, p.8).

Nonspeaking children are especially at risk for developing good turntaking skills. For example, Yoder and Kraat (1983) reviewed several studies on interaction between communication display users and other persons, and reported that nonspeakers have fewer opportunities to communicate, communicate less frequently, and are allowed only one utterance per turn. Thus, these nonspeakers either were given fewer turns or did not claim turns; when they were given turns, these turns were very brief.

MacDonald and Gillette (1984a) note that the turn is a unit that allows communication to develop from noninteractive to interactive behavior and then from nonlinguistic to linguistic communicative behavior. Interaction through turntaking is an excellent goal for an adaptive play program. MacDonald and Gillette (1984a,b,c) describe intervention procedures for turntaking with actions and with communication, including targets (e.g., increasing turntaking length), potential problems (e.g., turn dominance by adult), and training strategies (e.g., imitate action turns). Table 8–2 presents strategies for turntaking with actions, including samples of related adaptive play tasks.

Early Peer Interaction

The previous sections have been concerned with promoting interactions between disabled children and their significant

Table 8-2. Turntaking with Actions: Adaptive Play Tasks

Materials	Task
Small fun toys (e.g., wind-ups, bubbles); wrap tissue paper around one toy, then place another toy on top and wrap another sheet around both toys; continue until there are as many toys as there are children	One child takes the wrapped packet, unwraps the top toy, uses it briefly, then passes the packet on to the next child, who repeats the process (Jeffree et al., 1977)
Object-in-the-can switch (see Burkhart, 1982); battery-operated toy attached to switch; several objects to drop in the can (artificial fruit, colored blocks)	Set the switch so that it will not activate until several objects are dropped in; each child puts an object in, then pauses to see if the toy is activated
Large mailing tube, or tube from wrapping paper; string; assorted small toys	Suspend tube with string; seat one child at each end of tube and have them send toys back and forth
Tennis ball pass-through (see McLean et al., 1981, for instructions)	Similar to tube pass-through task, except that partners do not need to problem-solve the task of lifting the end of the tube to send the toy
Fine motor toys with repeated opportunity for action: simple puzzles with knobs bus or boat with room for peg "people" stacking rings	Partners take turns inserting, stacking, etc., until task is completed; materials may need to be adapted as suggested in Chapter 4

others, such as parents, teachers, and other caregivers. It is also extremely important to increase appropriate peer interactions from an early age, rather than waiting until children are older. This includes interactions between disabled children and between disabled and nondisabled children. For example, Harris (1982) reported that nonspeaking students (ages 6 to 7) rarely interacted with their nonspeaking peers. A questionnaire sent to job placement personnel in sheltered workshops revealed that a major concern relating to job tenure in workshop settings was the worker's appropriate interactions with co-workers while on the job (Foss and Peterson, 1981).

Disabled children may also have problems interacting with their nondisabled peers. As mentioned previously, merely integrating children does not ensure interaction; training and teacher intervention may be necessary to promote interaction. Jeffree and colleagues (1977) offer these suggestions for enhancing peer interaction: (1) the child should practice an activity with parents (or teachers) first; (2) adults should be as "tough" as other children will be (e.g., do not accept the negative behaviors, hitting, whining, that peers will reject); (3) ideally, the activity should require two people, so that one person cannot succeed alone; and (4) both children should be active all the time. For children with severe physical disabilities, optimal positioning is a crucial consideration, as the child may not be able to move toward other children, or even to turn his or her head to look at a child seated directly to the side. Advance planning can reduce this barrier, as suggested in Table 8-2. Wehman (1977a) reviewed the literature on teaching cooperative play and social interactions to severely disabled individuals and suggested the following general strategies:

- Pair a child with an adult trainer; teach in a variety of play situations
- Pair a child with a higher functioning, developmentally disabled peer who does engage in appropriate play
- Pair a child with a nondisabled peer who engages in appropriate play
- Pair two equivalent (disabled) peers; have one or more trainers provide training
- Integrate a group of severely disabled children with nondisabled peers
- Use any of the foregoing combinations, giving various types of reinforcement, such as edibles, points, or praise for instances of cooperative play
- Manipulate the environment before play sessions by selecting toys, room size, or background music to promote cooperative play

(Wehman, 1977b, p. 26)

One common theme from literature reviews is that interaction cannot be expected between children with disabilities and their disabled or nondisabled peers without some intervention from adults. Strain and Kerr (1979) suggest that this intervention can come in two forms: (1) teacher prompting of the isolate child, plus social reinforcement of appropriate responses; or (2) prompting or training peers to initiate interactions. Research by van den Pol, Crow, Rider, and Offner (1985) indicated that teacher aides were able to arrange the play environment to enhance social interaction when given instructions (to "get handi-

Table 8-3.   Early Peer Interaction Strategies

General Strategy	Sample Activities
Facilitate peer-peer play for traditional early childhood games; ideally, facilitators should be from various disciplines (PT, OT, SLP, SpEd), as this is an excellent opportunity for demonstrating potential training opportunities (Ex., PT: show optimal positioning to increase trunk extension; SLP: show ways to incorporate sound production into tasks)	Peek-a-Boo: Adult can sit behind one child and prompt each to hide the partner (e.g., with a blanket), to pull the blanket off at the appropriate time, and to point to the "discovered" partner Pair-Up Patty-Cake: Adults can encourage children to pat each other's hands, rather than playing with an adult Tickling: Adults can show child that he or she can tickle a friend and request tickles vocally, verbally, or gesturally
Develop enticing play areas, similar to learning centers used for preschool children without disabilities; toys or location can be altered to provide optimum opportunity for children to use toys together	Wall of Toys: Affix objects to wall in a corner Hide-Out: Set a large box on its side and outfit it with toys dangling from roof, hanging on walls, a variety of surfaces; place two children at box entrance Activity Frame: Attach novel items to activity frame and place one child on each side (e.g., in TumbleForm Chairs) Playboard: Place one playboard between two students (e.g., side-lying)
Devise adapted games suitable for children with moderate physical disabilities	Pull-Apart: Cut two lengths of dowel or broomstick; place small toys or Cheerios in plastic tubing that fits loosely over sticks, joining them together; when children pull from ends, toys or Cheerios will fall out (Jeffree et al., 1977) Push-It-Down: Have one child sit at the top of a slide and push toys down to a peer at the bottom; preferably, the peer should request specific toys, after sender has listed his or her "wares"
Develop adapted games suitable for children with severe physical disabilities	Stack 'n' Knock: Stack toys up in a very unbalanced tower (include noise makers) and have children knock them down Race-Car Crash: Have children activate switch causing battery-operated car to knock down pile of toys or blocks Send-It-Over: Attach small toys to roof of battery-operated vehicle; have one child use a switch to send toy to a partner

capped and nonhandicapped kids involved in common activities and prevent playing alone by prompting toy play and group participation"), and provided feedback on the social interaction of students. This strategy of instruction plus child-focused feedback to paraprofessionals may be a very realistic one for classroom application. Strain and Kerr (1979) review several additional studies, suggesting that, although teacher prompting (e.g., "Go play with your friends," "You can play house together") can increase social interaction, this prompting must be faded gradually, based on the child's interaction behaviors, to achieve lasting change. With regard to peer training, Strain and Kerr note that the peer must be taught to expect that some of their initiations will be rejected by the isolate child; thus, the importance of repeating attempts to play must be emphasized. Table 8–3 suggests specific settings, toys, and events that can facilitate early peer interactions. Strategies using puppets or dolls with disabilities are elaborated in the following paragraph.

Anecdotal evidence (Heekin and Mengel, 1983a; Musselwhite, 1983) suggests that dolls with disabilities, such as the New Friends dolls, can also enhance social interactions between disabled and nondisabled children, through peer modeling. The dolls can model appropriate interactive behaviors and can also serve as a "magnet," drawing nondisabled children to disabled children. Presumably, puppets — especially puppets with disabilities — can perform the same function (e.g., I.D. Kids, Bodi-Puppets from the Super Sense Kits; see Chapter 15). Adults can manipulate puppets or dolls to have them interact with special needs children while nondisabled children are in a position to observe. For example, a doll or puppet can join a physically disabled child in a tea party at a small table; leaving one or two seats open can entice nondisabled children to join the activity, at which point the teacher can gradually fade out of the situation. This procedure can incorporate several of the suggestions given by Wehman (1977a), such as manipulating the environment and including disabled and nondisabled children in a variety of activities.

To summarize, Strain and Kerr (1979) assert that "Social isolation represents a pattern of behavior that cuts across most, if not all, categories of exceptionality" (p. 197). This social isolation is certainly not conducive to developing optimal communicative interaction skills. However, research suggests that interaction can be facilitated through strategies such as those presented in this chapter.

Chapter **9**

Object Interaction Skills

The previous chapters were concerned with developing interactive skills with people through adaptive play. The present chapter will cover strategies for enhancing a variety of object interaction skills in the context of adaptive play. Early sensorimotor training involving objects (e.g., means-ends, object relations in space) can be introduced simultaneously, following assessment (e.g., Dunst, 1980; Uzgaris and Hunt, 1975), and using appropriate training items (e.g., Dunst, 1981).

The first stage of object interaction is activation, discussed previously. The child who is activated to attend and respond to toys and other objects through use of the senses will be ready to engage in higher-level object interactions. Three additional stages of object interaction will be covered: exploratory play, conventional object use, and manipulative or constructive play.

EXPLORATORY PLAY

Description and Rationale

Exploratory play is an extremely important component of an adaptive play program as it allows children to learn a variety of different schemes for interacting with objects and an opportunity to practice a variety of fine motor patterns. Miller (1984) notes that the sequences of play schema development and fine motor development in normal infants appear to interact. For example, the development of controlled release of objects (involving voluntary control of wrist extension and finger flexion and extension) is seen in the "letting go" play schema, in which objects are repeatedly placed into containers. Exploratory play offers the chance to learn or practice both the fine motor skills and the play schemas while learning about the properties of various objects. Early communicative interaction goals, such as developing joint activity, can be practiced simultaneously. Exploratory play also allows the child to further develop the control initiated in the activation stage.

Wehman (1979c) describes four substages of development in exploratory play: (1) orientational responses (included here under activation); (2) locomotor exploration; (3) investigatory exploration; and (4) searching behavior (the search for new stimuli and situations, allowing a repetition of the exploratory substages). Many children with severe disabilities do not develop all of these exploratory behaviors naturally. For example, severely physically disabled children may be unable to engage in locomotor exploration, and severely cognitively delayed children may fail to investigate objects, or may end the object interaction without searching for new stimuli. Thus, intervention will be necessary to enable many children to productively explore objects.

Assessment of Exploratory Play

Most play scales (e.g., Lowe, 1975; Lowe and Costello, 1976; Nicholich, 1977; Westby, 1980) begin at the level of conventional object use or symbolic play. However, several parameters for examining early play behavior are suggested in the literature. Table 9–1 presents a summary of factors that can be considered in an observation of exploratory play. This can be accomplished in a checklist format, or via quantitative data, depending on the information needed and the time available for assessment. The manipulations noted are those identified through task analysis as manipulations used in a wide range of fine motor tasks across all skill domains (Musselwhite and Thompson, 1979). Therefore, they are generic manipulations that will allow children success in exploring and later using objects.

Strategies for Enhancing Exploratory Play

Several factors can influence the initiation and continuation of exploratory play. Features inherent in the toy can encourage or discourage interaction. For example, Bambara and colleagues (1984) found that reactive toys influenced their severely handicapped subjects to engage in manipulative activity for a substantially longer amount of time. In Chapter 4 it is suggested that a variety of general features may enhance types of play, including exploratory play.

Table 9–1. Factors to Consider in Assessing Exploratory Play

Toy	Self-Initiated?	Duration	Manipulations*	Appropriate?	Comments

Instructions:

Present toys in sets of four, listing toys in the left column; scatter toys to determine child's movement and searching behaviors. Summary information will include data or statements on the following information:

Toy Preference: Independence of Play:
Average Duration: Range of Manipulations:
Appropriateness of Play:

*Code: L, lift; Sh, shake; Sq, squeeze; Pl, pull; Ps, push; Ro, rotate; Sl, slide; T, throw; Re, repeat.
For further assessment ideas, see Wehman (1979c).

For severely physically disabled children, toy access is an important consideration relative to promoting exploration of objects. Chapter 4 also presents suggestions for increasing access to toys through strategies such as placing toys on trays; providing the child with a Velcro "mitt" to allow access to toys with Velcro strips; attaching toys to playboards; suspending objects from Activity Frames; and affixing toys to surfaces such as walls. Riddick (1982) offers numerous additional ideas, such as using roly-poly toys with weighted bases, which will not roll out of the child's reach. Items can also be attached to quilts by means of small Velcro loops for the child who spends a portion of the day lying on the floor.

The factors considered in the exploratory play assessment (Table 9–1) can also be targets for intervention. Sample adaptive play goals related to those factors are the following:

Increasing the Duration of Play. Wehman (1979b) suggests that the common problem of lack of sustained play can be remedied through more frequent and structured reinforcement of desired play goals. For example, a physically disabled child could be given reinforcement such as music for continuing to wear, look at, and make attempts to manipulate a puppet bracelet for a predetermined length of time. Jeffree and colleagues (1977) note that preferred "toys" for young children are items from Mom's purse. They theorize that this is because Mom "plays" with those items, thus setting up a model and making them appear desirable. One implication is that adults should use children's toys in a playful manner.

Encouraging a Diversity of Manipulations. Children can be encouraged to interact with objects using a variety of different play schemas, rather than being limited to one schema, such as mouthing, or using objects stereotypically, such as banging. This transition from sensorimotor exploration (acting in the same way on all objects) to differential object use is crucial. Traditional prompting procedures (verbal prompt, model, partial or full physical assists) can be used to introduce varied manipulations. To teach generic use of these manipulations, each should be taught in relation to several objects (shaking either a bell or rattle); in addition, it is helpful to demonstrate that a single object can be used differentially (e.g., a rattle may be used for banging or shaking). Lear (1977) provides numerous suggestions for interacting with play materials in a variety of ways through the senses (sight, hearing, touch, taste, and smell).

Increasing Range of Toys Manipulated. Wehman (1979b) notes that interaction with only one toy may lead to satiation with the toy and restrict the range of fine motor actions developed. Wehman recommends the following strategies to increase the range of play materials: (1) use the Premack Principle, in which the preferred toy is removed and others are offered; if the child manipulates them briefly (e.g., for 2 minutes), the preferred toy is returned; (2) remove the preferred toy and introduce toys with similar stimulus characteristics (size, color, reactivity, action required) to those of the preferred toy; (3) remove the preferred toy completely during play time and demonstrate manipulations on totally new toys.

Reducing Dependence on Prompts from Others. Williams, Brown, and Certo (1975) note that severely disabled students are often referred to as "externally controlled" because they rely on prompts and cues from caregivers. If the assessment indicates that students succeed in exploratory play only with direct prompting from persons in authority (parents, teachers), these cues should be faded out systematically; in this way children can begin to learn internal control, even at this early stage of adaptive play.

CONVENTIONAL OBJECT USE

Description and Rationale

This stage is also termed functional object use and appropriate play. Sample behaviors at this level are hugging or patting a doll, bringing a spoon to the mouth to eat, and bouncing or rolling a ball. Lyon, Baumgart, Stoll, and Brown (1977) suggest that severely disabled students need to be taught basic functional object use skills: (1) to develop or improve independent functioning; (2) to allow students access to less restrictive developmental environments; and (3) to promote the development of vocational and community living skills. In addition, research has demonstrated that appropriate object use skills in for the form of appropriate play can reduce stereotypies or repetitive movements of any part of the body (Flavell, 1973; Hopper and Wambold, 1978).

Lyon and colleagues (1976) caution that functional object use skills, like other generic skills, should be carried out in a variety of natural settings in which severely disabled students might be expected to function. Examples would be domestic settings, such as a private residence or group home, and public facility settings, such as consumer centers (e.g., restaurants, shopping centers). Teaching functional object use skills through adaptive play leads easily into recreation-leisure settings that the student will encounter in the future.

As with exploratory play, substages of development can be identified. Conventional object use begins with self-utilization in natural contexts, using objects with simple manipulations. Examples would be using a spoon for self-feeding and activating simple toys such as pushing a car or ringing a bell. More complex manipulations would follow, such as "reading a book" or scribbling with a crayon. The child would next move toward symbolic play, by extending actions toward others (e.g., brushing Mom's hair), and beginning to combine objects (e.g., using the doll and the blanket together) (Lowe, 1975). Research (e.g., Tilton and Ottinger, 1964; Weiner, Ottinger, and Tilton, 1969) indicates that the category of combinational toy play is highly important in discriminating the toy play behavior of various subgroups. The nondisabled group demonstrated the greatest number of combinations, followed by the retarded group, with the autistic group performing the least number of combinations in their toy play.

Assessment of Conventional Object Use

Unlike "appropriate" use, which may be somewhat subjective, conventional object use is typically straightforward. It can be assessed through structured observation in which a student is presented with a variety of objects and the manipulations are observed. The simple form designed by Chappell and Johnson (1976) and presented in Table 9–2 can be used for this purpose. This form offers an opportunity to observe the child's unprompted response, as well as the verbally cued response. An intermediate level of modeling the desired response could be added to provide additional information.

Strategies for Promoting Conventional Object Use

Conventional object use skills are highly appropriate targets for adaptive play sessions, with conventional use of various objects modeled by a sibling, parent, trainer, peer, or doll. It may be helpful to gather daily living items (spoon, brush, doll, blanket, washcloth, and so forth) into a brightly decorated "Fun

Table 9–2. Observation Form: Conventional and Symbolic Play

Object	Verbal Directive	Level of Development			Comments on Observations
		1	2	3	
Doll	Make Dolly sleep on floor.				
Ball	Throw ball to Dolly.				
Spoon	Feed Dolly with spoon.				
Box of Kleenex	Blow Dolly's nose with Kleenex.				
Plastic phone	Make Dolly talk on phone.				
Doll hat	Put Dolly's hat on her head.				
Wash cloth	Wash Dolly's face with wash cloth.				
Hand mirror	Show Dolly her face in mirror.				
Toothbrush	Brush Dolly's teeth with toothbrush.				
Cup	Give Dolly drink in cup.				
Hair brush	Brush Dolly's hair with brush.				
Small pillow	Make Dolly sleep on pillow.				

Levels of Development:
  Level 1: Sensorimotor Exploration
  Level 2: Imitative Self-Utilization of Items
  Level 3: Primitive Play Application

From Chappell, G.E., and Johnson, G.A. (1976). Evaluation of cognitive behavior in the young nonverbal child. *Language, Speech, and Hearing Services in Schools, 7*(1), 27. Reprinted with permission.

Box" to reduce the logistics of locating items, and to provide the child with consistency and expectations. Obviously, novel items should be added to the box at intervals, and specific objects should be changed so that the child does not become stimulus-bound — assuming, for example, that all washcloths are thick and red. Turntaking with actions (MacDonald and Gillette, 1984b) is an excellent structure for teaching conventional use of objects while simultaneously teaching early interactive skills. The trainer can also follow the substages listed previously in modeling object use, beginning with self-utilization of easily activated objects, moving to more complex activations and then to applications to others, and finally moving to the early combinational play that signifies the transition to more symbolic play.

Wambold and Bailey (1979) present a highly replicable study on appropriate toy play with children having severe to profound cognitive delays. They found that the key factors enhancing success in independent, appropriate play were the following: (1) a comfortable play area; (2) appropriate toys (including a wide range of traditional toys and home-living items); (3) prompting of inappropriate behaviors, with interventions keyed to the needs of individual children (example: model, pause; if still inappropriate, physically prompt, pause; if still inappropriate, substitute another toy); (4) encouragement from the teacher for appropriate play; and (5) allowing self-directed action on the part of the children (to minimize the influence of the teacher and encourage self-regulated behavior).

Lyon and colleagues (1977) and Musselwhite and Thompson (1979) note that children with severe physical disabilities may require compensatory strategies to use objects conventionally. One strategy would be to adapt the objects, such as adding a built-up handle to a spoon or putting a lid on a cup to reduce spillage. A second strategy is to prosthetize, such as fitting the child with a headstick to permit dialing a telephone, or affixing Velcro strips or magnetic buttons to the items and providing the child with a mitt having corresponding Velcro strips or metal washers to permit gross manipulation (Faulk, 1984). Physical and occupational therapists can be consulted to assist in developing compensatory strategies and materials.

MANIPULATIVE OR CONSTRUCTIVE PLAY

Description and Rationale

This set of play skills, referred to as skillful play by Jeffree and colleagues (1977), includes activities involving the use of "tools," stacking, threading, object placement, graded fitting, shape matching, and construction (e.g., using blocks). One feature that all of these tasks have in common is increased eye-hand coordination in comparison to the activities listed previously. These are typical fine motor development activities that lead to the development of skills such as pincer grasp, bilateral hand usage, and improved eye-hand coordination. This is probably the area on which attention is most commonly focused during traditional play programs.

Assessment of Manipulative or Constructive Play

Typical classroom assessment scales cover most of the activities involved in manipulative or constructive play (e.g., Sanford and Zelman, 1981). More in-depth evaluation can be found in formal or informal scales used by physical and occupational therapists.

Intervention for Manipulative or Constructive Play

Persons intervening in manipulative or constructive skill development should be cautioned in several respects. First, it is wise to *consult with an occupational or physical therapist* regarding appropriate manipulations for a particular child. For example, a hemiplegic child will need to be assisted in a different manner from a child with general "low tone," such as a child with Down's syndrome.

It is also crucial to keep in mind the *generic nature* of these skills. That is, test items are often highly specific regarding materials (e.g., will work a one-piece form board; will drop a 1 inch cube into a container) so that they will provide a clear, replicable testing opportunity. However, the goals derived from these test items do not limit the child to using these materials. In fact, teaching directly to the test would be highly inappropriate, as it would make the student stimulus-bound, thus inhibiting generalization. The suggestions in Chapter 3 relating to naturally structured tasks (see Table 3–4) are highly valuable for focusing on generic training of manipulative or constructive skills. For example, if a goal is to string beads, the generic skills intended include pincer grasp (to hold the string), bilateral hand usage (the bead must be held in the other hand), and object placement through eye-hand coordination. An alternative play task for introducing these same goals would be to use electrical wire to thread colored or decorated spools to form a snake (Lear, 1977) or to put small rubberized cars together by means of miniature pegs. The natural environment can also be explored for opportunities to practice these manipulative tasks. For example, one life-oriented stacking task enjoyed by many children is to make a sandwich using bread, cheese, and meat. Clearly, these alternatives are not always of equal difficulty to the test items, and more formal training using objects such as pegboards will likely be necessary. The concern is merely that training not be limited to use of test-related materials. Riddick (1982) and Jeffree and colleagues (1977) suggest specific motivational toys for establishing stimulus generalization for skills such as graded fitting, stacking, and shape matching.

A third concern regarding intervention with manipulative and constructive play skills is that the *playful* and *communicative elements* be maintained. This can be done through turntaking, animation, and use of a conversational tone of voice. For example, the play partner should be alert to the need to change tasks to avoid extreme frustration or boredom and should give directives conversationally ("Put it *in. Now!*") rather than falling into a rote pattern of robotic instructions ("Put in . . . good . . . put in . . .").

In summary, play is an obvious context for introducing or practicing a variety of object interaction skills. For children with severe disabilities, the focus on play may help to avoid the frustration that can accompany difficult tasks.

RESOURCES

Books and Articles (see Appendix A). Dunst (1981); Jeffree et al. (1977); Lear (1977); Riddick (1982); Wehman (1979c).

Chapter 10

Symbolic Play Skills

RATIONALE AND DESCRIPTION

Symbolic play is sometimes labeled creative play, or representational play. As described in the previous section, the transition to symbolic play comes as the child begins to use objects in a "pretend" manner, such as pretending to eat from an empty spoon. The investigation of symbolic play skills in children has been an area of great interest to researchers, with much of the current research based on the work of Piaget (1962). Several scales of symbolic play have been introduced, based on this research (Lowe, 1975; Lowe and Costello, 1976; Nicholich, 1977; Westby, 1980). It is important to consider symbolic play skills because of the assumed relationship between symbolic play, language, and cognition.

Jeffree and colleagues (1977) suggest that imaginative play helps children to (1) develop thought and language, as they add something to a situation or allow one object to represent another; (2) understand others, as feelings and roles are explored; (3) develop creativity and learn to devise their own amusements; and (4) come to terms with the self, an especially important goal for for many disabled children. The area of symbolic play offers excellent opportunities for telescoping goals in a number of domains. For example, during a tea party, children can learn or practice skills such as social (turntaking, sharing); communication (requesting, acknowledging, commenting); fine motor (pouring, using pincer grasp to obtain small foods); self-help (feeding self, washing dishes); gross motor (walking or crawling to sink); and cognitive (1:1 correspondence in handing out napkins, sequencing events). This allows joint participation by children at a variety of developmental levels. Symbolic play routines are also an ideal format for integrating disabled and nondisabled children. Thus, for the child who is cognitively ready, symbolic play can provide an enjoyable framework for learning experiences in a highly social setting.

A number of investigators have followed Piaget's lead in examining the development of symbolic play in nondisabled children. For example, Lowe (1975) observed 244 children at seven age levels between 1 and 3 years, using miniature replicas of everyday objects in four standard play situations. She found a rapid development from the appropriate use of a small number of objects to comprehension of all elements of the sets presented. Although activities initially centered on the child's own body, a transition to doll-oriented activities was observed at approximately 21 months. Lowe notes that this is the same age when children normally begin combining words.

Nicholich (1977) suggested that play analysis can be used as a means of assessing language potential in disabled children. She observed the free play and conversation with mothers of five nondisabled children observed monthly in their homes over a one year period and reported that "despite differences in age at attainment and frequency of pretend play, all five children did progress to the point of planning extended pretend games" (p. 98). Differences in symbolic play in various groups of disabled children have also been explored. For example, Wing and colleagues (1977) rated symbolic play and other symbolic activities of 108 mentally retarded or autistic children. They found that (1) no child demonstrating symbolic play had the complete autistic syndrome; (2) symbolic play that was flexible and varied in theme (not stereotyped) did not seem to occur in retarded children below a mental age of approximately 20 months; (3) children with stereotyped play appeared to have a better prognosis for achieving some degree of independence as adults than did the autistic children with no symbolic play, and (4) children with Down's syndrome were especially likely to have symbolic play. Comparisons between children with and without language impairments have also been made. Terrell and colleagues compared the symbolic play of normally developing children (chronological age 16 to 22 months) and language-impaired children (chronological age 32 to 49 months), all of whom had productive language skills at the single-word utterance. They found that the language-impaired children were developmentally advanced in their symbolic play relative to their younger, language-matched peers. However, the language-impaired children demonstrated deficits in their symbolic play relative to age norms. This suggests that symbolic play and language may not be based equally on cognition. It also indicates that the knowledge and concepts used in play are not necessarily translated into verbal expression. Thus, as Terrell and colleagues (1984) assert, "in clinical intervention with some impaired children it may be appropriate to direct primary attention to verbal expression of the meanings and relations already evidenced in play" (p. 428).

ASSESSMENT OF SYMBOLIC PLAY SKILLS

Singer and Singer (1977) suggest that initial assessment take the form of observation of a child for at least 10 minutes while he or she moves through groups during free play; at this point the adult should look for patterns of interaction and behavior. Next, the observation form by Chappell and Johnson (1976), presented in Table 9–2, can provide an initial screening of the general level of a child's play skills. If this screening indicates that the child is functioning at the symbolic play level, a further analysis will be desirable. Several symbolic play observation forms are available (e.g., Hanna, Lippert, and Harris, 1982; Lowe and Costello, 1976). Westby's checklist (1980) is given in Table 10–1 because it can readily be completed through structured observation and parent or teacher reporting, and it allows combined assessment of correlated language levels. A yes or no checklist is also included in the book by Jeffree and colleagues (1977), in their section on imaginative play.

INTERVENTION IN SYMBOLIC PLAY

This section is concerned primarily with strategies to enhance the development of symbolic play skills, although ideas for promoting related skills will also be suggested. Initially, the facilitator must identify the current stage for each child to determine appropriate play materials and situations. Thus, goals should be to extend the child's play behaviors at the present stage, to encourage generalization and prevent stereotyped play, or to introduce behaviors gradually from the next stage.

Four components should be considered in attempting to facilitate symbolic play and related skills.

Choose Materials Carefully. The strategies listed in Chapter 4 can help in choosing appropriate materials. For young children,

Table 10-1.   Symbolic Play Scale Checklist

Play	Language
Stage I: 9 to 12 months ____ Awareness that objects exist when not seen; finds toy hidden under scarf ____ Means-end behavior — crawls or walks to get what he or she wants; pulls string toy	____ No true language; may have performative words (words that are associated with actions or the total situation) Exhibits following communicative functions: ____ Request (instrumental) ____ Command (regulatory)
Stage II: 13 to 17 months ____ Purposeful exploration of toys: Discovers operation of toys through trial and error; uses variety of motoric schemas ____ Hands toy to adult if unable to operate	____ Context-dependent single words — for example, child may use the word "car" when riding in a car, but not when he sees a car; words tend to come and go in child's vocabulary Exhibits following communicative functions: ____ Request ____ Protest ____ Command ____ Label ____ Interactional ____ Response ____ Personal ____ Greet
Stage III: 17 to 19 months ____ Autosymbolic play — for example, child pretends to go to sleep or pretends to drink from cup or eat from spoon ____ Uses most common objects and toys appropriately ____ Tool use (uses stick to reach toy) ____ Finds toys visibly hidden (when placed in box and box emptied under scarf	Beginning of true verbal communication. Words have following functional and semantic relations: ____ Recurrence ____ Agent ____ Existence ____ Object ____ Nonexistence ____ Action or state ____ Rejection ____ Location ____ Denial ____ Object or person associated with object or location
Stage IV: 19 to 22 months Symbolic play extends beyond the child's self ____ Plays with dolls: Brushes doll's hair, feeds doll bottle, or covers with blanket ____ Child performs pretend activities on more than one person or object — for example, feeds self, a doll, mother, and another child ____ Combines two toys in pretend play — for example, puts spoon in pan or pours from pot into cup	____ Refers to objects or persons not present Beginning of word combinations with following semantic relations: ___ Agent-action ___ Action-locative ___ Action-object ___ Object-locative ___ Agent-object ___ Possessive ___ Attributive ___ Dative

Table 10-1   (continued)

Stage V: 24 months
____ Represents daily experiences; plays house — is the mommy, daddy, or baby; objects used are realistic and close to life size
____ Events short and isolated; no true sequences; some self-limiting sequences — puts food in pan, stirs, and eats
____ Block play consists of stacking, knocking down
____ Sand and water play consist of filling, pouring, and dumping

____ Uses earlier pragmatic functions and semantic relations in phrases and short sentences
The following morphological markers appear:
____ Present progressive (ing) on verbs
____ Plurals
____ Possessives

Stage VI: 2½ years
Represents events less frequently experienced or observed, particularly impressive or traumatic events:
____ Doctor-nurse-sick child
____ Teacher-child
____ Store-shopping
Events still short and isolated; realistic props still required; roles shift quickly

Responds appropriately to the following wh-questions in context:
____ What
____ Who
____ Whose
____ Where
____ What . . . do
____ Asks wh-questions — generally puts wh-word at beginning of sentence
____ Responses to why questions inappropriate except for well-known routines like "Why is the doctor here? Baby sick"
____ Asks why, but often inappropriately, and does not attend to answer

Stage VII: 3 years
____ Continues pretend activities of Stages V and VI, but now the play has a sequence. Events are not isolated — for example, child mixes cake, bakes it, serves it, washes the dishes; or doctor checks patient, calls ambulance, takes patient to hospital and operates. Sequence evolves — is not planned
____ Compensatory toy — reenactment of experienced events with new outcomes
____ Associative play

____ Uses past tense such as, "I ate the cake . . . I walked"
____ Uses future aspect (particularly "gonna") forms such as, "I'm gonna wash dishes"

Table continued on following page

Table 10-1   (continued)

Stage VIII: 3 to 3½ years

_____ Carries out play activities of previous stages with a doll house and Fisher-Price toys (barn, garage, airport, village)

_____ Uses blocks and sandbox for imaginative play; blocks used primarily as enclosures (fences and houses) for animals and dolls

_____ Play not totally stimulus bound; child uses one object to represent another

_____ Uses doll or puppet as participant in play

Descriptive vocabulary expands as child becomes more aware of perceptual attributes

Uses terms for the following concepts (not always correctly):

_____ shapes

_____ sizes

_____ colors

_____ texture

_____ spatial relationships

_____ Gives dialogue to puppets, dolls

_____ Metalinguistic language use, such as "He said . . ."

_____ Uses indirect requests such as, "Mom lets me have cookies for breakfast"

_____ Changes speech depending on listener

Stage IX: 3½ to 4 years

_____ Begins to problem-solve events not experienced; plans ahead; hypothesizes "What would happen if . . ."

_____ Uses dolls and puppets to act out scenes

_____ Builds three-dimensional structures with blocks which are attempts to reproduce a specific structure child has seen

Verbalizes intentions and possible future events:

_____ Uses modals (can, may, might, will, would, could)

_____ Uses conjunctions (and, but, if, so, because)

Note: full competence for these modals and conjunctions does not develop until 10 to 12 years of age

Stage X: 5 years

_____ Plans a sequence of pretend events. Organizes what he or she needs — both objects and other children

_____ Coordinates more than one event occurring at a time

_____ Highly imaginative; sets scene without props

_____ Full cooperative play

_____ Uses relational terms (then, when, first, next, last, while, before, after)

Note: Full competence does not develop until 10 to 12 years of age

From Westby, C.E. (1980). Assessment of cognitive and language abilities through play. _Language, Speech, and Hearing Services in Schools, 11,_ 154–168. Reprinted with permission.

realistic props that are close to life-size are necessary. The play scales cited previously can also assist in selecting materials. For example, children at Stage III (Westby, 1980) will not be ready to use miniature props, a readiness that will not evolve for several stages. For children at higher cognitive levels, extremely realistic props can hinder creativity, as children will have less opportunity or need to use one object to represent another. In addition to traditional play materials (dolls, dollhouses, daily living sets), miniature play sets such as a tree house or castle, puppets, and dress-ups can greatly enhance creative play. Singer and Singer (1977) provide an extensive listing of toys and materials ideal for imaginative play.

Prepare the Situation. Jeffree and colleagues (1977) recommend setting the scene in advance, especially while the child is out of the room, to enhance motivation. For example, the children can return from swimming to find a toy shopping center waiting for them. Clearly, it is also important for children to help set up a situation at times, so that they can learn the entire sequence and have an opportunity to change the setting as desired. For a situation that becomes routinized, secretly adding unexpected materials for the children to discover and incorporate can increase participation. Examples are a plane hidden in the silo of a play barn; new jewelry concealed in a purse in the dress-up box; and a small stuffed dog stuck in the garage of a plastic play house. A final suggestion for setting the scene is to take children on outings (to a restaurant, park, supermarket, zoo) to provide themes for later symbolic play (Jeffree et al., 1977).

Facilitate Play. Singer and Singer (1977) suggest that the adult will have three roles relative to developing imaginative play: first, the adult should be an onlooker, observing the child as recommended in the assessment section. The adult should also be a participant in modeling routines, following the lead of children, and verbalizing what is happening. This will involve commitment from the adult, who should be at child's-eye level, and should become involved in the activity. The caution at this point is to model options but to avoid being highly directive or overly routinized. Wing and colleagues (1977) suggest that children with stereotyped play may need a more structured and organized approach, but with flexibility built in. Finally, the adult can move to a stimulator role, in which symbolic play is initiated for one child alone or for a group of children, with the adult promoting the activity but fading involvement as soon as possible. Specific strategies for accomplishing this are the following: (1) set up a situation, as recommended previously, and entice children to join in the play, directing their attention initially to play possibilities ("Look, Erica, Bear's having a tea party. He has muffins!"); (2) begin a symbolic play routine, such as doll play with a

Table 10-2.   Modifications to Overcome Obstacles to Symbolic Play

Obstacle	Sample Modification
Child displaces toy set when attempting to manipulate it	Use a pegboard as a playboard, affixing the major piece (e.g., schoolhouse) with bolts or a C-clamp Attach smaller pieces (e.g., desk, swing) with screws and bolts, affixing moving vehicles to routed tracks (using wing nuts), so they can be moved (see Carlson, 1982, for specifics) Use a Shuffletown play set, in which "people" are permanently attached on movable tracks
Child can move arm, but cannot grasp miniature "person" or uses a palmar grasp that obscures "person"	Affix "person" to dowel, or screw ribbon or Velcro strap to head of "person" and tie onto child's hand (See Carlson, 1982, for specifics)
Play set "people" are too small for child to manipulate	Substitute larger handmade play set with weighted Table-Top puppets (Renfro, 1984; Sullivan, 1982)
Child can make gross movements, but cannot grasp objects	Use a Velcro mitt (Faulk, 1984); affix Velcro to glove or band fitted to head, hand, foot, knee, elbow, etc.; affix other side of Velcro to doll, ball, or stuffed animal, or choose fabric that sticks naturally to Velcro For use with a metal sets (e.g., tea set) child can wear fabric mitt with washers sewn on, and high-power button magnets can be glued to tea set pieces (Faulk, 1984)
Child cannot manipulate objects independently, due to severely impaired motor skills	Prepare a communication display with vocabulary appropriate for activity — Ex., Sesame Street Clubhouse: include characters (Big Bird); locations (upstairs); actions (slide); comments (look); social language (thanks, my turn); allow child to "direct" action by means of display

child, gradually fading input until child is playing alone; (3) initiate a play situation with two or more children, with adult seated behind children, interacting only as necessary to continue the activity.

Adapt Materials and Situations. Most suggestions and curricula for development of symbolic play skills are directed toward children who are nondisabled or mildly to moderately disabled. Clearly, symbolic play is a crucial area of development for children with severe physical disabilities, especially if cognitively they are at the appropriate age level. Several of the adaptations of materials suggested previously, such as clamping dollhouses to surfaces, will be applicable here. However, several additional adaptations will be needed. Sample modifications are presented in Table 10–2. The following chapter presents specific strategies for facilitating language in symbolic play contexts.

RESOURCES

Two sources of further information on the topic of imaginative play are included in Appendix A. Singer and Singer's book (1977) is written for use with nondisabled children; however, it presents an excellent background to the area, including activities for developing the adult's imagination. The book by Jeffree and colleagues (1977) is intended for use with disabled children. It includes a yes or no chart to determine at what point in the process training should start, with play activities provided for (1) dawning imagination (very early activities); (2) pretend play (games and make-believe); and (3) role-playing (pretending to be another person).

Chapter 11

Early Communication Through Speech

DESCRIPTION AND RATIONALE

This chapter is not an attempt to produce a communication curriculum or to advance new theories on oral communication development; rather it presents strategies for integrating adaptive play into existing communication therapy programs. In addition, many of the ideas suggested in this chapter are appropriate for use by significant others in a child's life to enhance generalization of training. These adaptive play strategies are directed toward the development of functional communication through oral speech in the natural environment. Several recent training programs reflect this play orientation in teaching communication skills (e.g., Ausberger, Martin, and Creighton, 1982; Fewell and Vadasy, 1983; Hanna et al., 1982).

The three-dimensional view of language developed by Bloom and Lahey (1978) is used as a framework for this chapter. This concept has both theoretical and applied validity, and it can easily be understood by persons working with children with special needs. The three components are content, form, and use.

Content. Content refers to words or signs, and the relations between words or signs, that represent meaning in messages. Elements of content are (1) object knowledge (particular objects such as Daddy and White House and classes of objects such as chairs); (2) object relations (this cookie, big ball); and (3) event relations (causality, such as eating because one is hungry; time, such as yesterday). The topics of language are also included in the content category. A child with a disorder in content might have difficulty in concept development, or he or she might demonstrate "empty" speech, talking around a topic.

Form. Form includes (1) phonology (units of sound); (2) morphology (units of meaning that are words or inflections, such as "-ing"); and (3) syntax (the way in which units of meaning are combined with one another, or word order). A child with a disorder in form might communicate well but use only one- and two-word utterances, although chronologically and developmentally more complex forms would be expected.

Use. Language use has two major aspects: (1) the goals or functions of language (why people speak); and (2) the rules for deciding how to use language (the ways in which context causes alterations in language form or content). Children with a language use disorder may use language intrapersonally rather than interpersonally; that is, they may speak as if for themselves, without regard to the listener.

Bloom and Lahey (1978) caution that there is extensive interaction among these three categories for both normal and disordered language. Although the three components may be defined in isolation, most assessment or intervention tasks will relate to a combination of two or three components. The three components will be discussed further in considering strategies for assessment and intervention.

ASSESSMENT ISSUES

The philosophy of language development and intervention will guide a speech-language pathologist in selecting appropriate tools for assessing early prelanguage and language skills. Bloom and Lahey (1978) review existing tests as they relate to the identification of content, form, and use disorders as well as the interaction of these components. They also suggest various methods for describing deviant language according to the three categories (1978).

Several existing language assessment tools may be of special interest in describing early language development.

• *Developmental Communication Curriculum Inventory* (Hanna et al., 1982): Includes a teacher-child interaction section and a teacher and caregiver interview to assess objectives of function, form, and content.

• *Infant Scale of Communicative Intent* (Sacks and Young, 1982): Examines receptive and expressive skills from birth through 18 months.

- *Ecomaps* (MacDonald and Gillette, 1984d): Assesses language through conversation, focusing on the child–significant other dyad.
- *PALS Developmental Assessment Tool* (Owens, 1982): Investigates a range of presymbolic and symbolic behaviors, and provides for structured observation of client–caregiver interaction.
- *Nonverbal Communicative Behaviors Scale* (Dunst, 1978): Developmental checklist for assessing nonverbal items at perlocutionary, illocutionary, and locutionary act stages.

These brief descriptions merely indicate the areas and orientations of assessment for each tool. Further information is contained in Appendix A. For any comprehensive intervention program, it will be necessary to supplement formal assessment with informal procedures.

INTERVENTION THROUGH ADAPTIVE PLAY

The three phases of early communication intervention described by Wilcox (1984) are used to structure this section. They are (1) nonverbal intervention, with the goal of establishing intentional communication in the form of gestures or vocalizations or both; (2) initial verbal interaction, with the target of developing a core lexicon; and (3) expanded verbal skills intervention, with the purpose of developing more complex communicative skills. At each phase, potential goals for content, form, and use are identified, with sample adaptive play intervention strategies described.

Nonverbal Intervention Strategies

Many of the goals at this level are included in other chapters of this book (e.g., turntaking with actions, functional object use). The *Program for the Acquisition of Language with the Severely Impaired* (PALS) (Owens, 1982) includes numerous nonverbal items on the *Developmental Assessment Tool* and in the manual, as does the *Developmental Communication Curriculum* (Hanna et al., 1982). Other sources for nonverbal communicative behaviors are Bloom and Lahey (1978) and Dunst (1978).

Content Goals

The precursory goals of language content suggested by Bloom and Lahey (1978) center on (1) developing object relations and intraclass relations; and (2) developing interclass relations. Specific strategies are proposed for each.

Object Relations and Intraclass Relations. Bloom and Lahey recommend both teaching the child to search for objects that disappear (recurrence) and teaching the child to cause objects to disappear, with several specific subgoals provided for each step. These goals demonstrate to the child the themes of recurrence and object relations (between the child and the object). Clearly, object play is the appropriate medium for working on these goals, with the child and adult taking turns hiding and searching for objects. A variety of objects, barriers, and containers should be used, so that the activity remains playful, rather than rote. In addition, these activities should be incorporated into everyday life, such as hiding behind the diaper while changing the child; hiding the musical bear under the child's blanket at naptime; hiding a brush in one of three pocketbooks while teaching self-help skills; and dropping objects into boxes after they are used during functional object use training.

Interclass Relations. This goal involves helping the child learn that he or she can act on different objects in similar ways (exploratory play), in prescribed ways (conventional object use), and in relation to each other (combinational use). These phases help the child to learn the relations between objects that can later be coded through communication (dog sleeping, doll on chair, kiss baby, and so forth). Bloom and Lahey (1978) describe general procedures for training these object play skills to help the child see the relations between objects. For example, at each stage, the child should be allowed to watch the adult acting on the objects in the specified manner, then should be offered a turn at manipulating the objects. In Chapter 9 are presented numerous ideas for helping children with disabilities move from the exploratory stage through the conventional use stage to the combinational stage of object interaction.

Form Goals

Precursory goals of language form suggested by Bloom and Lahey (1978) are (1) imitating movement; (2) imitating vocalization; and (3) more closely approximating the adult model. Adaptive play strategies can be useful for all goals.

Imitating Movement. Turntaking activities can provide an excellent format for facilitating movement imitation. Bloom and

Lahey (1978, p. 403) outline the typical progression: (1) copy a child behavior immediately after it is produced (child yawns, adult follows suit); (2) gradually increase a time delay between the child's movement and the adult's imitation (child pushes block, adult pushes block 30 seconds later, one minute later, and so forth); the subgoal is to elicit imitation of movement that is in the child's repertoire, although it has not occurred in that play session; (3) combine child's behaviors in new ways, forming novel patterns from familiar movements (reach arms out, then bring together in a clapping movement); (4) introduce new behaviors that are somewhat similar to old behaviors (if child has been patting her lap, encourage her to pat adult's hands instead).

It must be stressed that, although the progression will be the same across children, the specific movements used as targets will vary, depending on the movements the child produces to be imitated. For children with physical disabilities, this goal may need to be modified to allow for adapted movements, such as focusing on head movements, gross body movements, or eye gaze patterns. The Ecological Communication System (ECO) treatment model, Turntaking with Actions (MacDonald and Gillette, 1984b) offers excellent intervention strategies for teaching movement imitation within a highly interactive context. It can be practiced across settings and trainers through adaptive play. For example, parents and siblings can play follow-the-leader, incorporating appropriate movements into the game, and using traditional early games such as "So Big" and "Peek-A-Boo." Therapists can be made aware of the level of movement imitation (e.g., combining old movement forms) and can incorporate these into therapy (reach and pull switch while doing exercises with a ball).

Vocal Imitation. A similar progression should be used for vocal imitation. Schumaker and Sherman (1978), in a chapter directed to parent intervention, suggest a hierarchy of vocal imitation training and provide specific training techniques at each stage. For some special needs children, it will be necessary to increase vocalizations in general as a first step. They define vocalizations as "any sound a child makes with the vocal apparatus, excluding crying and reflexive coughs, sneezes, and hiccups" (1978, p. 291), and recommend that adults provide verbal praise ("Good boy") and tactile stimulation (rubbing the infant's cheek) following any vocalization. The second level is termed mutual imitation or imitation chains, and involves imitation of a sound made by the child, to encourage vocal imitation from the child. The remaining levels are similar to those for motor imitation, with the children (1) imitating vocalizations in their repertoires following increasing delay periods; (2) imitating combinations of previously made vocalizations; and (3) attempting imitations of sounds differing slightly from previously made sounds.

Play can provide the background for facilitating vocal imitation. For example, Bricker and Dennison (1978) suggest that play, especially action play (tickling, swinging, vigorous rocking) may elicit vocalizations that can be imitated by the adult, and for which the child can be reinforced. Child movements can also be imitated, with "sound effects" added to encourage vocal imitation. Therapists can use a modification of this strategy. For example, the physical therapist can accompany specific, frequently occurring movements with sounds already in the child's repertoire, such as "oooo" as the child practices protective reactions while seated on a large ball; "whee" as a child goes down a slide; "hey" as the child moves on a scooterboard; or "uh-oh" as the child sits down unexpectedly. Similarly, sounds can be used by siblings to routinely accompany familiar interactive games, such as Peek-A-Boo ("hi") or Ride-A-Horse ("a-a-a").

More Closely Approximating the Adult Model. This goal indicates that the child will produce sounds, word attempts, or sign attempts that approach the adult model, although an exact match is not expected at this stage. Thus, the child should begin to approximate aspects such as adult intonations and sound production.

Varied intonational patterns follow naturally from the animation that is an integral part of play. Although the child may not learn the function of differing intonational patterns at this stage, he or she can be exposed to and encouraged to imitate varying patterns of intonation.

Play can also be an ideal medium for facilitating *sound production*, expanding on the association of sounds with actions and objects at the previous stage. For example, Musselwhite (1985) has used English phonemes to represent actions or objects, with simple songs encouraging production of those phonemes. Table 11–1 presents target phonemes, representative objects, and associated actions. In this way, sound production can be practiced in context, rather than in isolation ("Say /p/ . . . good . . . again . . ."). MacDonald and Gillette (1984a) caution

Table 11-1.   Sound Production Ideas

Phoneme	Sound Used	Props	Gestures
/p/	"puh-puh"	boat	make boat go in "water"
/b/	"bye-bye"	—	wave bye-bye
/t/	"t-t-t-t"	clock	index finger "ticks"
/d/	"d-d-d-d"	drum	beat drum
/k/	"kuh-kuh"	chicken	arms flap like "wings"
/g/	"guh-guh"	cup	drink from cup
/m/	"mmmmmmm"	spoon	rub stomach
/n/	"no-no-no"	doll	shake finger
/s/	"ssssss"	snake	make snake's fangs with fingers
/ʃ/	"shhhhhh"	doll, blanket	finger on lips
/t͡ʃ/	"ch-ch-ch"	train	make train go
/z/	"zzzzzzz"	bee	follow bee with finger
/l/	"la-la-la"	wind-up radio	"conduct" music
/w/	"wuh-wuh"	dog	make dog bark
/r/	"rrr-rrr"	race car	rev car up
/h/	"ho-ho-ho"	Santa Claus	pat large belly
/f/	"ffffff"	angry cat	show your "claws"
/v/	"vvvvvvv"	—	follow fly with eyes

Note: An attempt was made to select sounds made by familiar objects; thus, "bye-bye" was chosen to represent the phoneme /b/ rather than an infrequent environmental sound such as a jack-hammer.
From Musselwhite, C. (1985). *Songbook: Signs and Symbols for Children* (p. 87). Asheville, NC: Author. A song accompanies each phoneme in this songbook.

against correcting sound production for children who are in the "fragile stages" of developing communicative habits, being concerned about discouraging sound production in general. Thus, offering models in the context of play and providing corrected imitations and expansions of a child's attempts (without labeling the child's attempt as "wrong") will be a more productive approach.

Use Goals

The precursory language use goals identified by Bloom and Lahey (1978) and Wilcox (1984), although differing in labels, describe similar nonverbal communication functions. Bloom and Lahey recommend that the child should (1) develop reciprocal gaze patterns; (2) regulate the behaviors of others; and (3) call attention to objects and events.

Reciprocal Gaze Patterns. Bloom and Lahey stress that "It is not expected that the child will sit still and maintain eye contact in the absence of other activity, instead, the goal is the frequent exchange of gaze in the context of other interpersonal activities such as greeting, showing, giving, and pointing" (1978, pp. 396–397). The joint activity routines suggested by MacDonald and Gillette (1984a) can provide a useful framework for fostering reciprocal gaze in the contexts listed previously. Several factors may enhance the development of reciprocal gaze within play activities:

1. *Animation:* The adult should show animation, to get and maintain the child's interest, as recommended in Mac- Donald and Gillette (1984a, pp. 4–5) and summarized in Chapter 8.
2. *Positioning:* Initially, the adult should be at a child's eye level — too often adults sit in a large chair and attempt to interact with a child sitting in a small chair. Reciprocal gaze should also be encouraged in a variety of child-adult positioning patterns — in real life, the child will not always be seated directly across from the communication partner.
3. *Delay:* If the pace is too fast, as it often is for children with disabilities, the child may not have time to read cues to take his or her turn through reciprocal gaze.

Calling Attention to Objects and Events. As Wilcox (1984) notes, the child must begin to understand that his or her activities are of interest to the adult. She recommends that the adult initially follow the child's lead, making simple, one- to two-word verbal expansions of the child's nonverbal interactions (child pats baby, adult says "Pat baby," or "Nice baby"). Wilcox asserts that the adult should give unconditional attention for several sessions, after which contingencies can be placed on attending. Thus, the adult will gradually begin to withhold attention to elicit appropriate attention-getting behaviors, such as eye contact, gestures, or vocalization. To maintain the interaction, it is important to use "creative stupidity," so it is not obvious that attention is deliberately withheld (which would suggest punishment), but instead it appears that the adult is "busy."

Regulating the Behavior of Others. This goal requires that the child establish a clear signal indicating that assistance is needed to obtain objects or events. "Environmental engineering" is helpful, so that items or events desired by the child are available, but unobtainable. For example, the adult can wind up a toy for the child that he or she cannot activate alone, or a tantalizing toy can be put in a see-through, tightly closed container or on a high shelf which the child cannot reach. Wilcox (1984) recommends intervention procedures similar to those in the previous step. Initially, the adult must anticipate the child's need for assistance and comply. Again, several unconditional sessions will be needed to assist the child in recognizing that the adult can be of assistance. Then the adult can withhold assistance until the child gives a signal, such as pointing to the desired item, gesturing to indicate the desired action, holding the object out to the adult, or vocalizing. Care must be taken to keep these sessions playful rather than frustrating for the child. It may be necessary to model or prompt behaviors that will be accepted as requests for assistance.

Initial Verbal Intervention

The distinction between content, form, and use categories becomes increasingly blurred as communication skills develop, with increasing overlap between categories. Following the treatment model of Wilcox (1984), the overall goal at this phase is to establish a core lexicon. This phase is intended for children who demonstrate intentional communication (as presented in the previous phase) but do not use conventional forms (words, signs, symbols) to code their intentions. This section covers oral communication only, with augmentative communication development presented in Chapter 12.

Content Goals

The development of a *core lexicon* is the primary content goal at this phase. This refers to a small, functional vocabulary that can be adapted to the needs of an individual child. Several authors have suggested guidelines for developing a core lexicon (Bowerman, 1976; Holland, 1975; Lahey and Bloom, 1977). Musselwhite and St. Louis (1982) reviewed the literature and summarized primary strategies for matching a core lexicon to the individual child: (1) client preference — at least a few of the entries should have high motivational value for the child; (2) frequency of occurrence — this would yield entries to which the child has repeated exposure and, presumably, opportunities for coding; (3) coding a variety of communicative functions — entries that can be used in a variety of ways at the single-word level are useful targets; (4) ease of demonstration in context — for children with poor receptive language skills, entries that are difficult to demonstrate would have low priority; (5) ease of production and discrimination — features such as the number of sounds and syllables in an entry can influence ease of learning; (6) efficiency — for future applications, it is important that entries can be combined with others to code a wide range of ideas about the environment; thus, highly specific words that combine poorly should be restricted. The clinician must also consider those messages the child is already coding nonverbally, so that the child can be taught to code them verbally.

Once a target core lexicon has been selected, the adult should again present several unconditional sessions, in which the child's nonverbal communicative acts are coded using words from the core lexicon. For example, in coding attention-getting, the child points to an object, the adult codes "look"; in coding behavior regulation, the child holds out a wind-up toy for activation and the adult codes "on"; or the child vocalizes and points to the baby (doll) on a shelf, the adult codes "baby." Initially, the adult must also respond by actions to the child's nonverbal requests. At this point, the adult requires contingencies (a conventional word approximation paired with the nonverbal signal) before complying with the communicative function expressed by the child. For some children, it may be necessary to accept a vocalization as an intermediate step before words are produced. Use of the *delay procedure* (Halle, Alpert, and Anderson, 1984; Snell and Gast, 1981) can also enhance word production. Briefly, the adult sets up a situation that has been coded numerous times for the child. For example, the adult produces a box and shakes it to indicate that something is in it, then pauses for a predetermined time while looking expectant, to facilitate verbal coding of the function (request to "look" or to "open").

Again, the framework for this intervention is interactive play, with the adult following the child's lead. For children with motor disabilities, the toy modifications suggested in Chapter 4 can enable the child to be an equal participant.

Form and Use Goals

Form and use goals at the initial verbal level are difficult to separate. First the form goals for nonverbal interaction must be refined. For example, closer word approximations should be reinforced, although the emphasis should still be on communication, not on articulatory correctness.

With regard to intonational patterns, the adult can model a variety of patterns to discriminate various language functions; thus, form and use can be taught simultaneously. Table 11–2 presents a list of eight early-developing communicative functions (Lucas, 1980). Although there are numerous lists of language functions, this list is concise and describes early communicative functions.

Children with severe disabilities may not be exposed to as wide a variety of language functions as nondisabled children, especially in residential settings. For example, Tizard, Cooper, Joseph, and Tizard (1973) found a large percentage of directives used by the institutional staff they studied. The same may be true in traditional teaching settings. For example, if a teacher views "putting in" as a play and learning opportunity, rather than as a rote teaching task, communicative models will reflect this. A variety of intonational patterns will be used, depending on the function, rather than the unvarying pattern typical of adult teaching directives. Samples for the word "in" are in⟶(repetitive teaching directive); in⟶ (requesting); in⟍ (commenting on action); in⟶(questioning whether the toy is in the container). This strategy of varying intonational patterns according to function should be taught expressly to all significant others. A good medium for teaching is to role-play simple play routines, asking adults to guess, from the intonations and accompanying gestures, what the functions are for single-word utterances, such as the following:

- *Go:* Sample uses are to request action ("let's go"); assertion ("it's going now"); or request information ("Time to go?").
- *Baby:* One-word functions could be assertion (parent pointed and said "doggie," child is responding "No, it's a baby"); request for information (something is hiding under the blanket, and child asks "Is it a baby?"); request for object ("I want the baby"); or calling or summons ("Come here, baby," spoken to a real baby).
- *More:* Sample uses at the one-word level are: request for action ("I want more tickles!"); request for information ("Is there any more?"); or statement of information ("There's more juice in here").

Thus, adults should display for children with delayed language various forms, including intonation and gestures, for

Table 11-2.   Early Communicative Functions

Function	Context	Examples
Requests for Objects	Child knows that someone has an object that he or she wants	"Want cookie"; "May I have a cookie?"; "Gimme glue"
Requests for Actions	The child believes that the action of another child or adult is needed	"Go away"; "Me up"; "Would you please pour the juice?"; "Help me"; "Tie my shoe"
Assertions	The child says something he or she believes to be true; he or she does not think the listener knows this	"That doggie"; "No, it's a car"; "That's the biggest horse ever"; "Daddy's car"
Denials	The hearer or someone in the context does something that the child does not accept; the child believes that the hearer must be told to keep the action from continuing	"I don't wanna"; "no dirty" (meaning that she doesn't want to wash); "no juice" (to indicate that she does not want the juice there)
Requests for Information	The child believes that additional information about the context is needed	"Time go?"; "Daddy home?"; "Why do birds die?"; "How come we go to school?"
Callings	The child wants to call attention to the next utterance, to the immediate area, or to get attention	"Morning"; "Hey, you", "Yoo-hoo"; "Look"; "Sue"
Stating Information	The child has something to tell that is not common knowledge to the speaker and hearer; the only way the hearer would know this is by the child telling the hearer	"Mommy bakes cookies"; "I found a dollar bill"; "My brother is a meany"; "I found my dog"
Rule Ordering	The child believes that something needs to be told to the hearer to change the actions of that person	"You're not 'spose' to play with matches"; "Stop pulling the swing"; "Mine"

From Lucas, E.V. (1980). Semantic and pragmatic disorders (pp. 198-200). Reprinted with permission of Aspen Systems Corporation.

coding a variety of communicative functions at the one-word stage. Again, a play context is highly appropriate for training, although these strategies should be carried over into all settings.

Expanded Verbal Communication

Once the child is using approximately 10 words communicatively, expansion can begin. Interactions between the content, form, and use categories are readily apparent at this point.

Content, Form, and Use Goals

At this point, the specific ordering of communicative goals becomes less clear-cut; for example, for clinicians following normal development, the normal child's language begins to expand in multiple directions once a core lexicon is established. This section presents exemplary adaptive play strategies for targeting several communicative goals. Although content, form, and use are combined in this section, the elements of each addressed in the various tasks are specified.

Social Routines. There is an increasing awareness of the role that social routines can play in language evaluation and treatment (Gunter and Van Kleek, 1984). Routines refer to interactions in which children participate in a sequence of events and the accompanying verbal exchanges are similar each time the routine occurs. Initially, these involve caregivers, but they expand to include all individuals with whom a child comes in contact. Gunter and Van Kleek (1984) identify four major formats of interaction: (1) nonverbal games (peek-a-boo) and verbal games (rhymes, jokes, fantasy); (2) social amenities and courtesies (please–thank you routine, greetings and departures, pardon or excuse me); (3) description of everyday activities (verbal accompaniments to caregiving routines such as toileting, dressing, and bathing, and later routines for storytelling and narration); (4) formats and scripts (routines for situations such as mealtime, reading circles, and community activities).

MacDonald, Gillette, Bickley, and Rodriguez (1984) present a number of conversation routines designed to turn everyday activities into language teaching conversations. Their sample routines demonstrate progressive routines for interacting with children who are nonlinguistic as well as those who are at the two- and three-word level. Table 11–3 presents a sample routine for their module.

Communication scripts and other social routines offer children an opportunity to learn an entire set of behaviors, including verbal behaviors, appropriate for a situation. It is important to note that the focus is on developing conversation during a situation, not on simply describing the activity. A variety of content, form, and use goals can be modeled within a single communication script, with language put on display so that the child can gradually assume responsibility for performing the routine. Although redundancy should be built into the general presentation of a routine, specific elements such as language forms and content should be varied. Thus, the adult can demon-

Table 11-3.   Sample Conversation Routine: "In and Out," Turn-taking with Communications

Sample Goal: To take turns with child with increasingly higher levels of communication using "in and out"

Suggestions for communications:

1. Body language: gestural, facial, mime
2. Sounds: "Ooo," "Ahh," "Yuk"
3. Single words: in, out, me, you, Mommy, hi, bye, Daddy, block, toy, bead
4. Two words: block out, Mommy hi, me in
5. Three to five words: My block out, Mommy toy bye-bye, My bead fall in
6. Six words: My block is stuck in box, Me and Mommy made bead go bye-bye

Sample script with useful strategies and common problems:

Child's level: Linguistic 1 to 2 words

Not Like This	*Like This*
You: (take marble out of bag) "Look."	You: (take marble out of bag) "Look."
Child: (takes marble out) "Look."	Child: (takes marble out) "Look."
You: "You took it out." MISMATCH	You: (drop marble in bag) "Fell in."
You: "Let's put them back in."	MODEL MESSAGE FOR CHILD
You: "In." (drop marble in) TURN DOMINANCE	Child: (Feigns dropping marble)
	Child: (laughs and hides it in hand)
Child: (keeps marble and rolls it on floor)	You: "Uh oh, not in." RESPOND TO CHILD'S BEHAVIOR AS COMMUNICATION
You: "Don't you like turns?"	
You: "Not much, huh?" DEAD-END CONTACT	You: "All gone?" CHAIN
	Child: (Laughs and holds out marble) "Look, Mommy."

From MacDonald, J.D., Gillette, Y., Bickley, M., and Rodriguez, C. (1984). *Conversation routines* (pp. 27–28). Columbus, OH: The Ohio State University. Reprinted with permission.

strate a variety of communicative options to the child, so that the child will not develop stereotyped speech. For example, a routine for outdoor play can include a subroutine for getting and putting on coats, but the specific forms for the requesting and thank-you routines will vary to avoid the rote request ("I want coat, please"). Although many routines can and should be practiced across natural settings, they can be introduced in a play setting. Table 11–4 presents sample play situations and targets potential social routines for each, with sample strategies for encouraging the routines.

Matrix Training. Once children are beginning to use combinations to code linguistic functions, activities can be built around a matrix to facilitate response generalization. Previous research on generalized instruction-following (Striefel et al.,

Table 11-4. Introducing Social Routines

Play Situations	Sample Preparation and Facilitation Strategies	Potential Routines
Shopping at the grocery store	Let "clerk" hide several items in the store area. The buyer should be instructed to purchase those items, and helped to see the need to request information. The clerk should be prompted for direction-giving regarding location of items Both should be helped with greeting and departure routines and please and thank-you routines as appropriate	Request for information: "Do you have eggs?" "Where's the milk?" "How much is it?" Direction-giving: "On the bottom shelf" Greeting and departure Please and thank-you
Snack preparation and eating	One group can first be shown how to prepare a simple snack, with each child completing his or her own portion (e.g., skewering cheeses, olives, and meats on toothpick) This group can be paired with new children and asked to be the teachers Facilitators can prompt use of language as well as physical models for instructing peers Facilitators can show peers how to ask for clearer instructions	Request for information: "Where are the toothpicks?" Request for objects: "Need olives" Request for actions: "Hold it" Give information: "They're behind you" Give directions: "Put on two olives" Please and thank-you

1976) and generalized productive verb-noun phrase usage in manual language systems (Karlan et al., 1982) has demonstrated the efficacy of using a systematic combination matrix. This strategy consists of teaching a small number of possible combinations of elements (e.g., nouns, verbs) from a matrix to promote novel combinations of elements that were not taught together. Figure 11-1 shows several sample training matrices. Each matrix can be used within a play activity, with the adult modeling and prompting production of the target combinations. Other possible combinations that have not been taught should be probed to determine the extent of generalization. Following are sample play activities for use with the matrices in Figure 11-1.

Hiding Game. A major content goal could be to code locative state, using the form "preposition + location." The adult facilitator can choose a target combination ("in box") and instruct one child to hide there while another child (or a doll or puppet) turns his or her back. Next, another child can be asked to tell where the child is hiding; since one child (or doll) is not watching, there is communicative intent for the speaker to share this information. The linguistic form can also be displayed through a song (e.g., "Chad is hiding, . . . in the box") to serve as an additional, nondirective model.

Tea Party. A primary content goal can be to code action, using the form "agent + action." Children and animals can participate in a tea party, with the adult putting target combinations ("bear cook," "Katie wash") on display as the actions are performed nonverbally. To use the matrix framework, the facilitator will need to be subtly directive ("Table's dirty. Let bear help") so that target combinations will be enacted. A sample technique for making the communication meaningful is to pretend to be busy, then to call out a "real" question to prompt the target response ("What's bear up to?").

Outdoor Play. The content goal of action can again be taught, through the form of "action + object." A game format can be used, with the adult facilitator whispering instructions to the first child ("throw Frisbee"), who carries out the task, then directs the next child in line to repeat that same action. Thus, the child received a model in the form of instructions, and must now use the form "action + object" to instruct a peer. This has the added benefit of encouraging peer-peer exchange at an early communicative level.

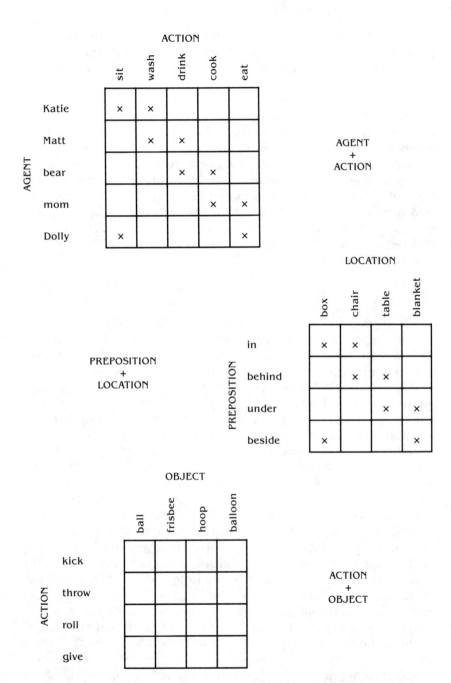

Figure 11-1. Sample matrices for use with play activities. These are merely samples; matrices should be expanded and modified to meet the needs of groups. The spaces marked with "X" indicate targets to elicit for efficient training.

It is clear that the social routines and matrix training approaches can be combined in a single session. For example, during the tea party, the primary target for data-keeping might be production of the form "agent + action" to code the content category of action. However, the social routines of greeting and departure can be used as each agent (child, animal, doll) comes to or leaves the party. The routine of answering questions is developed through the elicitation strategy ("What's bear doing?"), and the routines of requesting objects (food, drink, silverware) and please and thank you are practiced during the snack portion. In addition, adults can model social routines (requesting information, such as asking about the bear's actions) that are currently above the child's linguistic level. Social routines can be inserted into other matrix training activities as well, to allow telescoping of learning.

Use Goals

Many goals of use at the two- to three-word level were incorporated into the social routine and matrix training strategies. This section focuses on the application of referential communication games for more advanced students (Glucksberg, Krauss, and Weisberg, 1966; Robinson and Robinson, 1976). These games provide children with practice in decoding messages (in listening and later in reading) and in coding messages (in speaking and writing). In addition, a working relationship is established between the message sender and the message receiver. Barrie-Blackley (1978) describes six steps to follow in setting up a communication game. First, the facilitator must *determine the type of information to be conveyed.* To enhance enjoyment and effectiveness, the game should be both meaningful and related to other aspects of the child's life. For example, following a doll play activity, the game could deal with caregiving activities such as feeding, washing, or dressing dolls or animals. Detail and sequence categories to be included will depend on the child's developmental level and the targets of intervention. Examples are color; shape; space (above, in); material (plastic, wood); physical quantities (little, heavy); and number (one, ten). Second, the facilitator should *control the difficulty level* of the game by specifying the units of information. An information unit can be defined as a single action carried out on a single object. The amount of detail contained within each information unit must be specified. For developmentally young children, a small number of details is used, indicating that a small number of choices will be presented. For example, if there is only one doll and one washcloth, the instruction for doll-washing will be simple, whereas if there is both a large doll and a small doll, or a red washcloth and a blue washcloth, the sender will need to include more detail to provide a clear message. Another way to vary the difficulty is to control the number of information units given before the participants check their progress. For example, "wash the baby" is one unit, but a second unit, "now put the bib on" could be added. A third rule is that the *message sender and the message receiver should not be able to see each other;* thus, some type of barrier should be placed between them. However, for young children, a barrier may be distracting; a substitution may be to ensure that the message sender and message receiver cannot see objects of the partner because they are hidden (in a box, behind a screen). This has the added advantage of allowing face-to-face communication, so that partners can more readily discriminate communication breakdown through facial expressions, gestures, body posture, and so forth. The fourth rule is that the *message sender should perform the action.* After completing the action, the *sender tells the receiver what to do.* This provides salience to the message. Fifth, the message receiver is taught to *respond to the message,* by acknowledging it or expressing misunderstanding. This will need to be modeled or prompted for young children ("Matt, tell her to say it again"; "Janet, tell him he's talking too fast"; "Chuck, tell him you don't have a bib"). The final rule is that the sender can give the next direction only after the message receiver has *confirmed receiving the message.*

Clearly, communication games can involve highly complex goals of content, form, and use. However, they can also be modified for facilitating more simple goals. For example, the outdoor play activity described in the section on matrix training involves elements of the communication game, such as performing an activity, then directing a peer to perform it. A true communication game will also include some form of barrier, so that the receiver can perform the actions only through the verbal directions of the sender. A strategy for altering the outdoor play game so that it will conform to the rules is to supply each partner with identical materials (ball, Frisbee) and a walkie talkie. One partner can then go out of sight of the other (around the corner, back to back) and instruct in ways to manipulate the various objects ("roll the balloon"). Table 11–5 presents sample communication games that are based on content, form, and use goals, and are appropriate for developmentally young children.

Table 11–5. Sample Communication Games

Sample Goals	Materials and Set-Up	Sample Conversation
	Doll Play Task	
C Self-help topic F Action + object U Informing, directing, requesting info, acknowledging	Standard barrier Two sets of each: doll brush dog washcloth cup spoon	S: Informs ("I have doll"); commands ("You get doll") R: Acknowledges ("I have it") S: Commands ("Find washcloth") R: Acknowledges ("Got it") S: Commands ("Wash dolly") R: Requests information ("Where?") S: Gives information ("Wash dolly's face") R: Acknowledges ("O.K.")
	Snack Task	
C Colors, long or short F Modifier + noun U Describing (color, size)	Standard barrier Snack bowls containing: olives (green, black) cheese (yellow, white, red) toothpicks (long, short; yellow, red, green)	S: Informs ("I have olives and cheese") R: Requests information ("What do you have?") S: Informs ("Olives and cheese and toothpicks") R: Commands ("Get a long toothpick") R: Requests information ("What color?") S: ("Red toothpick")
	Dressing Up Dolls Task	
C Clothing items F Prepositional phrase used as modifier (dress with flower) U Command, request info, describe, acknowledge	Standard barrier with hole that can be plugged Matching sets from My First Paper Dolls (Golden) On each side, set up: boy, girl, dog, cat, hat, 2 dresses, 2 suits	S: Informs ("I have the girl") R: Commands ("Get your girl") S: Acknowledges ("I got my girl") R: Commands ("Find the dress") R: Requests information ("Which one?") S: Describes ("The dress with the rainbow on the front") (Note: When dolls are dressed, the plug can be removed so partners can view them to determine if the task was carried out correctly)

Code: C, Content; F, form; U, use; S, sender; R, receiver.
For additional strategies, see Glucksberg and colleagues (1966) and Robinson and Robinson (1976).

To summarize, play can be used as a framework for a wide range of communication intervention activities. This does not mean that random playing is recommended, but only play incorporating carefully identified communicative goals.

RESOURCES

Assessment. Bloom and Lahey (1978); Dunst (1978); Hanna et al. (1982); MacDonald and Gillette (1984d); Owens (1982); Sacks and Young (1982).

Intervention. Ausberger et al. (1982); Bloom and Lahey (1978); Fewell and Vadasy (1983); Hanna et al. (1982); Owens (1982).

Chapter 12

Early Augmentative Communication

DESCRIPTION AND RATIONALE

A wide range of terminology has been used relative to the area of communication intervention for nonspeaking people. The following list presents several terms that are used in this chapter, as defined by the Position Statement on Nonspeech Communication (1981):

- *Augmentative Communication System.* This refers to the total functional communication system of an individual, including (1) a communicative technique (e.g., manual signs, physical communication boards); (2) a symbol set or system (e.g., pictures, Blissymbolics, signs of American Sign Language); and (3) communication-interaction behavior (e.g., demands or requests, conversation).
- *Unaided.* All techniques that do not require any physical aids, such as speech, manual (signs or gestures), and facial or body communication are considered unaided.
- *Aided.* This refers to all techniques in which some type of physical object or device is used, including physical communication displays, mechanical typewriters, and electronic devices and prostheses.

Although the previous chapter (Chapter 11) covered oral speech alone, it should be noted that augmentative communication can also be used as a facilitator of oral communication (see Silverman, 1980, pp. 40–42, for a review of studies). For example, Musselwhite (in press, b) notes that gestural cues (through manual signs) can be used to prompt a variety of language components, including language *concepts* (beside, after, many), *forms* (plural "-s," auxiliary verbs), and *functions* (requesting information, initiating communication).

ASSESSMENT ISSUES

Assessment of nonspeaking children for potential use of an augmentative communication system is an extremely complex procedure that is typically undertaken by teams, including specialists from disciplines such as speech-language pathology, physical therapy, occupational therapy, special education, psychology, social work, and rehabilitation engineering. The members included on a team will depend on factors such as the age and needs of the child, with additional members required in some situations.

A number of tools have been developed recently to assess various behaviors relative to augmentative communication. Sample tools are *An Assessment Battery for Assistive Device Systems Recommendations: Part 1* (Meyers, Grows, Coleman, and Cook, 1980); election criteria for determining candidacy for an augmentative communication system (Shane and Bashir, 1980); *Non Oral Communication Assessment Forms* (Montgomery, 1980); *The Non-Oral Communication Assessment* (Fell, 1984); and *The Nonspeech Test for Receptive/Expressive Language* (Huer, 1983), The Formal Pre-Sign Motor Assessment (Dunn, 1982, pp. 76–78) can be used for assessing potential for unaided communication. Each of these assessment tools is described in Appendix A. Assessment cautions in augmentative communication include the need for a team approach, the wide range of areas to be assessed, and the rapid of growth of information in the field, meaning that materials can become outdated in a short period of time.

INTERVENTION STRATEGIES USING ADAPTIVE PLAY

Numerous ideas have been presented throughout this book for incorporating adaptive play and augmentative communication into various activities, such as symbolic play routines. This chapter focuses on early augmentative communication goals that can be facilitated through adaptive play, and on potential communication barriers that may be ameliorated to some extent through adaptive play strategies.

Early Augmentative Communication Goals

Some of the goals described may be considered precursory to augmentative communication. Both unaided and aided system goals are presented as they relate to adaptive play.

Unaided Communication

Nonverbal Intervention. Many of the early goals for users of unaided communication systems will be similar or identical to those for speakers. For example, the goals described in Chapter 11 for *Nonverbal Intervention* are appropriate for unaided communication users. Motor imitation will be a more central goal for the potential unaided communication user. Child factors such as hearing impairment or cognitive delay may of course require modifications in training strategies. Strategies presented in Chapter 9 should be emphasized for potential signers.

Early Sign Intervention. Some differences in goals will be apparent as the child moves to the phase corresponding to the "early verbal intervention" phase, as signs or gestures will be used in addition to or in place of words. Strategies for selecting a *core lexicon* of signs have been suggested by Dunn (1982), Fristoe and Lloyd (1980); Musselwhite and St. Louis (1982); and Reichle, Williams, and Ryan (1981). For example, the feature "ease of production and discrimination" assumes great importance in selecting early signs. Some selection features, such as child preference, will remain the same.

To some extent, the procedures suggested by Wilcox (1984) for facilitating single word production will apply to single sign production. Goossens' (1983) presents an outline-format summary of instructional procedures for teaching gestural communication systems to nonspeakers, based on an extensive literature review. Three sample training strategies that can be incorporated into adaptive play are the following:

Time Delay. Table 3–5 summarizes the general time delay procedure, which can be applied to teaching signing in adaptive play contexts. The adult facilitator will first model the target response (e.g., sign MORE) and, if necessary, physically prompt the child to produce it within an appropriate context. The adult sets up a situation (tickles the child, then stops) in which the sign is appropriate and expected, then delays for a predetermined length of time (e.g., 10 seconds) while looking at the child expectantly. If the child completes the behavior (signs MORE), the adult praises and immediately provides the natural consequence (tickling), whereas failure to produce the behavior yields predetermined prompts (verbal, gestural, physical). This procedure can be used within many play contexts, such as outdoor play (delay help in pushing swing); doll play (delay giving child play materials automatically); and turntaking games (delay pushing toy through the tube). This delay procedure puts emphasis on the situation as the elicitor of a sign; eventually, the facilitator will want to expand the situation-evoked component by strategies such as reducing proximity to the child and reducing eye contact (so the expectancy is not so obvious).

Manipulating Iconicity. Goossens' (1982, 1983) reviewed a number of studies suggesting strategies to make the iconicity (guessability) of signs more apparent to the learner. Several of these strategies can be highlighted through play activities. The first set of considerations deals with manipulating the *symbol* aspect of the association between the sign (WALK, BABY, BIG) and its referent (the act of walking, a doll, the relative size of the item). One sample manipulation involves adding facial movement or expression with or without sounds simultaneously with sign production. For example, during a tea party, the adult could add lip-licking to the sign HUNGRY and eating noises to the sign EAT. Manipulations can also involve slight changes in signs to make them more apparent, such as making the hands clearly "walk" for WALK. The *referent* aspect can also be modified. For example, the movement of the referent action can be exaggerated, as in enlarging BIG. It may also help to choose prototypical referents that clearly mirror the visual image or configuration of the sign. For example, a "Fun Box" filled with enticing items to encourage requesting OPEN could be a box with flaps, to demonstrate the movement of the sign (opening the flaps). A related modification would be to use the referent as a prompt to physically mold the handshape of the sign. For example, the child's hands can be placed on the box and he or she can be helped to open the flaps. A variety of other play materials (doll, cup, bib) can be used in this manner. Although these strategies could also be accomplished in a nonplay setting, many of them (e.g., enlarging signs, adding facial expressions or sounds) are ideally suited to a spirit of playfulness.

Music. Music can also be used with adaptive play to facilitate sign acquisition; in fact, many traditional songs combine gesture with melody (e.g., "Itsy Bitsy Spider"). Musselwhite (1985) reports on a number of studies and anecdotal reports that have supported the use of music in training unaided communication. For example, Jameson (1984) investigated the use of melody in sign acquisition with four trainable mentally handicapped preschoolers. Probe data measuring generalization across time, place, and person consistently favored the use of melody, signs were acquired more quickly with melody, and subjects were more likely to verbalize signs introduced with melody than those introduced without melody. Early signed songs should meet several criteria (Musselwhite, 1985): (1) ease of acquisition (simple, short songs); (2) acceptability to children and staff; (3) teaching opportunities (e.g., communicative goals for content, form, and use); and (4) opportunities for generalization (interactive component within song, opportunities for later practice) (see Chapter 16 for further ideas).

In terms of form in unaided communication, the focus will be on enhancing the clarity of sign production. Dunn (1982) describes motor skills that are involved in accurate sign production, and Shane and Wilbur (1980) identify the primary motor components that predict success in expressive signing. Attention can be given to the primary locations (chest, hand, face), handshapes (flat hand, index finger, curved hand, fist, thumb touch), and motions (linear, handshape change, rotate or twist, repeat, circular, arc, hold) used in a core vocabulary of signs appropriate for use by nonspeaking individuals. Table 16–2 in Chapter 16 presents sample art activities that can be used to facilitate the motor components of sign production. These motor components can also be incorporated into other play activities, such as toy play (e.g., index finger isolation in dialing a toy phone) or social routines (e.g., handshape change while doing the "Open-Shut" rhyme). Sample pre-sign activities and adaptive teaching techniques are presented in Dunn (1982).

Expanded Sign Intervention. Signing fits well into the matrix training and social routine tasks covered in Chapter 11. However, if signing skills are to be extended through communication games, procedures will have to be modified so that each player can see the signs made by the other. For example, a simple task would be for the sender to sit at the top of a small indoor slide, with the receiver sitting at the bottom. The sender can have a box of play materials (baby, ball) that he or she will first describe; the receiver will next request one object, which will be located and sent down via the slide. As with the games described in Chapter 11, the game can be made more complex by increasing the detail within an information unit. For example, the box can contain several balls of different colors, sizes, or materials, so that the receiver must specify which one is to be sent. Since players can see each other, signing communication games are more difficult to arrange for increased complexity. However, children who have good impulse control (so that they won't "peek") could use a barrier off to one side to hide the objects being manipulated, then move from behind the barrier for signed communication.

Aided Communication

Aided communication, especially for the child with severe physical disabilities, involves numerous skills to be taught. The sequence presented for oral communication will be followed: however, the timing for acquisition of skills such as scanning can be highly variable.

Nonverbal Intervention. It is important to focus on all areas listed in the *Nonverbal Intervention* section in Chapter 11. That is, a diagnosis of severe cerebral palsy should not preclude attempts at movement imitation and vocal imitation. Although the child may not develop adequate vocal skills for intelligible speech, he or she might be able to use vocalizations productively for purposes such as summoning attention, answering questions eliciting yes or no answers, or giving feedback (similar to "uh-huh"). Similarly, although motor skills may not be sufficient for conventional signing, a limited number of conventional or idiosyncratic signs may be developed to provide rapid, "portable" communication for basic needs as a supplement to aided communication. For example, movement imitation training may demonstrate that the child has adequate skills for production of gross motor signs from DuffySign (Duffy, 1977) or may identify movements that can be used as idiosyncratic signs.

The reciprocal gaze patterns established in this phase will be especially important for aided communication users. Strategies presented in Chapter 7 should also be considered as precursory augmentative communication goals.

Initial Aided Communication. The task for the aided communication user becomes extremely complex, as the nonspeaker must learn skills, such as a means to indicate, elements for a symbol set or system, alternative output forms, and interaction patterns for optimum communication using an atypical medium. Sample adaptive play strategies will be suggested for the first three goals listed here.

An early goal will be to develop some type of *indicating* message entries. Table 12–1 presents brief descriptions of the three basic means of indicating — direct selection, scanning, and encoding — with sample adaptive play activities designed to enhance each. It should be noted that the three methods are not of equal ease in terms of cognitive and motoric demands. Encoding is typically believed to be the highest cognitively, whereas direct selection through pointing requires the highest physical skill.

Table 12–1. Adaptive Play Activities to Enhance Means of Indicating

Means of Indicating	Description	Sample Play Strategies
*Direct Selection**	User indicates the message elements by directly pointing in some manner	Play "You can't get it" to develop reaching, then extend this to pointing
Hand Pointing	Fist or knuckle used to point	Have child "catch" cars or puppets on tray
Finger Pointing	Index, middle finger, or thumb used to point	Have child poke clay or other material in compartments of fishing tackle box; hide pressure switch under pictures, so that pointing activates toy
Handstick	Appliance held by child or attached	Let child choose objects with magic wand
Mouth, wand or headstick	Appliance attached to controlled part	Have puppet or doll model use of appliance
Eye gaze	Eye-pointing to objects or symbols	Play "I'm Looking at . . ." with child trying to match your gaze
Scanning	Message elements are presented one at a time; user indicates desired elements	Begin with decision-making (Chapter 7) Use computer scanning learning games** Play 20 Questions with nondisabled peers
Encoding Color-number	Pattern or code of signals is used to indicate message elements; Sample: two-movement encoding	Teach color-matching through games such as "I Spy," board games, and toy sorting tasks
Morse Code	Dots and dashes represent alphabet	Introduce Walkie-Talkies with help

*See Fothergill et al. (1978) for a discussion of various means of indicating.
**For current listings of computer programs for learning skills such as scanning, consult the International Software/Hardware Registry, Trace Center, 314 Waisman Center, 1500 Highland Avenue, Madison, WI 53706.

Aided communication users must also develop a *core lexicon* of graphic symbols. Musselwhite (in press, a) provides a summary of various symbol sets and systems available. Suggestions for selecting early symbols are presented in Carlson (1981) and Musselwhite and St. Louis (1982).

Goossens' (1982) reviewed the literature on instructional procedures for aided communication and identified several general and specific manipulations that have been found to enhance symbol learning. Sample suggestions are presented for incorporating several findings relative to the iconic dimension through adaptive play. In manipulating the *symbol* aspect of the symbol-to-referent association, changes can be made that do not alter symbol structure. For example, the facilitator can animate or interact with cardboard or wooden cutouts of symbols in a manner that suggests their typical action sequence or function. An example would be "jumping" the Blissymbol for jump, or placing the Picsym for "sit" on a toy chair. Some manipulations will alter symbol structure, such as embellishing symbols by colored "helping lines" or coloring in parts of symbols (e.g., grapes), then comparing them to a referent that is a replica (plastic grapes) or a prototypical referent (vineyard grapes). Picsym system (Carlson, 1985) uses many helping lines, which are lightened or dotted, and the Blissymbolics Communication Institute (1984) has recently developed *Picture Your Blissymbols*, which consists of graphic enhancements of Blissymbols designed to illustrate the meaning of selected Blissymbols for introductory purposes. Both of these systems are very play-oriented, and are highly suited to inclusion in play activities. The *referent* aspect of the symbol-to-referent association can also be manipulated by using exemplars that best mirror the configuration or the symbol, and by embedding the symbol in a picture of its referent, or on a referent. For example, Carlson (1982) describes symbol toys that present Picsyms on the items they represent (doll, block, ball).

Perhaps because symbol learning reminds adults of traditional picture tasks, symbol learning can often become rote and meaningless. Incorporating symbol learning into play activities can help promote intent and motivation, so that symbol training does not degenerate into a series of "point to . . ." sessions. Numerous strategies for promoting symbol acquisition have been presented throughout this book, especially in Chapters 10 and 13 (the section on providing parent support).

Another goal that can be enhanced through adaptive play is that of experimenting with various *output* types. Children can play with visual output by means of cathode ray tubes in computer games, and they can experience light-emitting diode (LED) output through playing with calculators. Exposure to vocal output using synthetic speech can be gained from experimenting with simple computer games using speech synthesizers. An introduction to pre-recorded speech can be offered through an adaptive switch and a tape recorder. Initially, the child can just "babble" by activating the tape, but gradually interactive play-oriented programs can be initiated using loop tapes and a set of vocabulary items, with the child using a scanning mode of selection.

Expanded Aided Communication. The goal of expanding aided communication does not imply that all messages must be expanded in length, but that successful communication be enhanced. Thus, although "use a complete sentence" might be an appropriate admonition for a nonspeaker in an occasional training session, typically it would not be an appropriate response to a request for a cookie. The strategy of using naturally structured training tasks is extremely important for aided communication users, who may already face great frustrations in communication attempts.

Adaptive play can provide a focus and a motivation for true communication, as opposed to stereotyped or "show" speech. Strategies for expanding aided communication will be discussed within the context of overcoming barriers to communication.

Barriers to Effective Communication

The few existing studies on interaction in augmentative communication indicate that nonspeakers (1) are not given as many turns to communicate, (2) typically produce only one utterance per turn, (3) receive and produce a limited repertoire of communicative functions, and (4) communicate infrequently with their peers (Harris, 1982; Shane, Lipschultz, and Shane, 1982; Yoder and Kraat, 1983). After reviewing research and anecdotal reports, Musselwhite (in press, a) identified four categories of barriers to effective communication interaction: (1) the communication techniques and symbols selected; (2) altered conversational patterns; (3) altered temporal patterns; and (4) altered conversational forms and functions. Each of these areas will be described briefly, with adaptive play intervention strategies suggested where appropriate.

Communication Techniques and Symbols Selected

Techniques, such as scanning, may interfere with eye contact. The concern is that nonspeakers may have eyes trained to the communication display, thus missing out on face-to-face interaction. A simple game of "gotcha" can be played between an adult and child who are sharing information via a joint communication display. A prearranged signal (e.g., stomping foot) can be used each time one partner catches the other forgetting to reestablish eye contact between messages. Silly penalties can be applied to make the exercise more motivating. This game has the added advantage of requiring the adult to model turns on the child's communication display.

Symbols, such as abstract Picsyms or combined Blissymbols, may be difficult for partners to interpret. The strategies suggested previously for training a core lexicon can be applied to communication partners as well. In addition, simple rules for forming symbols can be explained to people at an appropriate development level.

Altered Conversational Patterns

Speaker and listener *roles and turntaking protocols may be drastically altered.* This can give a decided power advantage to the listener and interfere with effective interaction. Communication games, as described in Chapter 11, can provide an ideal format for equalizing turntaking. Initially, the partner should be a speaking child, with the nonspeaker serving first as the receiver but rapidly moving to the role of sender. The rules for setting up games will vary if the nonspeaker cannot manipulate objects on his or her side of the barrier. In addition, a total barrier cannot be used unless the child is using a vocal output communication aid. A sample game could involve dual sets of "peel and stick" pictures. Before the game, the nonspeaker could use his or her communication board to indicate to the teacher where to place the picture pieces. The completed picture would then be set on a stand in view of the sender (nonspeaker), with the matching set (with no items affixed) on a stand in front of the receiver. The sender would use his or her communication display, which

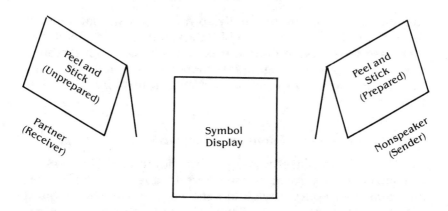

Figure 12-1. Communication board set-up for symbol-board user. The Symbol Display is jointly visible, while each Peel and Stick display is visible to only one participant. Sample Peel and Stick sets, such as a Uniset House, Farm, or Zoo set, are available from The Speech Bin, 8 Beechtree Lane, Plainsboro, NJ 08536.

would be jointly visible, to instruct the receiver in making the picture match the original. Figure 12-1 depicts the spatial arrangement of this communication game. Because the speaker must rely on the nonspeaker, roles and turntaking are more equalized.

Altered Temporal Patterns

Real conversational time, or production of message at approximately the rate of oral communication, is necessary for some functions, such as commenting on fast-moving action. Some aided communication users may find this impossible. One way to reduce the impact of this problem is to have *multiple displays* that are readily accessible in all settings and include messages appropriate for functions such as quick comments. For example, a display for use while watching or playing computer games might include entries such as WOW!, GOTCHA!, or UH-OH placed around the perimeter of the screen.

Slow rate can yield problems such as loss of listener attention, listener interruption, or shift of topic. Rate of indicating may be enhanced for some children through practice with symbol-aided songs (Musselwhite, 1985). The child can indicate key words through "rhythmic pointing" (Brodsky, 1983), with the tempo speeded up gradually so the child can maintain the pace. Since time pressure can often result in slower rate, due to increased tension and more errors, play can be a nonthreatening medium for encouraging rate increase. The facilitator must be alert to the child's level of tolerance in responding to time pressure.

Altered Conversational Forms and Functions

The need to make messages brief to allow rapid message transmission may force nonspeakers to *abandon polite forms and humor.* Although the child need not procede each request with "please," knowledge of how to use such social routines when necessary (e.g., to "soften" a request) is important. The strategies described previously for using social routines are applicable to aided communication users as well.

Research has demonstrated that communication partners may produce a proportionally *large number of requests and directives.* This has implication for direct training of partners. Peer partners might be more motivated to join into play-based activities than to sit in on lecture-style training sessions. The facilitator can model additional communication functions appropriate for use with nonspeakers, such as information-sharing and commenting. Communication activities involving matrix training are an appropriate format for putting a variety of functions on display. The nonspeaker should be encouraged to communicate directly with the peer, to avoid casting the adult in the role of primary communication partner or translator.

To summarize, adaptive play activities can serve as nonthreatening, enjoyable opportunities for learning and using augmentative communication skills. Knowledge of potential barriers to effective communication can be used to identify early goals, so that some of the barriers can be avoided.

PART IV
DEVELOPING SUPPORT
FOR ADAPTIVE PLAY

Chapter 13

Initiating a Toy Lending Library

It is extremely important that adaptive play skills be practiced and enjoyed in all environments. Thus, if the child spends a large portion of the day away from home, specific efforts must be made to ensure that play skills learned in a school or center setting are used also at home with parents and other caregivers. This may be difficult if the family does not own adaptive play materials that are appropriate for their child. One way to deal with this problem is to offer a toy lending library so that parents and other caregivers may check out play materials that are suited to the needs and interest level of their children.

RATIONALE FOR BEGINNING A TOY LENDING LIBRARY

The toy lending concept derives from the Lekotek concept; "Lek" is Swedish for play, "-tek" is the Greek suffix connoting library. The first Lekotek was begun in Stockholm in 1963, and currently there are Lekoteks in over 30 countries. The primary goal of a Lekotek is to facilitate the integration of the disabled child into his or her family, and thus into society. A Lekotek is considerably more than a toy lending facility, as it offers counseling and resource services to families and communities in order to assist in the integration of disabled children into the mainstream. All Lekotek leaders receive specific training in play and counseling methods. Lekoteks also have extensive toy libraries attached to their programs, to assist in promoting play for children with disabilities. (See Lekotek, Appendix B, for more information.)

There are numerous excellent reasons to organize a toy lending library for disabled or nondisabled children. This section will focus on development of a toy lending library for children with special needs to meet the following goals:

Focus for Parent-Child Interaction. A well-chosen toy may provide the basis for a successful interaction between caregiver and child, especially for a caregiver who seems to have difficulty initiating appropriate interactions. A toy that allows the child to demonstrate competence may also enhance the parents' impression of their child's ability to learn.

Logistics. It is unrealistic to assume that each family will be able to purchase a number of stimulating, age-appropriate toys that offer opportunities for learning; in addition, many toys needed by children with severe physical disabilities are not readily available or must be produced or adapted by hand.

Generalization of Learning. The literature on training severely disabled children has documented that generalization cannot be expected to occur automatically (Brown et al., 1976). Therefore, skills taught in classroom environments should be practiced in other natural environments, especially the residential setting (home, institutional cottage).

Focus for Sibling- or Peer-Child Interaction. Too often children with special needs are isolated from their peers or siblings because they are unable to participate in normative play activities. If adaptive play materials of high interest to nondisabled children are selected, the nondisabled child may be engaged in the play process with the disabled child. This works especially well if the disabled child masters use of the adaptive play materials first and can serve as "teacher" to the sibling or peer.

Framework for Parent Training. Closely related to the previous considerations is the idea that appropriate materials can provide a framework for enjoyable parent training activities. An example would be the use of an "object-in-the-can" switch described in Chapter 5 to aid in teaching and practicing skills such as direction following ("Get the apple and put it in"), turntaking, release of objects, and cause-effect relationships.

Development of Lifetime Leisure Skills. It is hoped that early introduction of appropriate adaptive play materials in the home environment can reduce the "learned helplessness" often seen in adult severely disabled people. In addition, the sheer enjoyment value of play must never be forgotten.

STRATEGIES FOR BEGINNING A SMALL-SCALE TOY LENDING LIBRARY

A number of decisions must be made in planning a toy lending library. One question that must be considered initially is whether several organizations should join resources to form a community-wide toy lending library, or whether individual facilities should form their own toy lending libraries, focusing on the specific needs of each facility. As with many questions, there are advantages and disadvantages on each side. Table 13–1 summarizes potential advantages and disadvantages. A compromise solution may be to develop a community-wide toy lending library with facility-based satellites; the satellites could check out an assortment of materials from the larger library or develop their own inventory, with the community library serving as a resource and clearinghouse for information and materials. Regardless of the delivery mode selected — community-wide or facility-based — many of the subsequent decisions will be the same.

Several excellent resources are available to assist planners in developing a toy lending library (see the *Resources* section at the end of this chapter). This section summarizes useful approaches and highlights additional strategies that are especially useful in initiating a small, low-budget toy lending library.

Gathering Support

The first step for the organizer will be to gather support for a toy lending library from administrators, staff, parents, and community. This can be handled in a variety of ways, depending on the group. Several ideas are presented here for engaging the support of the various groups named. The unifying element in each of these approaches is advance planning. That is, each group must be convinced from the outset that this is a well thought-out, achievable, worthwhile objective.

The *administrators* must first agree that the project is appropriate and manageable. This may best be accomplished in terms of a short proposal, listing the goals (modified from those presented in the *Rationale* section of this chapter); a plan of action (specifying support needed from the administration in terms of space, personnel, materials, and funds); and a timetable (when each component will be completed). This proposal

Table 13 – 1.   Choosing a Facility-Based or Community-Wide Toy Lending Library

Facility-Based Library	Community-Wide Library
Advantages	*Advantages*
Logistics — users will be on-site and can check out materials easily	Large inventory of play materials
Person(s) checking out materials will likely be familiar with child's interests and needs	Potential for hiring professional staff
Child's teachers or therapists can select materials to support goals	Large inventory of support materials and more opportunity for information-sharing
	Opportunity to meet parents whose children are at different facilities
Disadvantages	*Disadvantages*
Potential for duplication of services	Less personalized service
Smaller pool to draw from in stocking, staffing, and maintaining library	Added difficulty in using library resources, owing to travel needs

can be very brief and should require as little attention from administrators as is feasible; however, its presentation will demonstrate the advance planning that has gone into this project.

Gaining support from the facility *staff* will ensure smoother operation of the toy lending library, as staff members can play an important role in checking materials in or out and encouraging parents to make use of the library. In addition, staff members can be especially helpful in recommending toys to be included in the toy lending library and appropriate materials for specific children. Staff support can be enlisted through discussion at staff meetings or informal gatherings (break time) with ideas enlisted from staff members from the beginning of the process.

Perhaps the most important supporters of the toy lending library will be the *parents* of the children for whom the library is intended. Although their primary role is to check out toys often and to use them with their children, parents can also be helpful in all phases of the development and operation of a toy lending library. The idea can be presented as a program at a parent-teacher organization meeting. The program might include aspects such as the following: a speaker from an existing toy lending library; a display of toys that would be included in the inventory; a description of the benefits of a toy lending library; brief presentations from professionals (special educator, speech-language pathologist, physical and occupational therapists) indicating the skills that can be enhanced through play at home; and a brainstorming session to develop ideas for beginning and maintaining the toy lending library.

After the other groups have been engaged in the organizational process, *community* support should be developed. Community groups can aid a toy lending library in numerous ways, such as collecting toys, donating new toys, making toys, making toy bags, or volunteering to work in the library (cataloging, cleaning, repairing toys, serving as librarian). Community support can be gained through a variety of approaches, including writing a mini-grant proposal to community agencies such as Junior League (see *Child's Play*, Vol. 1, No. 5, p. 7, for excellent ideas); inviting representatives from groups to visit the toy lending library; and making a presentation to a civic group, including many of the same components as suggested previously for a parent-teacher program.

Finding a Location

As programs grow and expand, finding available space may become a major concern. Some excellent suggestions for providing space for a toy lending library can be found in the resource *Toys Help* by the Canadian Association of Toy Libraries (1981). Several desirable features of a potential space are easy access from the outside, for the convenience of patrons; minimal interference with ongoing activities, such as classrooms; space for children to sit and play while parents check out toys; attractiveness, including good lighting and an attractive display of toys; and room to grow. Facilities that plan a small toy lending library will typically not be able to provide an entire room for that purpose. However, a closet opening onto a hall may be available if materials are shifted; this can be modified to meet library needs through adding shelves, lighting, and so forth. If a separate space is not available, von Levetzow (1981) recommends building or purchasing an enclosed toy storage unit that can be kept in a classroom and opened during check-out times. Additional ideas on storage can be found in Liman's publication, *The Spacemaker Book* (1977). Another possibility is to use a mobile unit, such as a van (see von Levetzow, 1981, for addresses of currently operating mobile units). The space needs of a small toy lending library are not great, as much of the inventory will be checked out to patrons at any one time. As von Levetzow notes, "Sometimes one has to begin an innovative idea in this

modest way and expand as it becomes more successful"
(1981, p. 4).

Selecting Toys

Toy selection must be made with great care, especially if the
initial inventory of toys will be small. The toys chosen will depend to a great extent on the needs and interests of potential
borrowers. For example, if the population includes many severely physically disabled children, adapted battery-operated
toys and switches may be important items to include. A number
of published toy lists are available, and can be extremely helpful
in narrowing down choices (e.g., Beesley and Preston, 1981; Riddick, 1982; Sinker, 1983; Toy Libraries Association, 1983; Webb,
1978). Each of these resources describes a variety of toys, cate-
gorizes areas of skill learning, and specifies manufacturers.
Note that toy guides can become outdated and that a toy guide
prepared in one country may list toys difficult to locate in another country. Jeffrey (1981b) suggests that selection guidelines be used in conjunction with published toy lists. Chapter 4
includes a summary of selection guidelines for general use,
which can be adapted to the needs of a toy lending library.

Collecting Toys

A low-budget toy lending library will need to explore creative
options for developing and maintaining an inventory. The following strategies have been used successfully at small toy lending libraries:

Grant Proposals. A proposal for a grant to initiate a toy library can be sent to government agencies or foundations (see
Catalog of Federal Domestic Assistance, 1979, Appendix A, and
The Foundation Center, Appendix B, for starters). As suggested
previously, financial support from community groups may be
enlisted through presenting mini-grant proposals. For example,
a proposal can be sent to service groups such as the Junior
League or local universities or churches. (Several excellent suggestions for writing funding proposals are presented in *Child's
Play,* Volume 1, No. 5, p. 7.)

Toy Drive. A new and used toy drive can be organized by the
facility or by a community group. This can be initiated by a feature newspaper article describing the project and examples of

needed materials. The crucial element of a toy drive appears to be intense follow-up. The following example illustrates strategies for organizing a toy drive. A class of sixth graders at a public school agreed to collect toys for a developmental day center as part of a bartering project (see Chapter 14). The steps they took were the following: (1) inform the students and parents of the upcoming toy drive (through the monthly school newsletter); (2) organize into teams, to canvass grade levels; (3) inform students, through a letter read and posted in each classroom, of the specific types of toys needed; (4) deposit marked boxes ("Toys for Irene Wortham Center") in each classroom; (5) set up a grade level contest for the most appropriate, useable toys collected; (6) gather toys, judge contests, and award prizes (kindergarten, cookie party; fourth grade, coupon for free french fries); (7) sort, clean, and deliver all appropriate toys to the toy lending library. This strategy proved extremely effective in terms of both the quantity and the quality of the yield; the steps could be modified to meet the needs of each situation. It is crucial to be selective in accepting used toys; toys that are not appropriate should be given to an appropriate agency, and toys not in good condition should be discarded.

Discounts on Large Orders. A number of toy manufacturers (Tomy, Child Guidance, Little Tyke) offer discounts on large orders. In addition, discounts are available to educators on small orders (over $25) of specific toy assortments from Johnson and Johnson Child Development Products (see Appendix B).

Pool Buying. Related to the previous suggestion is the idea of pool buying, with several organizations joining together to order materials. This practice can help toy lending libraries meet the high minimum orders of many manufacturers. Pool buying can also reduce shipping costs. (See *Child's Play*, Volume 1, No. 5, for specific information and addresses on pool buying.)

Trading Stamps. Although this is not feasible for stocking an entire toy lending library, collecting trading stamps (Green Stamps, Top Value Stamps) from parents or civic groups can add to the inventory.

Handmade Toys. Many toys and other materials appropriate for the needs of severely physically disabled children are not readily available commercially or are quite expensive, owing to the small market. Parents or service organizations such as the Telephone Pioneers may be enlisted to make specific materials, such as battery-run toy adapters and adaptive switches. In Chapter 14 are suggested strategies for encouraging groups to make materials for a facility.

Organizing Toys

Once a base of toys has been established, it will be necessary to prepare these toys for check-out. This involves several steps, which are outlined in the following section.

Toys must first be assessed to ensure that they are clean, working, safe, and appropriate for the intended borrowers. At this point, wooden toys should be given a polyurethane coating (preceded by a nontoxic sealer, if unpainted). Concern should be given to making all toys appear attractive and inviting, to encourage borrowers to use them, and to avoid abusing them.

Next, toys should be categorized and catalogued, according to the category system selected. Each facility can choose the category system that best suits its needs. Table 13–2 presents a relatively simple category system used by the Canadian Association of Toy Libraries. That organization recommends identifying items by number, with a category number followed by a decimal point and the number of pieces. For example, an abacus with 16 pieces would be labeled D4.16, where D = Discrimination, 4 = fourth toy in category, and 16 = number of pieces. A second copy of the same toy would be labeled D4.16(2). The number for each toy should be recorded in a master catalogue.

Once toys are categorized and catalogued, they must be marked with the catalogue number. Several possibilities for marking toys are the following: using permanent, nontoxic markers, wood-burning pencils, or adhesive stickers.

Careful consideration must be given to procedures for storing toys. This is important so that toys can be displayed attractively and with easy accessibility while protecting them from damage or loss of pieces. Von Levetzow (1981) offers several suggestions for reinforcing existing containers (using tape or covering with clear plastic) or transferring toys to suitable containers (such as opaque freezer boxes or see-through drawstring net bags, hung from hooks). She also suggests that pictures of toys should be retained from original boxes to affix to substitute containers or to use in a pictorial catalogue.

Table 13-2.   Toy Categories

A for *Activity*	a. Suitable for nonwalkers as well as walkers
	b. Suitable for walkers and climbers only
B for *Baby Play*	a. Sense stimulating toys
	b. First handling and pushing toys
C for *Coordination*	a. Fitting, threading, screwing, turning, hammering, steering, and balancing skills
	b. Insets and jigsaws
	c. Construction
D for *Discrimination*	a. Visual: matching, sorting, grading
	b. Auditory: music appreciation
E for *Expression*	a. Creative
	b. Fantasy
	c. Language
F for *Figures* (Shapes and Measurement)	a. Geometric shapes and sizes
	b. Numbers and scoring
	c. Measuring time, weight, etc.

G for *Games and Amusement Toys*
H for *Homemade Toys*
I for *Instrumental Aids*
R for *Reading Aids and Books*
T for *Tapes*
TP for *Tape Players*

From von Levetzow (1981, pp. 4-7). Adapted from Wroe, 1979, Organising a Toy Library, the British Institute on Mental Handicap).

Distributing Toys

This section includes procedures that will be followed in the check-out process. Several strategies can make this job more manageable.

First, a record system must be established to keep track of toys and borrowers. The Canadian Association of Toy Libraries (1978) suggests several options for record-keeping (see also von Levetzow, 1981). This might include a toy card with general and specific information concerning the toy (identifying and descriptive information, special uses of the toy) and a family card (including a description of the child's needs, a listing of the toys the child checks out, comments regarding progress).

Toy lending bags — sturdy and attractive drawstring bags — can be used for transporting toys to and from the toy lending library. Von Levetzow (1981) notes that this helps to identify the toys as borrowed ones, keeps them separate from other toys, reminds the family to return them, and provides a link between library and home. These bags are an excellent choice for a simple bartering project.

Each toy lending library must determine its own check-out policies. This will include a number of decisions, such as the following: (1) who may check out toys; (2) length of borrowing; (3) charges for borrowing, loss, damage, or overdue toys; (4) hours of operation; and (5) how toys will be selected (parents, children, teachers, therapists, or a combination of these). With regard to the final consideration, the toy selection for an individual child will depend on the goals for that child; if the primary goal is enjoyment and general learning, the child and parents are likely the best judges. However, if specific intervention goals are to be practiced through use of toys, input should be provided by teachers, therapists, or other professionals working with the child.

Providing Support to Parents or Caregivers

Dunst (1983) examined the relationship between different degrees of social support available to families and the following factors: (1) parental well-being; (2) family integrity; and (3) child characteristics. A group of 136 parents enrolled in the Family, Infant and Preschool Program (FIPP) at Western Carolina Center (Morganton, NC) completed both a Family Support Scale (Dunst and Jenkins, 1982) and the Questionnaire on Resources and Stress (Holroyd, 1978). Compared with parents in low and medium support groups, parents with high degrees of social support available reported (1) that their physical and emotional health was better; (2) that their families were more integrated units; and (3) that their childrens' behavior was less troublesome and the impact of their childrens' disabilities was less pervasive. Interestingly, there were no significant differences between the children of the parents in the three different support groups in terms of a number of child measures (chronological age, mental age, intelligence quotient, social age, social quotient, birth order, number of siblings, sex, and diagnosis). Therefore, Dunst asserts that "evidently, having support available makes the difficult job of rearing a handicapped or mentally retarded child seem less difficult" (1983, p. 34).

A toy lending library can be one excellent way to provide support to parents of children with disabilities, both directly and indirectly. Indirect support comes through contacts parents may make while visiting the library and general support of their parenting efforts through provision of appropriate adaptive play materials. In many cases, it will be helpful to provide more direct support for specific goals by providing training in conjunction with the toy lending library concept. This section will suggest potential direct parent training to accompany the provision of toys to disabled children.

Parent training may take the form of workshops designed to help parents capitalize on the learning potential of play activities. For example, an occupational therapist could share ideas on developing the pincer grasp through play; a physical therapist could suggest play activities that encourage weight-shifting while seated; a speech-language pathologist could demonstrate techniques for encouraging production and repetition of vocalizations during physical play; and a special educator could present ways to learn color labels through game-playing.

Manolson (1984) suggests that adults take on many different roles when they play with children, including *the entertainer* (to get a child's attention); *the director* (to teach the child); *the observer* (when we're not quite sure how to join in); and, best of all, *the conversationalist,* "an equal partner in the activity, who initiates, responds, and encourages the child to take his or her turn" (p. 69). When professionals encourage parents to use their skills in teaching their children, all parental roles must be emphasized, so that the adult does not dominate the interaction. Manolson (1984) and MacDonald and Gillette (1984a,b,c,d) offer numerous training strategies that can be incorporated into group training workshops or training sessions with individual parents and their children.

Another parent training format that can be offered in conjunction with a toy lending library is the provision of print materials that provide general or specific ideas (or both) for toy use of skill acquisition. For example, the *Lekotek Guide to Good Toys* (Sinker, 1983) includes ideas for home use of selected toys that can be sent home with that toy. The Johnson and Johnson Child Development Toys each include an illustrated, 10 to 20 page "Play and Learning Guide" suggesting traditional and creative ways to use each toy at various developmental stages, and providing additional games or parent-made toys to further stimulate the child. A toy lending library can easily design print materials to accompany toys. Simple sign or symbol books can be prepared to help both the child and the parent learn signs or symbols associated with a toy. Booklets can list target vocabulary to model while using a specific toy, such as "more," "go," "truck," "in," and "push," accompanying a dump truck. Symbols or signs can be placed in spaces left where puzzle pieces have been removed, to facilitate pairing of symbols and signs with their referents. A simple picture or symbol communication board can accompany a toy such as a toy barn set (see Carlson, 1985, for an example). Finally, therapists can write suggestions for specific toys or for individual children. For example, the occupational therapist may request parents to encourage bilateral hand use through ball play and use of a jack-in-the-box.

RESOURCES

In this chapter were presented many reasons why a toy lending library can enhance life and learning for children with special needs. The following resources will provide additional support to organizations considering this undertaking:

Articles and Books (see Appendix A). *Good Toy Guide 1983;* Jeffrey (1981a,b); Manolson, (1984); MacDonald and Gillette (1984a,b,c,d); Riddick (1982); Sinker (1983); Webb (1978); and von Levetzow (1981).

Organizations (see Appendix B). Canadian Association of Toy Libraries; Lekotek of Evanston; Toy Libraries Association (Britain); and USA Toy Library Association.

Chapter 14

Enlisting Community Support Through Bartering

Community support can greatly enhance the success of an adaptive play program. However, under tight economic conditions, both financial resources and volunteers may be limited. Therefore, it may be necessary to explore a variety of "carrots" that may encourage individuals or groups to provide support. Another name for this process is bartering. This section will present several useable strategies for locating appropriate groups for bartering and for planning and executing bartering projects.

It is recommended that one person at the facility be designated as the "bartering agent." This agent must, of course, consult closely with his or her colleagues on issues such as setting goals; however, allowing one person to oversee the bartering projects will permit clear communications with potential bartering organizations.

SETTING GOALS FOR BARTERING

The first step in planning a bartering project is to delineate, in general terms, what you hope to accomplish. Following is a list of potential goals for bartering projects. It is unlikely that all of these goals would be reached within a single bartering project.

Increasing Public Awareness of Facility. Establishing a bartering project with a large community organization, such as the Girl Scouts, can make a segment of the public aware of the existence of your facility and the general types of services offered.

161

Enhancing Public Awareness of Specific Programs. A bartering project can be related to a particular program within a facility, such as adaptive swimming or a toy lending library, thus focusing attention on that program.

Increasing Public Awareness of Specific Disabilities. Through guided exposure, community participants in the bartering project can be helped to develop empathy and insight while reducing negative feelings regarding disabilities.

Providing Needed Materials for the Facility. With appropriate information or instruction, community groups can make adapted or individualized materials that are beyond the time or skill limits of facility staff.

Providing Financial Support for Specific Projects. Although asking for financial support from the community is certainly not novel, phrasing the request in the form of a bartering contract can yield increased support while reducing the sense of begging for money.

Allowing Students at the Facility an Opportunity to Interact with a Variety of People. If the bartering contract involves direct services, such as volunteering time as an aide, entertainer, or playmate, additional exposure to community people is provided.

CHOOSING TARGET GROUPS FOR BARTERING PROJECTS

A wide variety of community groups may be appropriate for bartering, depending on the goals identified. Primary types of organizations ideal for bartering projects are *scouts* and similar organizations (Boy Scouts, Girl Scouts, 4-H, Camp Fire Girls, and so forth, with a variety of age ranges); *church groups* (youth groups, circles, men's groups); *civic organizations* (such as Telephone Pioneers, Junior League, and Jaycees); and *student groups* (ranging from preschool through college age, drawn from classes, clubs, sororities, and fraternities).

When selecting a group to approach regarding a bartering project, it is important to keep the primary goals in mind. Additional factors may also be relevant in choosing a target group. For example, the bartering agent may have personal contact with a representative from one organization, making that group a more approachable target. Considerations such as logistics (location, meeting times of the organization and facility) may also influence the decision. Ideally, the bartering agent should identify several potential target groups, in case one group is unable or unwilling to participate. The next section suggests strategies for engaging the interest of the target organization.

MAKING THE MATCH

Considerable thought should be given to the manner in which the target group is to be approached with the idea of a bartering project. Musselwhite (1984) suggests several questions that may be helpful in setting up a trade:

1. *What do we need?* Sample needs are materials to be made (puppets, sign books), bought (specific toys), or collected (good used toys); volunteers to work directly with students or indirectly (staffing Toy Lending Library); financial support for specific projects (adaptive playground).

2. *What can we offer?* Potential offerings are expertise in a variety of areas appropriate for sharing in a classroom or program format (information on disabled children, introduction to sign or symbol use); opportunity to interact with disabled students; free services (speech, language, hearing screenings by qualified professionals).

3. *What do they want?* Sample needs of a target group are sensitivity training (using *New Friends* dolls and simulations); programs (for clubs, PTA groups); opportunity to fulfill requirements (badges for scouts, service requirements for church or civic groups); specific training (signs or symbols).

4. *What can they offer?* Primary capabilities of target groups are many hands, permitting completion of projects in far less time than facility staff could manage; creativity, so that materials are varied and interesting for the students; varied skills (sewing, woodworking, electronics, art).

It should be clear that the sample answers given to the foregoing questions depend on a variety of factors. The *age* of the target group will determine to some extent what the needs and capabilities will be. For example, very young children will have less skills for making materials of great use, other than for decoration. The *skill level* of the target group must also be considered in making a match. For example, members of the Telephone Pioneers of America are often highly skilled in electronics; therefore, they would be an excellent group to work on a project involving adaptations of battery-operated toys. A third factor to consider is the *time* the target group will be able to devote to the bartering project. Thus, it is important to know if scouts will work on the project only at their weekly 1 hour meeting, or if they will also work independently at home.

Once the target group has been selected, major goals have been identified, and needs and capabilities have been delineated, the bartering agent can begin to make the trade. It may be helpful to write up a sample bartering "contract," outlining potential goals, needs, and offerings for each group. This can be extremely informal, and flexible, with the primary purpose of giving the target group an idea of the benefits of a bartering project.

One highly effective method of making a match is to present an introductory program to the target group, sharing information about the facility, preferably through on-site visits, videotapes, or a slide show. The sample contract can then be presented and modified to suit both groups. Although this entire process may sound rather cumbersome, it is not greatly time-consuming, and advance preparation in the form of identifying needs and preparing a sample contract can yield a favorable outcome. An ongoing bartering project can be highly cost-effective, because the primary effort is spent in setting up the trade, with the benefits to the facility increasing progressively as the project continues.

SAMPLE BARTERING PROJECTS

The range of potential bartering projects is vast, from extremely simple one-time projects, such as making animal mobiles; to ongoing contracts, such as providing room decorations for all holidays; to skilled projects, such as adapting computers to accept single-switch access. Table 14–1 outlines sample activities that can be assigned to various scouting groups to fulfill portions of specific badges. This information should be helpful in working out a contract with a scout organization. Table 14–2 presents a list of sample projects. For each project, the following information is provided: the appropriate age group, skills

Table 14–1. Bartering Projects for Scouts

Scouting Level	Book	Sample Activity	Badge
Cub Scouts	Wolf Book	Use a secret code (p. 88)	Elective 1
		Learn the manual alphabet (p. 91)	Elective 1
		Make something useful with tools (idea: Activity Frames) (p. 99)	Elective 3
		Make a toy (p. 121)	Elective 9
	Bear Book	Make an electric buzzer game (p. 164)	Elective 4
		Do original artwork (p. 186)	Elective 9
	Webelos Book	Make a mobile (p. 41)	Artist
		"Do a good turn" (p. 77)	Citizen
		Make useful things of wood (idea: form board) (p. 82)	Craftsman
		Make puppets (p. 213)	Showman
Boy Scouts	Merit Badge Pamphlets	Paint wall or ceiling; repair furniture	Home Repair
		Read to young children or volunteer at a library	Reading
		Simulate disabilities and volunteer (at playground, tutoring, leading songs, helping with Special Olympics)	Handicapped

Table continued on following page.

Table 14-1   (continued)

Scouting Level	Book	Sample Activity	Badge
Brownies and Juniors	Worlds to Explore	Make sewing cards or dressing cards (p. 120)	Get Ready to Sew
		Paint furniture, make toys, or plant flowers (p. 144)	Friendship Ideas
		Make puppets (p. 256)	Plays with Puppets
		Make a book (p. 278)	Write It Down
Girl Scouts	Girl Scout Badges and Signs	Make a playground safer (p. 16)	Health/Safety
		Rainy day activities box	Child Care
	You Make A Difference	Volunteer 25 hours (can be repeated)	Community Service

Table 14-2. Sample Bartering Projects

Project	Age Range	Sample Group	Skills Needed	Time Required	Comments
Holiday decorations	3+	Preschool, primary	None	15 min +	Excellent first project
Signing or symbol booklets	10+	Upper elementary	Use of office machines	2 hr each	Students can copy pages, color, laminate, collate, and assemble books
Used toy drive	6+	Any youth group	None	1 hr	Large group simplest
Enrichment or entertainment	16+	College student	Talent (art, music)	1 hr/week	Student could earn class credit
Stickers for rewards	5+	Any youth group	None	15 min	Use marking pens to decorate mailing labels
Adaptive switches	10+	Civic group or older scouts	Soldering	2 hr	Requires careful supervision; do on assembly-line basis
Building adaptive playground	16+	Adult civic or church group	Carpentry	1 day	Should have detailed plans and supervisor
Activity frames	12+	Older scouts or civic groups	Simple woodworking	3 hr	Best done as assembly-line task

needed, time required, and comments regarding use of adaptations of materials. These lists are merely samples of possible bartering projects. The needs of the facility and the special abilities of the target group will suggest additional ideas.

In summary, bartering can yield useful materials that save the facility both time and money, which can then be directed toward other purposes that cannot be met through bartering. For example, bartering for holiday decorations can permit staff members to use their time and energy on direct student services, while still enabling the facility to have a festive, stimulating, morale-boosting holiday look. Similarly, bartering for production of adaptive switches can save considerable amounts of money, as well as time; this money can then be spent toward equipment that cannot be produced by hand.

Chapter 15

Promoting Mainstreaming Through Adaptive Play

Excellent adaptive play skills will be of limited value to a disabled child if he or she is never able to share these skills with nondisabled peers. This chapter will focus on the use of dolls, puppets, or stuffed animals with disabilities to enhance community awareness of disabilities and to support mainstreaming projects.

RATIONALE

Dolls, puppets, and stuffed animals are all within the everyday experiences of children. Parents and professionals can capitalize on the natural relationships between child and doll, child and puppet, or child and stuffed animal to teach information and model desirable attitudes and behaviors. Use of these props can provide a nonthreatening introduction to a disability awareness program.

KIDS ON THE BLOCK

The Kids on the Block, a troupe of disabled and nondisabled puppets, are well known through the media. They are performing puppets that share information on topics of social concern, including disability awareness. The Kids on the Block puppets are intended to be used to stage performances for children to enhance awareness of disabilities. They are not designed to be activated by children, either with or without disabilities. They are typically purchased by a community organization, such as Junior League, and made available to the public through puppet performances, with follow-up activities provided by the organizing group or the target group, or both (e.g., an elementary group).

At present, there are 26 Kids on the Block puppet characters, with programs available for 20 different topics. Puppets are divided into two groups, according to disability. Group A includes programs for cerebral palsy, mental retardation, learning disability, emotional disturbance, blindness, and deafness/total communication; a sibling is also part of the program. Group B provides programs for spina bifida, abuse, cultural differences, leukemia, diabetes, epilepsy, and prosthetic limbs. Six additional puppets represent concerns such as aging and teenage pregnancy. Considerable time and research goes into developing each puppet, with information solicited from national disability organizations to ensure optimum presentation of information. The cost for most of the puppets with disabilities is approximately $600 each. Various support materials are included for staging puppet performances (e.g., props, scripts, and cassettes), including an introduction to puppetry techniques and follow-up activities (educational materials such as Braille cards and a Teacher's Guide with discussion topics, simulations, and bibliographies). Considerable support services are available through the national Kids on the Block organization (see Appendix C).

BODI-PUPPETS AND SUPER-SENSE KITS

Bodi-Puppets (Renfro, 1984) described in Chapter 16, can also be used to enhance disability awareness for elementary school children. Seven washable Bodi-Puppets, each 45 inches high, can be worn by teachers or children in exploring individual differences. The multimedia program uses "puppetmime," a combination of puppetry and pantomime to introduce characters with six disabilities (hearing, visual, physical, cognitive, emotional, learning impairment) plus a robot who assists in the interactions. The starter kit (Zookie Robot plus 1 disabled character) costs $115, with additional kits costing $65 each. A super-sense kit is also available for children with disabilities.

Manuals specific to each disability include a wide variety of information (see Nancy Renfro Studios, Appendix C):

• *Techniques* and simple creative dramatic *activities* for using the Bodi-Puppet

- A *script* plus pictures reproducible as transparencies to introduce the puppet
- Related follow-up *questions* and child-based *simulation* and learning activities
- A *Puppetmime story script* for children to perform in several versions (scripted, play, or creative storyline)
- Bibliography of books and resources

SPECIAL FRIENDS

Special Friends are stuffed animals with mobility, sight, and hearing disabilities. These animals were developed to introduce nondisabled children to the special challenges of various disabilities, and to provide disabled children with a figure with which they can relate. These hand-washable animals were designed by an occupational therapist and are intended for use by teachers, therapists, other health professionals, parents, children, or anyone wanting a Special Friend. Seven animals are currently available, ranging in price from $15 to $24:

Monkey in wheelchair
Elephant with two hearing aids
Penguin with walking stick
Rabbit with prosthetic arm
Koala bear with glasses
Frog with leg cast

Order from Pediatric Projects, Inc., Post Office Box 1180, Santa Monica, California 90406.

NEW FRIENDS

New Friends are dolls with disabilities designed to serve as a vehicle for presenting mainstreaming activities to help young children understand and accept individual differences. The New Friends Program, developed by the Chapel Hill Training-Outreach Project, will be described in some depth because the program is comprehensive, highly flexible, and affordable.

Comprehensive. It encompasses dolls, parent and staff training, extensive support materials (staff training manual, teacher manual, slide or tape sets), and follow-up simulation activities.

Highly Flexible. Although careful guidelines are presented for use of the program, the dolls, scripts, and simulation activities can be modified to meet the needs of individuals or groups. The manual is divided into several units (vision, hearing, ortho- pedic, and so forth); the myths, stereotypes, and fears associ- ated with that general disability are explored in each unit, but only one specific condition is developed into a script. This script can be used as a model to develop other dolls to fit the needs of individual programs (e.g., a nonspeaking doll).

Affordable. A single doll pattern can be used to make all dolls needed; manuals and other support materials are inexpen- sive and portions may be reproduced if appropriate credit is given.

Potential Uses of "New Friends"

Although the program was designed "for teachers who wish to create classroom environments and experiences to help young children understand and accept individual differences" (Heekin and Mengel, 1983a), additional uses have been docu- mented (Musselwhite, 1983). These uses fall into three general areas, as described in the following sections.

Enhancing Awareness and Understanding

Use with Nondisabled Children. The primary use of New Friends is to provide an introduction to the concept of individ- ual differences for nondisabled children. This can be accom- plished through a variety of formats. Ideally, the New Friends Program can be incorporated into the general curriculum for preschoolers and primary grade students. Thus, while students are studying the senses of vision, touch, and hearing, informa- tion on the effects of impairments in those senses can be intro- duced through the dolls. Simulation activities, such as attempt- ing to manipulate small objects while wearing ski gloves or locating objects while blindfolded, can then follow naturally. Re- lated books and filmstrips suggested in the New Friends Manual can be provided for an in-depth or follow-up approach. Thus, ide- ally, the dolls and activities can be part of a gradually unfolding learning experience, with the dolls left in the classroom to allow extended, nonstructured interaction and exploration opportunities.

The New Friends dolls can also be used appropriately in other settings, including scout meetings, church or Bible school sessions, and other youth organization meetings. Although the visit by the dolls may be on a "one-shot" basis, it is recommended that the youth group leaders extend the exposure by planning related simulations, field trips, or projects. Involving these groups in making dolls for a school can be another effective way to promote awareness.

Community Awareness. Throughout the development of the New Friends Program, it became apparent that adults often had less understanding and acceptance of individual differences than did the students. This may be related to the relative recency of mainstreamed programs — when many of these adults were in school, the norm was separate and isolated learning environments for disabled youth. Therefore, the New Friends *Trainer's Manual* (Heekin and Mengel, 1983b) presents a variety of interactive workshop activities designed to help adults sort out and understand their own attitudes toward disabilities. In addition, a variety of simulation activities appropriate for adults are presented in the *Trainers' Manual*. (See Lessee, 1983, for additional adult-oriented simulation ideas.) These activities can be used, with the dolls, in a number of settings to enhance community awareness. Malls often have "health fairs" at which information is provided to shoppers. A display of dolls and printed information, accompanied by a series of simple simulations such as manipulating a wheelchair, could be an attention-getting and informative booth. Presentations to adult service organizations can use similar displays and activities on a small- or large-group basis. In addition, these presentations can be used as trading components in bartering for materials or services (see Chapter 14 for specifics on setting up bartering projects). Again, such organizations are a valuable resource for doll-making.

Using "New Friends" with Children with Special Needs

Understanding and Dealing With Disabilities. The New Friends dolls can be used to help children understand their own disabilities. This can be accomplished through role-playing or dramatic play. For example, the doll can explain why she must wear a long leg brace for an extended period of time, what is being accomplished through use of the brace, and so forth. A doll with a disability similar to one the student has can also serve as a "support group." For example, the doll can "talk" with the child about issues such as pain or frustration ("Sometimes I get so mad when people don't understand me — do you ever feel that way? This is what I do . . ."). This has been found especially helpful when a child does not have access to peers with similar disabilities. Adults can also provide information to a child through a doll. This approach is appropriate for a child who is concerned about a new medical procedure. For example, a doll with an A-frame brace can accompany a student to the hospital for hip surgery, with the following note pinned to the doll's dress:

> Hi. My name is Charlotte. I am Kizzy's New Friend! I wear an A-frame brace just like Kizzy. Please use me to show Kizzy what you are going to do because she's a little bit scared. Thank you!

Peer Modeling. New Friends dolls can serve as excellent peer models because they are so cooperative. Leonard (1975) has documented success in using puppets as models to put representative utterance forms on display for language-delayed children. The typical procedure is to have the doll model appropriate behavior, then to reinforce her, through natural consequences if possible ("You pointed to 'tickle.' Here I come!"). Following are some additional examples of behaviors that New Friends dolls can model: simple signs (OPEN, ON); switch use; turntaking; and use of adaptive equipment (headstick, parapodium).

Supporting Mainstreaming Efforts with "New Friends"

The New Friends Program has been an invaluable aid to both group and individual mainstreaming projects. The dolls and activities can be used to introduce mainstreaming, then can provide support to promote successful maintenance of the project.

Group Mainstreaming Projects. One simple arrangement for a group effort is to exchange students on a regular basis. For example, preschoolers from the Irene Wortham Center (a small developmental day center for children with cognitive and physical disabilities) and the Biltmore Baptist Child Care Center (a private, church-sponsored day center for nondisabled preschoolers) meet on a biweekly basis for several hours, alternating between the two centers. Before beginning the program, and when the student group at the Biltmore Baptist facility changes, several dolls visit the Biltmore Baptist center and act out appropriate scripts. Children are given an opportunity to ask questions and several simulations are introduced, such as "helping" the visually impaired doll explore the classroom. Students are taught a few simple signing songs they will use in the exchange project (Musselwhite, 1985), and are enticed by hearing of the activities they will encounter when they visit. For example, Jenny, a doll with short-leg braces, may announce: "We have a neat thing at our center. We fill it up with air and you can jump and jump and jump! I get to take my braces off when I jump. Would you like to come try it?"

The teachers are then left with the dolls, or make their own dolls for the children to keep and play with informally. Teachers are also asked to carry through with simulations, such as making a mural — without using hands! (Sixteen additional classroom-oriented simulations are included in the Kids Come in Special Flavors Classroom Kit; see Cashdollar and Martin, 1981, in Appendix A.) Related books or filmstrips are also appropriate to help prepare the nondisabled children for the first meeting (see Exceptional Children in the Regular Classroom Series or Azarnoff, 1984, for readings). Once the project is initiated, dolls can help by serving as models, leading circle time, and just being available for play experiences. Thus, they can help to provide a link between the two groups involved in the mainstreaming project.

Individual Mainstreaming Projects. New Friends dolls can also serve as excellent liaisons for individual mainstreaming efforts when a disabled child enters a school, play, community, or church group. The same basic steps are followed as for group mainstreaming, but dolls, scripts, and activities are modified to meet the needs of the individual child. Following is a case example of prepared entry for a child in a Sunday School class:

Introduction of Doll. The Sunday before the child, Luke, was to enroll, his mother, speech-language pathologist, and New Friend (Randy) visited the class of 4 year olds. Randy, like Luke, has cerebral palsy and a good sense of humor.

Demonstration of Personality Aside from Disability. Randy started the meeting by telling a joke and encouraging other students to tell jokes.

Mention of Disability. Randy then mentioned casually that he didn't walk and his arms "didn't work very well," but he had recently learned to operate battery-run toys through use of switches.

Building Excitement. Randy offered to bring the switches to Sunday School the next week, then "remembered" that he would be out of town.

Description of Child. Randy next announced that his friend Luke also knew how to make toys go with switches, and Luke could come the next week. Luke's abilities, disabilities, and interests ("He loves singing!") were described, and his mother passed around a picture of him.

Question Time. Students were encouraged to ask Randy or the adults about Luke or Randy.

Engagement of Students. The students were asked if they would like Luke to come visit the following week to teach them how to do the switches. This presented Luke as a "can-do" child, and the others welcomed him eagerly.

Although the specifics would need to be adapted to meet the needs and interests of each child, this introductory sequence has proved to be effective in several mainstreaming attempts. The key elements appear to be sharing factual information while engaging the student's interest — but not pity — at the same time.

To summarize, the New Friends dolls, materials, and activities can be used to support a variety of learning and mainstreaming experiences for disabled children, nondisabled children, and community members. The flexibility of the program allows it to be adapted to the needs of specific projects, and the low cost permits widespread applications.

RESOURCES

Appendix A includes annotated references to a variety of books, articles, and films for teaching people about individual differences.

Simulations. Cashdollar and Martin (1981); Heekin and Mengel (1983a,b); Lessee (1983); Renfro, Click, and Harp (1982).

Readings. Sources for additional readings are included in the above references and Azarnoff (1984); Exceptional Children in the Regular Classroom Series.

Organizations (see Appendix B). Pediatric Projects.

Manufacturers (see Appendix C). Kids Come in Special Flavors; Kids on the Block; Nancy Renfro Studios.

Chapter 16

Adaptive Play and the Arts

Play and various budding art forms, such as music and movement, are closely related for young children. Evans (1982) summarizes information from a review of more than 120 articles to document the benefits of arts programming for individuals with disabilities. These benefits are described for the art forms of music, drama, and dance, in relation to goals in the areas of social and personal development (group interaction, self-confidence), cognitive skills (language, academics), and motor skills (gross, fine). Both Evans (1982) and Sherrill (1979) assert that recent national legislation provides support for the inclusion of arts programming for children with disabilities. Public Law 94–142, the Education for All Handicapped Children Act, requires full educational opportunity for all handicapped children. As Sherrill (1979) notes, "full educational opportunity" is a rather broad term, which may or may not be interpreted to include experiences in the arts. The comments section of the *Federal Register*, August 23, 1977 (121a. 304), urges local educational agencies to include arts in programs for the handicapped and suggests that this could cover both arts appreciation and use of the arts as a teaching tool. In addition, the various educational programs and services (including art and music) available to nonhandicapped children must also be available to handicapped children served by that same agency. Sherrill (1979, pp. 13–20) provides an excellent summary and interpretation of this legislation as it pertains to arts and children with special needs.

This chapter presents ideas and resources for incorporating art as part of a general adaptive play program. The areas covered are music, movement, art, and puppetry. Additional suggestions for integrating these art forms into the curriculum are suggested throughout the book. Both general and specific ideas for implementing an arts program are presented by Dahood and

Lessee (1982) and Evans (1982). Strategies range from gaining interest on the part of educational agencies and visiting artists, to arranging for individual needs, to developing funding sources. A team teaching approach can support the focus on creativity and development of specific skills. This team may include a pairing of artists or dance, music, or art therapists and specialists such as special educators, physical or occupational therapists, and speech-language pathologists.

Although the emphasis in this chapter is on the therapeutic value of adaptive play in conjunction with the arts, the value of each art form in enhancing the child's self-esteem, creativity, and general quality of life must not be ignored. Each of these activities should be approached in an atmosphere of delight and exploration, to achieve both therapeutic and esthetic goals.

MUSIC AND ADAPTIVE PLAY

As Thursby (1977) observes, "Today we seldom find music classes where children only sit in neat rows and sing songs with the piano" (p. 77). Especially for disabled children, music is more often incorporated into other facets of learning. Adaptive play can likewise be included within the format of music to further extend the therapeutic benefits of both.

Benefits of Music for Children with Disabilities

Lathom and Eagle (1982a) recently sent a survey to music therapists employed by public and private schools or institutions serving a special-education population. The 164 respondents specified the following most frequently as goals for their music therapy programs: (1) to improve gross and fine motor skills; (2) to encourage cooperation with peers and adults; (3) to increase ability to follow directions; and (4) to encourage active participation. Other goals, listed somewhat less frequently, included eye contact with the speaker, eye-hand coordination, appropriate use of language, and auditory discrimination. Harvey (1980) reports that "music therapy research has demonstrated the use of music in facilitating: (1) academic behaviors such as math skills, (2) reading skills, (3) language skills, (4) activity level, (5) sensory awareness, (6) imitative behavior, (7) behavior problems, (8) social behaviors, and (9) self-help skills" (p. 202). Thus, anecdotal and clinical reports indicate that music therapy has a wide range of use with disabled children. Carter (1982) has delineated several more general uses of music with children having special needs:

- *A carrier of information:* For example, the song may carry information that will enhance concept development ("around," "more," "first").
- *A reinforcer:* for example, a child's favorite musical tape can be placed in a cassette recorder activated by a mercury head control switch; thus, the child can listen to the music only if he or she holds the head in a predetermined position.
- *A background for learning:* For example, the teacher would play relaxing music while the children are engaged in potentially stressful learning tasks.
- *A physical structure for learning activity:* For example, the rhythm, melody, and tempo of a song can provide a framework for learning skills such as fine motor movements involved in finger play.
- *A reflection of skills or processes to be learned:* For example, musical and nonmusical concepts can be paired, such as high or low and soft or loud.

Ways to Incorporate Adaptive Play into Music

Combining adaptive play and music can have the added benefit of increasing the spontaneity of the music; that is, music need not be reserved for a specified "music time," but it can be part of general play. Music can be an excellent carrier of information during adaptive play. For example, a song can be used to describe ("It is a ball"), to comment on objects or actions ("Baby's sleeping"), to command ("Give the ball to Kara"), to request ("More, more, I want more, I want more of that"), and to code a variety of other language functions. Vocabulary, whether signed, spoken, or indicated through symbols, can also be introduced or practiced through music; the effectiveness of this strategy will be enhanced if children are also encouraged to explore objects, actions, and relations presented by engaging in adaptive play. For example, if the child actually engages in the activity while his peers sing "Kiss the baby," the relationship between the words and the objects or actions will be underscored. Figure 16–1 presents a sample matrix that could be used to introduce the language form "agent + action" through a combination of music and adaptive play. Additional

MATRIX: AGENT + ACTION
Actions

	SLEEPING	WALKING	TALKING	JUMPING	SWINGING
ASHLEY	×	×			
JOANNA		×	×		
KARA			×	×	
JEAN-LUC				×	×
WES	×				×

Agents

Song: Adapt the children's tune "Are You Sleeping." Example:
KARA is TALKING, KARA is TALKING,
ON THE PHONE, ON THE PHONE.
SAY HELLO to MOMMY,
SAY HELLO to MOMMY,
HI, HI, HI. HI, HI, HI.

Figure 16-1. Agent + action matrix: Combining music and adaptive play. From Musselwhite, C.R. (1985). *Songbook: Signs and symbols for children.* Asheville, NC: Author.

skills, such as direction-following, object manipulation, and turntaking, can be introduced or practiced through use of the matrix. Also, matrices can be developed for putting other language forms on display, such as "action + object" (feed duck, pat dog) or "modifier + noun" (big car, happy baby).

The second major goal appropriate when combining adaptive play and music is that of providing a physical structure for learning. Several examples are presented in the following section.

One general avenue is to provide structure through words and melody. In addition to the previous examples, songs can be used to direct actions, such as "Look at me, see what I do, climb, climb, climb," with the child matching actions to words.

A second possibility is to provide structure through rhythm. Children can also attempt to match actions to the rhythm of the song, such as "Jumping, jumping, jumping, yes. Jumping, jumping, yes," with the child jumping (alone or assisted) each time the target word is spoken.

A third option is to offer structure through tempo. For example, a child using symbols to communicate can eye-gaze or point to symbols affixed to a "song strip" (e.g., a Plexiglas strip 6 inches by 2 feet) as a song is sung by others (Musselwhite, 1985). This can facilitate symbol identification skills and can increase the child's rate of indicating symbols.

Musselwhite (1985) suggests several general strategies for using music in conjunction with signing, symbols, and adaptive play.

Slow the Tempo. Although this seems obvious, it is crucial not to set a pace that disabled learners cannot match. This is a special concern if the song or tune is highly familiar. In addition, signing or symbol-indicating may require more time than singing alone.

Use Nondisabled Children as Peers. Musselwhite and Childs (in preparation) have found use of music and adaptive play to be a strong bond between nondisabled and disabled children in mainstreaming projects. It is helpful to teach songs to nondisabled children first, so they can provide a clear model. However, on occasion the disabled children should be taught a song first so they can teach it to their nondisabled peers to demonstrate their abilities and promote a more equal relationship among the children.

Use Dolls as Models. When nondisabled peers are not available, dolls such as the New Friends (Heekin and Mengel, 1983a,b) can provide an excellent substitute. These dolls can model symbol-indicating or limited signing plus social skills such as turntaking and motor skills such as jumping on command. Because the teacher is in full command of the doll, desirable behaviors can be assured.

Capitalize on Interaction. Perhaps the most important joining of adaptive play and music is in the area of interaction. Music can be used as a motivator for active participation in adaptive play. For example, music can encourage requests ("Who wants the hat?"), actions ("Get the hat and put it on"), and peer interactions ("Give the hat to Luke"). However, the potential for inter-

Table 16-1.   Rules for Song-Writing

Rule 1: The song should have fewer than 10 different words (function words such as articles can be excluded).

Rationale: Many traditional children's songs have twice this number of different words, making excessive demands on children with low-level cognitive or motoric skills.

Rule 2: Use simple, familiar vocabulary.

Rationale: Although the rule is obvious, many common songs do not adhere to it, including unnecessarily difficult words, such as "twinkle," "wonder," and "diamond."

Rule 3: The words should be highly repetitive.

Rationale: This helps reduce overload and allows the child to practice the words, signs, or symbols just presented. It appears to be related to ease of acquisition.

Rule 4: Use a tune that is simple or highly familiar.

Rationale: This will permit focus on interaction, communication, and so forth, reducing the demands on memory and musical ability.

Rule 5: Use functional words that are important learning goals.

Rationale: This feature distinguishes "educational" songs from nursery songs, which often have confusing or irrelevant messages (e.g., "Pop Goes the Weasel"). Songs can be built around target words or concepts.

Rule 6: If songs are to be used in augmentative communication, include iconic (guessable) signs or symbols.

Rationale: These signs or symbols can support ease of acquisition and rapidity of generalization.

Rule 7: Include audience participation during or after each song.

Rationale: This is a key element, as it promotes interaction and generalization. This makes it appropriate to repeat a song several times within a session (e.g., repeat "Get the Hat" as each child takes a turn at the dress-up box).

Adapted from Musselwhite, C.R., (1985). Songbook: Signs and Symbols for Children (pp. 21-24). Asheville, NC: Author.

action is highly dependent on two factors: (1) advance planning — the teacher needs to ensure that songs are chained together to promote interaction and involvement; and (2) careful selection of songs — most traditional children's songs, such as "Mary Had a Little Lamb" or "Twinkle, Twinkle, Little Star" do not provide opportunities for interaction. Table 16-1 suggests several rules for song writing, which may also be helpful in song selection.

The National Association of Music Therapists (NAMT) has recently published a series of manuals describing the range of music therapy services available to disabled children (Lathom and Eagle, 1982b). These manuals cover the following populations: mentally retarded, speech impaired, orthopedically hand-icapped, visually impaired, hearing impaired, deaf-blind, other health impaired, and multihandicapped. Each manual covers specific therapeutic strategies using music; many of these incorporate adaptive play as well. Most manuals suggest assessment tools or strategies and present case studies to demonstrate methods and results.

RESOURCES FOR ADAPTIVE MUSIC

A number of publications, organizations, and distributors offer supportive information on music for disabled children. The following is a brief summary of primary sources:

Books (see Appendix A and references). Brodsky, 1983; Evans (1982); Lathom and Eagle (1982b); Musselwhite (1985); Nocera (1979); and Ward (1979).

Organizations (see Appendix B). National Association for Music Therapy.

Companies (see Appendix C). Folkways/Scholastic Recordings.

MOVEMENT EXPLORATION AND CREATIVE MOVEMENT

This category falls between the realms of play and art. As used here, movement exploration involves learning how the body, and parts of the body, move in space. Traditional examples would be movement to songs such as "Head, shoulders, knees, and toes." Creative movement relates more to the art form of using movement for expression, such as expressing feelings; interpreting experiences, such as music or visual images; or conveying nonverbal messages through movement.

Benefits of Movement as Part of an Adaptive Play Program

Experience in movement exploration and creative movement can yield a number of positive benefits in general areas, such as group interaction and self-confidence. The following paragraphs summarize some specific benefits that can be seen in several areas.

Motor Development. Specific gross motor and movement objectives can be incorporated into movement activities, allowing for normative and pleasurable learning. Sample gross motor skills are walking with heel to toe, walking on tiptoes, lateral trunk bending, kneeling, balancing on one foot, running, and performing a broad jump or a standing jump. Potential movement or reflex development objectives include graded knee flexion vertically and laterally, hip extension, forearm supination, protective extension reactions, and facilitation of equilibrium responses (in standing and jumping). This clearly represents a wide range of skills, indicating that movement activities could be supportive for children at a variety of developmental levels and with differing impairments.

Communication. Communication goals can also be incorporated into movement activities such as direction-following ("get on knees"); sequencing (baby tree grows up); sound production ("shhhh" as the baby tree is sleeping); and singing (simple, functional songs to accompany portions of the activity); responding or commenting to questions or events throughout the activity; and concept development (fast-slow, high-low).

Teamwork. Professionals from a variety of disciplines (physical and occupational therapy, speech-language pathology, special education) and parents can carry out joint treatment sessions, with each person facilitating the movement, communication, and general participation of one child. This provides an opportunity for demonstrating therapy techniques in a time-efficient manner and opens up topics for information-sharing after the session.

Strategies for Enhancing Movement Exploration and Creative Movement

It is tempting to use movement activities designed for non-disabled children, such as the multitude of children's records that allow movement exploration. However, these activities, especially if prerecorded, are likely to result in frustration for the student and the teacher for several reasons. The first concern is with the *target movements,* which are typically too advanced or chained in a way that is difficult for children with disabilities. The second concern is the *speed.* This is a major problem if using prerecorded songs or instructions. Activities designed for nondisabled children simply do not allow sufficient pause time for children with special needs. For example, the "I'm going on a bear hunt" sequence, although fun for able-bodied children, can be extremely frustrating for the physically disabled child, who cannot make the movements as rapidly as the instructions demand, or for the language-impaired or cognitively delayed child, who cannot process the instructions quickly enough. If the child must rely only on motor imitation, major opportunities for learning are being missed. A third concern relates to *directions,* which typically are too complex in terms of length and vocabulary. Traditional children's songs or nursery rhymes often used for movement exploration (e.g., Ring Around the Rosy, Jack and Jill) can be meaningless to children who have difficulty processing language. Finally, the *goals* of traditional movement exploration and creative movement activities often do not mesh with those goals identified for children with disabilities. The sample goals identified previously would suggest that we focus on simple activities that stress quality of movement and allow for additional goals, such as those listed for communication.

Using and Adapting Existing Movement Programs

Several existing collections of activities for movement exploration or creative movement, or both, include some activities that are appropriate for children with more severe disabilities. Several of the activities suggested by Evans (1982) under the category of "dance" are applicable or can be modified for use with children who have moderate to severe physical or cognitive disabilities, and the creative movement lessons developed by Moran and Kalakian (1977) are designed for use with moderately disabled individuals.

In other cases it will be possible to adapt existing activities, especially if the students can "almost" keep up in terms of speed, complexity of directions, and level of movement required. However, this assumes that the goals meet the needs of the target group, an assumption that will not always hold true. Sample curricula from which activities may be drawn are: *Kids in Motion: An Early Childhood Movement Education Program* (Gilroy, 1985); and *Learning Through Play* (chapter on learning through movement, space, and time, Fewell and Vadasy, 1983). Each of the preceding references is intended for or includes adaptations for children with various disabilities. One booklet of the parent-oriented *Let's Play to Grow* series focuses on "fun with rhythm, movement and dance," for use at home. It may be necessary to adapt some activities further, using the principles of reducing speed, focusing on quality of movement, and decreasing complexity of instructions.

Traditional movement activities such as "I'm going on a bear hunt" can also be adapted for some groups. Sample adaptations are (1) make the directions shorter, simpler, and more repetitive ("Let's go. March. March, Stacy"); (2) focus on movement goals identified by therapists (for balancing on one leg, "climb" over a fence, shake "water" off each leg); (3) include visual aids (cardboard cut-outs of fence, high grass, river); (4) incorporate concrete materials (obstacle course with actual fence for climbing, log for jumping, tunnel for crawling through); (5) pair words with signs, especially for spatial concepts (over, around, through); and (6) accompany movements with sounds or words, to encourage speech ("Ch-ch-ch" during high-grass sequence, "up-up-up" during climbing sequence). Although not all of these modifications will be needed for each group, selected modifications can greatly enhance success.

Developing Movement Activities to Meet Specific Goals

In some cases, new activities for movement exploration or creative movement will need to be designed to meet specific goals. Ideally, these activities can be developed and field-tested jointly by several professionals. For example, the physical therapist or occupational therapist can identify gross motor and movement goals, with the special educator suggesting a target concept to serve as a framework, and the speech-language pathologist writing instructions at the appropriate level. A dance therapist can provide ideas for aiding creativity and promoting self-concept. The handbook, *Movement Education for Preschool Children,* while not specifically written for children with disabilities, provides general and specific planning ideas for setting up a movement program.

Table 16–2 presents a sample movement exploration activity combining a variety of goals identified for a group of children with moderate to severe cognitive delays and mild to moderate physical disabilities. It is recommended that this be considered a treatment session, with one-to-one hands-on assistance provided as needed. Thus, children who do not stand alone can still gain practice in the movement patterns through stabilizing assistance. The activity listed in Table 16–2 clearly violates the "rules" for creative movement activities to focus on specific

Table 16-2.   Sample Movement Activity with Telescoped Goals

Gross Motor Goals	Movement Skills
Standing on tiptoes Lateral trunk bending Equilibrium responses in standing	Graded knee movement (vertical and lateral)
Dialogue	*Directions*
Let's be trees.	Pause to encourage answering.
Who wants to be a tree?	Pause to encourage answering.
Be a baby tree. Sit down.	Children should tailor sit.
Put your head down.	Heads on knees.
SLEEPING, SLEEPING, SH, SH, SH	
SLEEPING, SLEEPING, SH. (#1)	Keep heads on knees.
Look up! Look!	Children should look up.
Look all around.	Children should look all around.
It's the sun.	
Hi, sun!	Encourage them to greet sun.
Get on your knees.	Children should kneel.
Hold out your branches.	Children should hold arms up.
REACH OUT, REACH OUT AND TOUCH THE SUN. (#2)	
Let's stand up.	Help children stand up without
Be a big tree.	using hands on floor.
Bigger! Bigger!	Children should stand on tiptoe.
LOOK AT ME, SEE HOW I GROW	Continue reaching up.
UP, UP, UP.	Children should bend down again.
LOOK AT ME, SEE HOW I GROW	Repeat movements.
UP, UP, UP. (#3).	
Uh-oh! Listen!	Cup hand behind ear.
It's the wind!	Open mouth wide — look surprised.
I'M BLOWING, I'M BLOWING,	Lateral trunk bending
WOOO, WOOO, WOOO, WOOO	from side to side.
BLOW ME DOWN! (#4)	Fall to floor.

Words in capital letters represent songs. Tunes are: #1, "Jumping, Yes" (Musselwhite, 1985); #2, "Reach Out and Touch Someone"; #3, Adaptation of "Old MacDonald"; #4, "It's Raining, It's Pouring."

movement and direction-following goals. However, creative movement exercises also have great value for children at more advanced levels of symbolic play. Thus, instead of being told to "be" a tree, the child can be asked to observe a tree and identify the various components of its movements. Activities at this level are suggested in Movement Education for Preschool Children (American Alliance of Health, Physical Education, Recreation, and Dance, 1980). These activities may be appropriate for use or adaptation for children with special needs, or they may suggest additional creative movement opportunities. An extension from movement into more structured dance may be possible for some students, following suggestions in sources such as Evans (1982) and Sherrill (1979), and incorporating the talents of a dance or movement therapist.

Resources

Books and Chapters (see Appendix A). Evans (1982); Fewell and Vadasy (1983); Gilroy (1985); *Let's Play to Grow* (1977); *Movement Education for Preschool Children* (1980); Moran and Kalakian (1977); and Sherrill (1979).

Organizations (see Appendix B). American Dance Therapy Association, Inc.; Let's Play to Grow; and National Committee Arts for the Handicapped.

ARTS AND CRAFTS

Description and Rationale

Arts and crafts refer here to art forms such as drawing, painting, and sculpting, as well as to craft projects such as tie-dyeing. Like music, the arts and crafts are a very typical part of an early childhood educational program for nondisabled children. However, for children with disabilities, art activities may be thought too difficult or too time-consuming for frequent use. Thus, if visual art is to be included, it may need to be simplified or adapted, with the goals telescoped into the activities.

In addition to obvious benefits in terms of self-concept development and creativity, arts and crafts can contribute to skill development in areas such as fine motor development (e.g., wrist rotation, refinement of grasp); cognitive development (means-ends, transformations); and language development (direction-following, describing artwork). However, to yield optimum benefit, this telescoping of goals into art activities must be preplanned.

Strategies for Intervention

If art is to be incorporated into the curriculum for children with special needs, several aspects must be considered. As with other areas, the instructions must be at the appropriate cognitive and linguistic levels and at a speed that facilitates processing. For example, an art activity can provide an excellent opportunity for practice in responding to two-part commands ("Get your paintbrush and bring me the red paint"), but it can be extremely frustrating if the child is currently unable to process two-part commands.

A second concern relates to the manipulations expected of the child. Many currently existing projects books intended for children with several disabilities present projects at a high level of difficulty for that population. Thus, adaptations will often need to be determined, and some available projects will be unusable for many special needs children.

It is important to maintain part of the focus on the process of the artwork. Too often, adults become so concerned about the quality of the product that they provide too much assistance, thus limiting both self-creativity and the opportunity to learn. One way to shift some of the emphasis to the process is to allow sufficient time for completing the task and to identify telescoped goals in advance. For example, art activities in Creative Experiences (Broughton, 1982) are related to goals on the Learning Accomplishment Profile (Sanford and Zelman, 1981). Table 16–3 suggests ways to use art activities to facilitate the primary motor patterns identified by Shane and Wilbur (1980) for use in expressive sign production.

Thus, art provides one additional tool for enhancing specific skills while engaging in enjoyable activities. Following are several resources for specific art projects and general information.

Resources

Books (see Appendix A). Amery and Cirardi (1976); Atack (1982); Broughton (1982); Campbell, King, and Robson (1975).

Organizations (see Appendix B). American Art Therapy Association; Let's Play to Grow; National Committee, Arts with the Handicapped.

THE ROLE OF PUPPETRY IN ADAPTIVE PLAY

In Chapter 15 are suggested ideas on presenting puppet shows (Special Friends, Kids on the Block) *for* disabled children, and *about* disabled children. This section will focus on the use

Table 16-3. Facilitating the Motor Components of Signing Through Art Activities

Motor Component	Sample Art Activities
LOCATIONS	
Chest	Have child wear Bodi-Puppet with Velcro strip attached at chest; add Velcro-adapted bows or pompons as decorations
Hand	Make smiley face on child's thumb and encourage wiggling
	Put rings on fingers and small soft items on palm and promote exploring with other hand
Face	Have child put on face makeup, using index finger and thumb to apply various colors; target key areas (corner of eye, corner of mouth, cheek bone, chin) to facilitate various elbow angles
Handshapes	
Flat Hand	Make palm prints with fingerpaint
Index Finger	Use finger as paintbrush, keeping paint in baby food jars
	Give each child a finger puppet
Curved Hand	Mold clay into ball shapes
Fist	Make pictures using the fist with a rocking motion
Thumb Touch	Do thumbprint art
	Place finger puppets on the thumb
Movements	
Linear	Mount paper on easel and encourage vertical, horizontal, and diagonal paint strokes
Handshape Change	Alter modeling clay from round to flat and back
Rotate or Twist	Do marble painting: place paper in shallow box, put paint on in spoonfuls, add several marbles, and have child rotate and twist box to produce painting
Repeat	Make puppet (walking puppet, hand puppet) jump or walk
Circular	Use cardboard or Plexiglas template with large circle cut out; let child finger paint circle to draw balloon, sun
Arc	Have child make puppet bracelet turn upside down
Hold	Instruct child to hold glued pieces together for 5 to 10 seconds

Motor components identified are from research by Shane and Wilbur (1980).

of puppets *with* and *by* disabled children. Renfro (1984) asserts that "Puppetry, which represents the integration of sculpture, design, movement, expression and other elements of the arts, has almost unlimited potential as a teaching and therapeutic tool" (p. 16). Thus, puppetry is presented last in this chapter on the arts, as it combines many of the beneficial features of the other art forms described.

Benefits of Puppetry for Disabled Children

Renfro (1984) and Sullivan (1982) suggest that puppetry can yield a wide variety of benefits for children with special needs, such as the following.

Developing Language and Communication Skills. Specific puppets are recommended for specific communication tasks, such as a snake puppet for exploring the letter "S" and a Bodi-Puppet (described in Table 16–4) for teaching sign language to deaf children. Numerous concepts, including spatial and temporal relationships, can also be introduced or practiced through puppetry.

Overcoming Emotional and Physical Isolation. Renfro suggests that story dramatizations can enhance group interaction. Another example involves setting up miniature environments (Table-Top Play, described in Table 16–4) to allow physically isolated children, such as children with limited movements or those in institutions, to explore new environments (neighborhood, barnyard, jungle).

Building Self-Esteem. Performing with puppets can allow children an opportunity to demonstrate capability and creativity.

Encouraging Emotional Release. Children can express fear, anger, and other potentially threatening emotions through puppets; alternatively, puppets can express those emotions for the children within a play situation.

Making Decisions. Disabled children often develop "learned helplessness," partially as a result of not being able to have control over the everyday decisions of life, such as which clothes to wear; Renfro asserts that puppetry offers numerous opportunities for decision-making, especially when constructing puppets (selection of basic puppet, materials, features, and so forth).

Supporting Physical or Occupational Therapy. Various types of puppets encourage different therapeutic movements. For example, Finger Puppets enhance fine motor movements, such as index finger isolation; Walking Finger Puppets promote eye-

Table 16-4. Puppet Types and Sample Activities

Puppet Type	Sample Activities
Buddy Puppets: Traditional hand puppet that serves as a ready-made friend and a bridge between reality and imagination Examples: furry mouse, bright clown	Introducing a story or activity (see Champlin and Champlin, 1981) Stimulating motor coordination: Puppet can lead movement activities such as "Simon Says" Understanding prepositions: Puppet can act out various spatial prepositions
Puppet Bracelets: Images of puppet characters (frog, sun, flower) are attached with a ribbon to the child's wrist	Enhancing eye-hand coordination: The strong visual image can stimulate visual attending while attempting hand movements Motivating motor movements: Repetitive movements can be encouraged by having the child move the puppet in various ways (Example: turn butterfly over to work on forearm suppination)
Bodi-Puppets: Life-sized puppets that can be worn by a child or the teacher in leading special activities	Engaging in creative dramatics: Children can act out roles through gross motor movements, or can become part of the scenery Stimulating movement activities: PT or OT can model desired movement while wearing Bodi-Puppet, or can ask child to move specific parts of puppet
Table-Top Puppets Play environment created through props and scenery on table top (Example: shoebox bus or store) Walking-Finger Puppets (paper characters glued to cardboard) Adaptor Stand Puppets (hand puppets placed on purchased stands or weighted plastic bottles, and pushed by child) Stand-Up Box Puppets (made from boxes and pushed on surface)	Learning about neighborhood settings: Daily living experiences can be acted out in a variety of settings (school, airport, hospital, library) People in your neighborhood: Community helpers can be discussed, including those often seen by disabled children, such as medical personnel Communication scripts: Social routines can be acted out through Table-Top Puppetry, as described in Chapter 11, focusing on situation-based routines

For puppetry patterns and activities, see Renfro (1984); Rottman (1978); and Sullivan (1982).

hand coordination; flexible Hand Puppets aid in small muscle dexterity, such as thumb and finger opposition; and Bodi-Puppets invite gross motor movements, such as trunk rotation. Table 16-4 includes several puppetry activities designed to enhance movements related to signing.

Strategies for Using Puppetry in Adaptive Play

When presented with the term "puppet," many adults tend to limit themselves in thought to traditional hand puppets. In fact, numerous puppet types are available commercially purchased or can be made from recycled materials. For many disabled children, hand puppets will not be functional, and alternative types of puppets will be needed. Table 16–4 provides descriptions of a variety of puppets, with sample activities for their use with children having a variety of special needs. A number of puppetry books are available; several books describing puppet-making and puppetry strategies for young or disabled children are annotated in Appendix A (see *Resources* at the end of this section for references).

One major strategy that will hold true regardless of the type of puppet used is to allow the child maximum possible *control.* If possible, this control should begin at the puppet-making stage; as Renfro (1984) suggests, children should be allowed to make as many decisions as feasible regarding the materials, colors, features, and so forth, of their puppets. Students should also be given control over the manipulations of their puppets; for example, a puppet attached to a physically disabled child's wrist or foot may be activated independently, whereas a traditional hand puppet could require considerable assistance from an adult. Table-Top Play (Renfro, 1984; Sullivan, 1982) offers an opportunity for a child to control the actions of a puppet, even if he cannot guide the puppet himself; for example, the child can instruct an adult (through speech, signs, symbols, eye-pointing) where to move a Stand-Up Puppet and what actions the puppet should accomplish. It is also suggested that a wheelchair be incorporated as a prop in a puppet show; for example, a large box can cover it to yield a "village square."

As mentioned in Chapter 15 puppets can be excellent *models* for feelings and skills. Uses of puppets (or dolls) are also suggested in the section on using music in adaptive play. Because puppets can be adult-controlled, as well as child-controlled, they are well suited to the task of modeling desirable behaviors and actions. One strategy is to have the puppet model a target behavior several times, engaging in an exciting interaction with the adult, until the child (who is observing the fun) shows that he or she is ready to join in. For example:

Introduce a dollhouse and prepare a symbol board representing four "people" or "animals" (e.g., mom, dog); four "places" (e.g., car, bed); four "actions" (e.g., jump, sleep); and four "things" (e.g., crayon, telephone). Have the puppet model decision-making and symbol-indicating several times, using considerable pauses and putting the language on display by using a "communication script" that emphasizes key words, forms, and functions. The session should be very animated, with the puppet clearly having fun selecting people or animals to play with, places to go, and so forth. Signs or speech could be substituted for symbols, depending on the abilities of the child. A sample script might be as follows:

Let me see. . . . Who do I (you) want? . . . I want . . . dog! . . . Yes, I'll get Dog . . . Here's the dog. . . . Hi, Dog. . . . How are you?

Where do you want to go, Dog? . . . Where go? . . . (Pretend dog is whispering in puppet's ear, or let dog bark) . . . Dog says "Go to bed" . . . OK, Dog, go to bed. . . . There you are . . . see? . . . Dog's in bed.

Now, Dog . . . What do you want to do? . . . What do? . . . (Let dog bark or whisper) . . . Oh. You want to jump? . . . Dog wants to jump! . . . Silly Dog! . . . You can't jump on bed! . . . Naughty Dog! . . . Look! Dog is jumping! . . . See Dog jump on bed!

What do you want to play with, Dog? What play with? (Let dog whisper or bark) . . . Dog says "Play with crayon" . . . I guess Dog wants to color . . . Here's crayon. . . . Dog has a crayon . . . in bed! . . . Be careful . . . . Don't color on wall!

In addition to serving as language models, puppets (or dolls) can also serve as *communication partners.* At times a child will need a direct model of desired verbal, gestural, or symbol-indicating behavior. A child who does not respond well to general statements ("I have muffins") or indirect statements ("Tell me if you want muffins") may require a direct model; however, direct models can lack communicative intent. Therefore, children can be directed to communicate a specific message (request, comment, directive) to a partner, such as another child or adult, or to a puppet or doll. For example, the puppet can be the "person" who is distributing muffins and the child can be instructed to "Tell Freddie, 'I want one.' " Since Freddie presumably does not already know that the child desires a muffin, this can yield communicative intent on the part of the child, whereas simply holding out a muffin and ordering "Say, 'I want one' " may seem unnecessary to many children. Similarly, a puppet can pretend to miss action that occurs, so that there is a reason to ask the child to describe that action ("cat sleeping"). In each example, using a puppet can allow the child to share information that appears "new," whereas direct imitation or reporting on events the teacher viewed directly may be obvious as "show speech," rather than true communication.

Champlin and Champlin (1981), in their book on using puppets with mentally retarded students, recommend using a "Jack-of-All-Trades" puppet, nicknamed a Jack puppet. This puppet can be used generically, to set the stage for routine activities such as story time or snack, to praise, ask questions, model, prompt, and otherwise enhance learning. They provide specific suggestions for practicing with a Jack puppet to develop the puppet's personality through voice and movements.

The goals listed previously suggest several additional training strategies. For example, if the goal is to reduce isolation produced by being in a limited environment, a Table-Top Play can help expand a child's horizons by introducing him or her to reality-based environments, such as shopping centers or public parks. Renfro (1984) suggests creating these table-top environments with throw-away items, such as cardboard tube "trees" with fringed paper foliage, arranged on a groundscape painted or drawn on mural paper. More advanced students can enact more elaborate stories, including traditional fairy tales, in which the action moves from one environment to another, such as moving a stand-up puppet from the woods to a cottage. As indicated in Table 16–4, Walking Finger Puppets and Stand-up Box Puppets are most appropriate for this type of play.

Age appropriateness must be considered in puppet use, as in other activities. The types of puppets selected, the voices they are given, and the roles they play can yield a match or a mismatch between functioning level and chronological age. Champlin and Champlin (1981) suggest that puppets representing real people, and used to act out biographies, can be an excellent age-appropriate learning tool for older students who function at preschool mental age levels and enjoy puppetry.

Resources for Adaptive Puppetry

Numerous resources are available on puppetry in general (see Renfro, 1984). The following are geared to the cognitive level of young children or intended specifically for children with special needs:

Books (see Appendix A). Champlin and Champlin (1981); Oatman (1984); Renfro (1984); Rottman (1978); Sullivan (1982).

Organizations (see Appendix B). Puppetry in Education; Puppeteers of America.

Companies (see Appendix C). Kids; Nancy Renfro Studios.

Chapter 17

Adaptive Play and Lifetime Leisure Skills

Thus far, this book has focused primarily on childhood-oriented activities, such as toy play skills. This chapter presents activities that can go beyond childhood, in terms of lifetime leisure skills planning. The first section covers adaptive swimming, the second focuses on adaptive playgrounds, and the final section provides an introduction to considerations that must be made in planning a lifetime leisure skills program.

ADAPTIVE SWIMMING

Swimming is one leisure activity that is accessible to many severely physically disabled people who are unable to participate independently in other sports. It can be initiated in childhood through adaptive play techniques. The American National Red Cross notes that individuals with disabilities may not have many "fun" experiences in life; therefore, the originator of their water safety program, Commodore Longfellow, suggested that instructors "entertain them hugely, while educating them gently" (*Manual for the Aide in Adapted Aquatics*, 1974, p. 1). It is fascinating to note that a relay team of disabled swimmers organized by the Association of Swimming Therapy (see Appendix B) successfully swam the English Channel in 1970; they were awarded the International Trophy for the fastest team that year (Martin, 1981).

Goals of Adaptive Swimming

The manual *Adapted Aquatics*, (1977) prepared by the American National Red Cross, separates the values of swimming into three general categories: (1) physiological values, including physical fitness (e.g., flexibility and cardiovascular endurance) and psychomotor development (e.g., speed, agility, and perceptual motor factors, such as balance and spatial relationships); (2) psychological values, such as experiencing success, enhancing self-image, and lessening the evidence of disability; and (3) sociological values, including peer-group interaction and normalization. Musselwhite and colleagues (1984) reported the following goals for an adaptive swimming program for disabled preschoolers:

- *To make children "water free":* Children should comprehend what water is, have control of all angles of rotation, and be comfortable if underwater
- *To facilitate normal movement patterns:* New movement experiences are possible for many physically disabled children, as they are not as dominated by abnormal reflex patterns while in the water
- *To increase the quantity and diversity of vocalizations, and to bring them under volitional control:* Speech sounds can be included in songs and games during training to take advantage of altered muscle tone while in the water
- *To provide opportunities for language development:* Direction-following ("Give the ball to Kizzy"), requests ("my turn"), and other communicative attempts can be highlighted
- *To enhance teamwork:* Team members can model, demonstrate, and describe therapeutic goals and techniques directly, with new skills tried out immediately in a relaxed atmosphere
- *To promote augmentative communication:* Signs and symbols can be introduced or carried out through a swimming program, with signs included in songs or symbols presented on plastic milk bottles, beach balls, or flotation rings.

Sample Adaptive Swimming Programs

This section will present an overview of two widely used adaptive swimming programs. Either of these can be an enjoyable and productive component of a comprehensive adaptive play program.

Adapted Aquatics: The American National Red Cross Program

This adaptive swimming program has three equally important aims: (1) safety; (2) fun; and (3) swimming (teaching or improving swimming skills). Both teaching methods and student activities are modified to meet the needs of individuals for whom traditional swimming instruction is not appropriate, owing to physical or cognitive impairments. Adapted methods include movement exploration (use of space, use of the body, and focus on quality of movement); keeping the "fun" in fundamentals, by teaching through games and stunts, with varying activities at different ability levels; and using behavior modification. Programs can be extended by reinforcing academics (e.g., spatial concepts) through aquatics or by offering competitive opportunities.

This Adapted Aquatics program is designed to be conducted in cooperation with community organizations serving the needs of disabled individuals. The Red Cross can provide support services in the following ways: training of instructors and aides; recruiting volunteers; and providing technical advisors and administrative leaders for programs. The amount of support offered will depend on the capabilities of the local Red Cross chapter.

Instructor training in adapted aquatics is offered to basic swimming instructors and water safety instructors. Other qualified individuals, such as therapeutic recreation specialists, adaptive physical educators, or physical therapists, can also take training in adaptive aquatics; however, Red Cross certificates can be given to students upon course completion only if the trainer is a certified Red Cross instructor. Red Cross instructor training in adapted aquatics is comprehensive, including technical information regarding a variety of physical and cognitive disabilities; disability simulation; teaching methods; and supervised practice teaching of students having a variety of disabilities. The Red Cross provides an Adaptive Aquatics textbook (1977) and a manual for the aide (1974) (see annotations of both of these in Appendix A). Volunteers are also an integral part of this adapted aquatics program, with volunteers serving support roles (transporting, dressing and undressing participants) and assisting as trained swimming aides.

The Halliwick Method of Adaptive Swimming

This adaptive swimming method was developed by James McMillan at the Halliwick School for Girls in England. Martin (1981) notes that "the method is based on known scientific principles of hydrodynamics and body mechanics" (p. 288). The program is organized into 10 stages:

1. *Mental adjustment.* Comprehending what water is, and becoming adjusted to the power of water and the reduction in the effects of gravity,
2. *Disengagement.* Freedom from flotation devices while learning about balance,
3. *Vertical rotation.* Movement around the horizontal axis of the body,
4. *Lateral rotation.* Movement around the longitudinal axis of the body,
5. *Combined rotation.* Using vertical and lateral rotation simultaneously,
6. *Use of upthrust.* Learning that water will push one up, so that the swimmer does not try to fight the water,
7. *Balance in stillness.* Developing balance in sitting position or supine (on back),
8. *Turbulent gliding.* Movement through the water by using turbulence, without direct propulsion,
9. *Simple progression.* Reduced turbulence, with minor propulsive movements initiated,
10. *Swimming movement.* Beginning instruction in swimming strokes, once the learner is fully prepared.

The Halliwick Method is often used with severely physically disabled children, as the progression of stages allows very gradual building of skills. In addition, the emphasis on features such as various planes of rotation makes this approach appropriate for therapeutic use, by physical and occupational therapists, therapeutic recreation specialists, and other professionals. Training is always accomplished on a one-to-one basis, with the swimmer-instructor pair forming a unit within a group activity. Martin (1981) suggests that this enhances the social interaction possibilities with peers. The medium of games and imagery appropriate to the developmental level of the learners is widely used in this method.

The Association of Swimming Therapy is supportive of this program in Britain, providing instructor training and a film. At present, there are few written materials describing the program, with the exception of a brief article by Martin (1981). Several films or tape and slide programs are available from various organizations (see *Resources* at the end of this section).

Using Music in Adaptive Swimming

The addition of music to an adaptive swimming program can enhance attending, direction-following, communication attempts, and enjoyment. Games can be accompanied by specific songs, to help provide a structure of familiarity for young or cognitively delayed children. For some children, it will be possible to use traditional children's songs, such as "Ring Around the Rosy" for circle activities and "Row, Row, Row Your Boat" for turbulent gliding activities. However, in many cases, it will be preferable to make up songs that provide a clearer message and are simple enough for young children to follow. For example, vertical rotation activities of moving from upright to supine (on the back) to upright can be accompanied by the following song, sung to the tune of Brahm's Lullaby:

> GO to SLEEP, "Shhh, Shhh." GO to SLEEP, "Shhh, Shhh."
> GO to SLEEP in your BED. (Repeat)
> WAKE-UP, "Hi, hi." WAKE-UP, "Hi, hi."
> WAKE-UP and SIT up.

The addition of sounds ("Shhh") and signs (words in capital letters) can further enhance communication development. Rules for writing songs for disabled children and additional examples of songs appropriate for inclusion in an adaptive swimming program are presented in Musselwhite (1985).

Resources

A variety of resources were described in the previous sections and are summarized in the appendices of this book:

Books, Articles, Films (see Appendix A). *Adapted Aquatics* (1977); *Manual for the Aide in Adapted Aquatics* (1974); Harris (1978); Martin (1981); Newman (1976); *Swimming for Disabled People* (three tape and slide programs); *Water Free* (film).

Organizations (see Appendix B). American Alliance of Health, Physical Education, and Recreation; American National Red Cross; Association of Swimming Therapy (Britain).

OUTDOOR PLAY

For nondisabled adults, many of their most pleasant memories of childhood will involve outdoor play. For children with disabilities, however, opportunities to play outdoors may be limited. This is especially true for children with severe physical impairments, as the logistics of outdoor play may seem prohibitive. Therefore, for many children with special needs, outdoor experiences may be limited to sitting in a wheelchair on a patio.

Wehman (1976) advocates use of the natural environment (e.g., playing in leaves or snow) for play, as described in Chapter 4. An example of training in the natural environment would be to drop objects off a bridge into a stream, leaning to watch them come out the other side (object release, visual tracking, lateral rotation). This section outlines ideas for beginning and using an adaptive playground as an opportunity for play and learning.

Adaptive Playgrounds

Adaptive playgrounds can yield benefits in a wide range of skill areas, as illustrated in Table 17–1. To derive the optimum gain from an adaptive playground, several features should be considered.

Safety is a primary consideration for any playground, but even more so for a setting to be used by children with special needs. Each piece of equipment should be explicitly evaluated for safety, with modifications made to reduce risks. For example, rails can be added to slides and stairways, the height of platforms can be lowered, and slides can be built into hills, thus reducing the risks of falling.

Accessibility is of prime concern, to ensure that the playground will be used. Ramps leading to play equipment and appropriate heights for easy wheelchair transfer are examples of strategies for improving access.

A third feature to consider is *normalization*. A playground that is esthetically pleasing will be more likely to invite use by children with and without disabilities. In many cases, typical equipment can be modified without needing to resort to equipment that is obviously intended for people with impairments. For example, a bottom can be added to a large tire swing, and fitted with padding if necessary, to allow use by moderately to severely physically disabled youth.

The *flow* pattern of the playground is another important factor. This refers to the flow from one activity to the next, to ensure widespread use of all equipment. In addition, if an adaptive playground is attached to a typical playground, ways of promoting flow between the two must be planned, if appropriate.

A major concern, if the playground is to be used as a learning environment, is the *potential for skill learning*. For example, a physical and occupational therapist should be included in the design process to make decisions, such as the use of steps or ladders and the types of swings best suited to the target group.

Table 17-1.   Benefits of Adaptive and Adventure Playgrounds

Skill Area	Sample Objectives	Potential Opportunities
Cognitive	Direction-following Motor imitation Concept development	Teacher gives series of commands Follow-the-leader Spatial terms (over, behind, through)
Social	Turn-taking Shared reference Parallel play	Waiting turn to swing, climb, slide Joint focus on monkey bar "show" Dumping and playing in sandbox
Gross motor	Reducing wide-leg gait Reciprocal crawling Hip rotation in walking	Walking on balance beam Tunnel of tires Alternating tire path

Fine motor	Motor planning while
	    propelling wheelchair
	Sensory integration
		Wooden barriers or pylons set on
		    cement rideway
		Tire swing and adaptive swings

Communication	Requesting actions
	
	Recurrence
	Promoting
	    vocalizations
	Two-word combinations
		Request turn to swing, push, and
		    so forth
		Request *more*
		Pair sounds with actions (Whee,
		    uh-oh)
		Pause to elicit two-word comments,
		    requests, commands (*push me,
		    more up*)

Self-help	Propelling wheelchair Climbing	Cement rideway Stairs to playhouse, ladders

Table 17-1 suggests areas to consider in planning an adaptive playground.

All of these considerations may be combined into the development of an adventure playground, adapted to meet the needs of children with disabilities. This is a play area where children are free to explore and experiment, with numerous learning opportunities and challenges, plus a large component of pleasure. Adventure playgrounds incorporate the existing environment. For example, a tree can be used as a post for a pulley, a site for a treehouse, or an attachment for a bench. Natural or artificial streams are well-loved components of many adventure playgrounds, and the existing terrain (hills, rocks) is often used rather than leveled. Large wooden play units such as forts or castles, and structures made from recycled materials (tires, railroad ties) are also trademarks of adventure playgrounds. Changeable structures also fit into the concept. For example, a patio can be marked with paint and supplied with moveable pylons to form an "obstacle course" for adaptive or traditional vehicles (wheelchairs, tricycles, wagons). At other times, the pylons can be removed and the surface can be used for playing games such as shuffleboard. Sample adaptive playgrounds are described and illustrated in "Meeting the playground challenge" (1983) and *Handicapped Adventure Playgrounds Association* (1978).

Thus, adventure playgrounds can be used to encourage integrated play and learning for children with a wide variety of disabilities. It should be recognized that this is a major undertaking, requiring devotion of considerable time, energy, and money. The resources for funding suggested in Chapter 13 will apply to designing and building adaptive playgrounds as well. The film "Principles of Playground Design" (1978) can be used in planning a playground. It can also be helpful in gaining support, as it depicts children with special needs using adaptive playground equipment.

Resources

There are numerous publications suggesting do-it-yourself equipment for adventure playgrounds (e.g., Hogan, 1974). Specific strategies for developing adventure playgrounds for children with disabilities are also available, as listed in the following sources.

Books and Pamphlets (see Appendix A). *Adventure Playgrounds for Handicapped Children,* (1978) and *Starting an Adventure Playground for Handicapped Children* (1978) (both from Handicapped Adventure Playground Association); Meeting the playground challenge (1983); *Movement Experiences for the Mentally Retarded or Emotionally Disturbed Child* (Moran and Kalakian, 1977); *Playgrounds for Free* (Hogan, 1974); *Principles of Playground Design* (1978).

Organizations (see Appendix B). American Alliance for Health, Physical Education, and Recreation; Canadian Association for Health, Physical Education, and Recreation; Handicapped Adventure Playground Association (Britain).

LONG-RANGE LEISURE PLANNING

Rationale for Long-Range Planning

This book has presented an overview of adaptive play. However, play is only the first step in the development of a repertoire of leisure skills. Bender and colleagues (1984) note that many adults with disabilities have disproportionately large amounts of leisure time, owing to more limited job opportunities. Thus, the trend of "enforced leisure" noted in Part I of this book may be extended rather than reduced with increasing age, especially for persons with severe disabilities. Bender and associates assert that this extensive leisure time may be both unfilled and unfulfilling. Thus, the play skills initiated through an adaptive play program should be expanded through development of a comprehensive leisure skills curriculum.

Development and Content of a Leisure Skills Curriculum

Wehman (1979a) presents general ideas related to design of a leisure skills curriculum for severely disabled students. Bender and colleagues recommend that the significant providers of leisure-related services for disabled people must encompass the following: (1) *schools*, with leisure education as an integral part of the total curriculum; (2) *home*, through parental awareness and involvement with school and community programs; and (3) *community*, with therapeutic recreation specialists serving as a resource and as a liaison for parents and teachers.

The range of potential leisure skills is extensive. Bender and associates (1984) have developed a taxonomy of leisure activities and experiences based on work by Overs, Taylor, and Adkins (1977). Table 17–2 shows the major categories in this taxonomy, plus sample subcategories and specific leisure activities or experiences. The extent of this classification suggests areas for training and underlines the need for a comprehensive, integrated program.

One consideration that should be made in selecting leisure activities for major emphasis is the life value in terms of both independence and integration. That is, leisure activities in which the individual can participate without assistance would be a priority, as would be activities that promote integration into the community. In some cases, these two needs may be met within a single activity, such as developing a collection independently, then sharing it with a group of people having the same interest.

McGill (1984) suggests that cooperative games can help to avoid the problems of inactivity and "spectatoritis," which can be prime concerns for people whose disabilities preclude success in traditional competitive games. Thus, these cooperative play activities can enhance integration into the mainstream, rather than widening the gap. As McGill notes, positive social in-

Table 17-2.   Classification of Leisure Activities and Experience: An Overview

Code	Major Categories	Sample Subcategories	Sample Tasks
1.0.0	*Play and Games* (10 subcategories)	High Active Games Low Active Games Table Games	Tag, keep away Frisbee, catch Pool, ping pong
2.0.0	*Sports and Physical Development* (17 subcategories)	Water Sports Snow Sports Team Sports	Swimming, polo Downhill skiing Softball, soccer
3.0.0	*Camping and Outdoor Activities* (7 subcategories)	Camping Alternatives Campfire Activities Outdoor Cookery	Day-trip camping Chopping wood Planning and cooking
4.0.0	*Nature Study, Appreciation, and Development* (4 subcategories)	Enjoyment of Scenery and Wildlife Raising, Caring for and Breeding of Plants	Home, outdoors, through books, TV Vegetable and flower gardening
5.0.0	*Hobby Activities* (9 subcategories)	Stamp Collections Model Collections Low Cost Collections	United States, foreign Autos, trains Buttons, bottles
6.0.0	*Craft Activities* (8 subcategories)	Paper Crafts Wood and Metal Working Handiwork Activities	Scrapbook Whittling Simple plumbing
7.0.0	*Art Activities* (8 subcategories)	Photography Dance Activities Drama Activities	Movies, slides Folk, tap, ballet dancing Puppetry
8.0.0	*Educational, Entertainment, and Cultural Activities* (11 subcategories)	Viewing Television Personal and Social Activities Civic Programs and Events	Sports News Entertaining, dining out Art museums, zoo

Adapted from Bender, M., Brannan, S.A., and Verhoven, P.J. (1984). *Leisure education for the handicapped: Curriculum goals, activities, and resources.* San Diego: College-Hill Press.

teraction can be fostered as participants share common goals. Although McGill's games are intended for children, the adaptations have been applied to adult games as well (Fluegelman, 1976, 1981; Weinstein and Goodman, 1980). Appendix B also lists several resources for more information on noncompetitive play for children and adults.

A number of programs or books are available for teaching selected components of a leisure skills curriculum, such as educational games for children with physical disabilities (Cratty, 1973); adapted aquatics (American National Red Cross, 1977); and basic locomotion, play equipment, and play vehicles skills (Watkinson and Wall, 1982). This book has presented introductions to a number of skills in this taxonomy, such as play and games, sports and physical development, and arts activities. Once these foundation skills have been deployed, more complex leisure activities should be addressed, with the guidance of a comprehensive leisure skills curriculum (e.g., Bender et al., 1984; Wehman and Schleien, 1981).

Resources

Books and Programs (see Appendix A). Bender et al. (1984); Fluegelman (1976, 1981); McGill (1984); Watkinson and Wall (1982); Wehman and Schleien (1981).

Organizations (see Appendix B). American Alliance of Health, Physical Education, and Recreation; Canadian Association for Health, Physical Education, and Recreation; New Games Foundation; Special Olympics.

Manufacturers (see Appendix C). Animal Town Game Company; Family Pastimes.

APPENDICES

Appendix A

ADAPTIVE PLAY: ANNOTATED BIBLIOGRAPHY

Adventure playgrounds for handicapped children. (1978). Order from Handicapped Adventure Playground Association, Fulham Palace, Bishops Avenue, London SW6 6EA, England; £1.00 (sterling), 32 pp.

This booklet contains specific ideas for designing community-based adventure playgrounds for disabled youth. They describe exemplary playgrounds, include aerial diagrams, and provide guidelines for setting up playgrounds. Needs in terms of structure, equipment, and staffing are specified, and strategies for financing this undertaking are suggested. The final section presents numerous references and resources.

Amery, H., and Civardi, A. (1976). *The FunCraft book of print and paint.* Order from Scholastic Book Services, 730 Broadway, New York, New York, 10002; $6.95, 47 pp.

Although this book is intended for nondisabled children, several of the activities are appropriate for many disabled children. For example, the ideas for finger, thumb, and hand prints can be incorporated into training sessions on the handshapes and movements for signing, and the wax rubbings can give children an added incentive for scribbling.

Atack, S. M. (1982). *Art activities for the handicapped.* Order from Communication Skill Builders, P.O. Box 42050-J, Tucson, AZ 85733; $6.95, 135 pp.

Step-by-step procedures are presented for projects such as drawing, painting, and modeling. The handbook illustrates ways to develop skills in areas such as cognition and fine motor development through art. A list of easily accessible materials is also provided.

Ausberger, C., Martin, M., and Creighton, J. (1982). *Learning to talk is child's play.* Order from Communication Skill Builders, P.O. Box 42050-J, Tucson, AZ 85733; $11.95, 112 pp.

This book is intended for parents, nursery school teachers, and others working with caregivers. It stresses the use of responsive language teaching through adult-child dialogues. Five sections present strategies for using commercially available toys in facilitating communication development: toys for reconstructing reality, toys for experiments with the world, perceptual motor problem-solving toys, representational toys (friends and playmates; the world around us).

Azarnoff, P. (1984). *Health, illness, and disability: A guide to books for children and young adults.* Order from Pediatric Projects, Inc., P.O. Box 1880, Santa Monica, CA 90406; $30.00, 300 pp.

This guide offers reference and ordering information on 1,000 books for children (preschoolers through teenagers) and adults on the following topics: disability, impairment, illness, medical treatment, and hospitalization. An annotated bibliography of fiction and nonfiction titles is presented, plus a detailed subject index. This can be extremely useful to adults attempting to suggest appropriate readings for children with disabilities or their peers, siblings, parents, or other family members.

Bender, M., Brannan, S. A., and Verhoven, P. J. (1984). *Leisure education for the handicapped: Curriculum goals, activities, and resources.* Order from College-Hill Press, 4284 41st St., San Diego, CA 92105; $18.50, 234 pp.

This book develops a strong rationale for the importance of leisure education for individuals with disabilities. A classification of leisure activities and experiences is presented, and the relationship of leisure education to existing curricula in schools is explored. Exemplary leisure learning units are provided for each of the eight major curriculum areas. Each leisure learning unit includes the following: overview, goal statement, short-term objectives, task analysis, assessment, lead-up and follow-up strategies, adaptations and modifications, and resources. Considerations for developing individualized instruction and evaluation are also presented.

Bloom, L., and Lahey, M. (1978). *Language development and language disorders.* Order from John Wiley and Sons, 605 Third Avenue, New York, New York 10158; $35.95, 689 pp.

These authors synthesize research findings in both normal and deviant language development, suggesting methods for identifying children with language disorders and describing their language. They then propose goals of language learning based on normal development and strategies for facilitating language learning. The correlates of language disorders (e.g., clinical syndromes) are also described.

Bricker, D. (1984). *Early communication: Development and training.* In M.D. Snell (Ed.), *Systematic instruction of the moderately and severly handicapped* (2nd ed.). Order from Charles E. Merrill Company, 1300 Alum Creek Drive, Columbus, OH 43216; $23.85, pp. 269-288.

A variety of communicative behaviors appropriate for teaching developmentally young children are covered in this chapter. Both general and specific teaching strategies are presented for six training phases, beginning with visual and auditory attention and ending with the establishment of multiword productions.

Bricker, D. D., and Dennison, L. (1978). Training prerequisites to verbal behavior. In M.D. Snell (Ed.), *Systematic instruction of the moderately and severely handicapped.* Order from Charles E. Merrill Company, 1300 Alum Creek Drive, Columbus, OH 43216; pp. 155–178.

A variety of behaviors thought to be preliminary to the development of formal language are covered in this chapter. Both general and specific training strategies are presented for the following skills areas: on-task behavior, imitation, discriminative use of objects, and word recognition.

Broughton, B. (1982). *Creative experiences: An arts curriculum for young children — Including those with special needs.* Order from Chapel Hill Training-Outreach Project, Lincoln Center, Merritt Mill Road, Chapel Hill, NC 27514; $12.00, 174 pp.

This curriculum is divided into four major sections: creative movement, drama, music, and visual arts. Each section contains activities correlated with the Learning Accomplishment Profile (LAP), with four skills presented in each of seven developmental areas (among them gross motor, language, self-help). Each activity includes description, related skills, materials, procedure (including a motivator to set the stage), suggested modification for five areas of impairment (hearing, vision, cognition, speech, and motor), and enrichment variations.

Burkhart, L. J. (1980). *Homemade battery powered toys and educational devices for severely handicapped children.* Order from Linda J. Burkhart, 8303 Rhode Island Avenue, College Park, MD 20740; $6.00 (add $1.50 for first class or UPS delivery), 57 pp.

This book presents complete "how-to" instructions for several switches (e.g., mercury head control switch, puzzle switch) and homemade battery toys (e.g., lighted peg board, happy face light). Suggestions are made for modifying battery toys to accept switch input.

Burkhart, L. J. (1982). *More handmade battery devices for severely handicapped children with suggested activities.* Order from Linda J. Burkhart, 8303 Rhode Island Avenue, College Park, MD 20740; $12.50 (add $1.50 for first class or UPS delivery), 160 pp.

This book is a wealth of information on the topic of switch-making. Chapter 1 presents step-by-step instructions for constructing 29 switches (e.g., cookie sheet switch, penny pincher, blow switch, pre-writing switch). Chapter 3 describes construction of four communication training devices (e.g., pointing training switch). Chapter 4 presents specific programming instructions for developing cognitive skills (e.g., cause and effect); communication skills (e.g., eye contact); motor skills (e.g., head control), and social and self-help skills (e.g., shared interactions). Six appendices cover topics such as how to solder and where to get supplies.

Campbell, J. H., King, M. P., and Robson, M. (1975). *Learning through art.* Order from DLM/Teaching Resources, P.O. Box 4000, Allen, TX 75002; $17.00, 200 pp.

More than 100 art activities are presented in this guide, designed to enhance basic motor, cognitive, and perceptual skills. The two sections cover both seasonal and nonseasonal activities. Each activity includes the following: a photograph demonstrating a sample completed activity; a materials list; advance preparation requirements, if necessary; directions; and adaptations for different developmental levels.

Carlson, F. (1982). *Prattle and play: Equipment recipes for nonspeech communication.* Order from Media Resource Center, Meyer Children's Rehabilitation Institute, University of Nebraska Medical Center, Omaha, NE 68131; $5.00, 63 pp.

This book is divided into two sections: The section on equipment covers the materials and instructions needed to make each project, whereas that on adaptations tells how to make changes to modify equipment to the needs of individuals. Examples of equipment included are looking board, symbol blocks, symbol stuffed toys, playboard, and handles for small toys.

Carlson, F. (1985). *Picsyms categorical dictionary.* Order from Baggeboda Press, 1128 Rhode Island St., Lawrence, KS 66044; $20.00, 190 pp.

This is intended for use by parents or professionals who have already had training in working with symbol users. The first section presents the rules for this open-ended visual language system, techniques for drawing Picsyms, and suggestions on making the symbols meaningful to children. The second section presents samples of Picsyms that may be copied for home or classroom use. Grids are presented for adding symbols to the system.

Cashdollar, P., and Martin, J. (1981). *Kids come in special flavors: Understanding handicaps.* Order from Kids Come in Special Flavors Company, Box 562, Forest Park Station, Dayton, OH 45405.

Two different kits are designed to help nondisabled people "try on a handicap" through simulations. The Classroom Kit ($35.95) includes resource book, equipment, and cassette for 16 action simulations with groups of up to 30 students. The Workshop Kit ($46.50) is designed to assist in presentation of a teacher-parent workshop designed to remove anxiety about mainstreaming.

Chance, Paul. (1979). *Learning through play.* Order from Gardner Press, Inc., 19 Union Square West, New York, 10003; $5.00, 60 pp.

This book, sponsored by Johnson and Johnson Baby Products Company, is a summary of a pediatric round table on play. Representatives are from fields as diverse as child development, psychology, education, medicine, folklore, and toy manufacturing. The book summarizes what constitutes play, types of play, functions of play, and what elements improve play. It is part of a series on early childhood development.

Charlebois-Marois, C. (1985). *Everybody's technology: A sharing of ideas in augmentative communication.* Order from Charlecoms Enr., P.O. Box 419, SUCC. Jean-Talon, Montreal, Quebec, Canada H1S 2Z3; $14.00 (including postage), 188 pp.

This compendium includes more than 150 descriptions and illustrations of homemade adaptations, including a number in the area of "Readiness Skills." This includes ideas for learning through recreation and play (adapted toys, basic skills, interface training).

Cherry, C. (1976). *Creative play for the developing child: Early lifehood education through play.* Order from Fearon Pitman Publishers, Inc., 6 Davis Drive, Belmont, CA 94002; $11.95, 260 pp.

This book is intended for use with nondisabled children. As such, it presents many concepts helpful in approaching normalization or initiating a mainstreaming project. The first section introduces a philosophy of play, including play guidelines for adults and children. In the second section, specific strategies are presented for creating the play environment, including physical influences such as colors, lighting, and odors and human influences such as size, nonverbal communication, and sex differences. The third section provides activities for implementing the creative play program in the following areas: movement experiences (gross and fine motor), construction experiences, natural and physical science, letters and numbers, creative expression, and forms of make-believe. Most activities are appropriate for children who are able-bodied and functioning above the two to three year cognitive level.

Dahood, K., and Lessee, J. (1982). *Celebration! Arts and the handicapped: A report and a guide to planning activities for disabled children and adults in dance, drama and the visual arts.* Order from Special Needs Service, Tucson Public Library, P.O. Box 27470, Tucson, AZ; 47 pp.

A report is presented on an intensive project by the Tucson Public Library in cooperation with the Arizona Commission on the Arts designed to promote arts programming. The project included a series of model workshops and special projects for children and adults with disabilities by professional arts organizations. Considerations are described for preparing artists, including sensitivity training and topics such as mainstreaming, age levels, and logistical problems. Planning strategies are presented to assist in initiating and operating an arts program. Workshop activities are described, including ideas regarding the role of dance, drama, and visual arts, as well as combined activities.

Downs, M. (1981). *Hearkit.* Order from BAM World Markets, Inc., P.O. Box 10701, Denver, CO 80210; $55.00

This kit contains a complete noisemaker system for screening hearing in infants and children. It includes a hearing development and communication questionnaire pad; an instruction guide; a score card pad; and several rattles packaged in a carrying case.

Dunn, M. L. (1982). *Pre-Sign Language Skills.* Order from Communication Skill Builders, P.O. Box 42050-J, Tucson, AZ 85733; $14.95, 105 pp.

This workbook assists educators in analyzing the motor components of signs, the motor skills a student can use in signing, and methods for sign instruction. It applies the perspective of occupational therapy to sign training for children with cognitive delay. The workbook can be used as a self-teaching tool, with periodic probes to assess learning. Many of the assessment and teaching worksheets included in the book may be reproduced for classroom use. Numerous examples and illustrations support the text.

Dunst, C. J. (1978). A cognitive-social approach for assessment of early nonverbal communicative behavior. *Journal of Childhood Communication Disorders,* 2(2), pp. 111–123.

This article presents a compilation of infant scale test items that assess nonverbal communicative behaviors. The developmental age for each item is listed, and items are classified according to the type of communicative act and the Piagetian stages represented. It can be used as a developmental checklist for determining behaviors that are and are not in a child's repertoire. Developmental progress can also be monitored through periodic updating of the checklist.

Dunst, C. J. (1981). *Infant learning: A cognitive linguistic intervention strategy.* Order from DLM/Teaching Resources, P.O. Box 4000, Allen, TX 75002; $22.00, 217 pp.

This program is intended for use by teachers, therapists, and child-care workers. It uses a Piagetian-based model in developing cognitive, social, and language abilities for prelinguistic children. Target populations are children who are at risk, developmentally delayed, or severely handicapped. The three phases are (1) response-contingent behaviors (e.g., reaching, visual tracking); (2) sensory-motor abilities (e.g., vocal imitation, means-ends behaviors); (3) early cognitive-linguistic abilities (e.g., symbolic play).

Evans, A. (Ed.). (1982). *Arts for the handicapped: A resource and curriculum guide.* Order from National Committee Arts for the Handicapped, 1825 Connecticut Avenue, NW, Suite 418, Washington, DC 20009; limited supply free, 198 pp.

Learning activities for disabled children are presented in five major areas: music, dance, drama, art, and media. Each activity includes instructional objective, materials and equipment, target population, training procedures, learning skills, and evaluation procedures. A major section is devoted to developing funding sources, and an extensive bibliography is provided.

Fell, A. (1984). *The non-oral communication assessment (NOCA).* Order from Alternatives to Speech, Inc., 1030 Duncan, Ann Arbor, MI 48103; $60.00.

This is intended for speech, occupational or physical therapists, and special educators. The target populations are individuals with severe physical, cognitive, or verbal disabilities. Three sections cover motoric functioning assessment for switching, motoric functioning assessment for pointing, and communication capacity assessment. Materials include a 180 page instruction manual and three sets of pictures as well as score forms.

Fewell, R. R., and Vadasy, P. F. (1983). *Learning through play: A resource manual for teachers and parents, birth to three years.* Order from DLM/Teaching Resources, P.O. Box 4000, Allen, TX 75002; $19.00.

This manual is intended for either parents or professionals. The first section summarizes natural learning and maturation and the second provides 192 simple, structured activities for infants and toddlers. Adaptations are suggested for children with motor, visual, or hearing impairments.

Fieber, N. (1983). Informal assessment of visual skills needed for non-speech development. *Working with pre-readers: Practical approaches.* Order from Meyer Children's Rehabilitation Institute, University of Nebraska Medical Center, Omaha, NE 68131; $6.00, pp. 149–172.

This article has two components. The first is a guide for functional vision assessment for infants and severely handicapped children. It assesses looking behaviors (fixation, focal distance, shift of gaze, visual field, and so forth) and discrimination behaviors (what the child sees). Each item tested includes function, specific test procedures, spontaneous student behaviors, and implications. The second component is a vocabulary of terms relating to the eye.

Fluegelman, A. (Ed.). (1976). *The new games book.* Order from New Games Foundation, P.O. Box 7901, San Francisco, CA 94120; $7.95, 193 pp.

This book provides an introduction to the concept of new games, with an emphasis on cooperative play. Most games included require moderate gross motor skills; the need for fine motor skills and eye-hand coordination is minimized. Although many of the games would need extensive modification or would be inappropriate for people with severe disabilities, the concept of this book can be used in designing cooperative games for children with special needs. The book *More New Games* (1981), by the same author, presents additional opportunities for creative group play.

Gilroy, P. J. (1985). *Kids in motion: An early childhood movement education program.* Order from Communication Skill Builders, P.O. Box 42050-B, Department 35, Tucson, AZ 85733; $11.95, 60 pp.

This program presents 20 minute movement education lessons, with a specific focus for each month (body part identification, rhythms, large group cooperative skills). For each lesson, the following information is presented: learning objectives, warm-up exercises, materials, and procedures. The lessons are open-ended, allowing children to experiment with movement exploration. The lessons are intended for children at a language age or interest level of 4 to 5 years; adaptations will have to be made for children who are cognitively or chronologically younger, or children with moderate to severe motor impairments.

Goetz, L., Utley, B., Gee, K., Baldwin, M., and Sailor, W. (1982). *Auditory assessment and programming for severely handicapped deaf-blind students.* Order from The Association for Persons with Severe Handicaps, 7010 Roosevelt Way, NE, Seattle, WA 98115; $5.00.

This manual was produced after three years of research and validation by the Bay Area Severely Handicapped Deaf-Blind Project. It offers strategies for assessing severely handicapped students who do not respond to conventional hearing tests. Assessment is inexpensive, requiring only readily available materials, such as lights and extension cords. The manual provides a vehicle for recording and analyzing data to present relevant information to the audiologist.

Granger, C., and Wehman, P. (1979). Sensory stimulation. In P. Wehman (Ed.), *Recreation programming for developmentally disabled persons.* Order from Pro Ed, 5341 Industrial Oaks Boulevard, Austin, TX 78735; $15.00, pp. 127–143.

This chapter emphasizes the importance of a multisensory approach to early intervention and suggestions for assessment and intervention in tactile, auditory, gustatory, olfactory, and visual stimulation. Assessment forms and suggested materials are provided.

Hanna, R. M., Lippert, E. A., and Harris, A. B. (1982). *Developmental communication curriculum.* Order from Charles E. Merrill Publishing Company, Test Division, Box 508, Columbus, OH 43216; $65.00.

This curriculum includes the following materials: curriculum guide, activity handbook, developmental communication inventory (package of 12), and parent handout (package of 12). It is intended to help extend the prelinguistic communication skills on which language is based. The curriculum uses play as a natural context for learning, with specific objectives divided into three domains: content (64 objectives); function (51 objectives); and form (64 objectives).

Heekin, S., and Mengel, P. (1983a). *New Friends teacher's manual.* Order from Chapel Hill Training-Outreach Project, Lincoln Center, Merritt Mill Road, Chapel Hill, NC 27514; $12.00, 156 pp.

This manual is intended to accompany the New Friends dolls, which are rag dolls with various disabilities. In addition to learning about the self and studying normal processes of sensation, movement, and so forth, six disability areas are covered (impairments in hearing, vision, movement, communication, learning, or behavior). Each unit includes suggestions for leading discussions, sample doll scripts, guidelines for answering questions, correlated classroom activities, and a resource list. Supportive chapters present suggestions for developing dolls, activities to involve families, and additional information concerning young children and disabilities.

Heekin, S., and Mengel, P. (1983b). *New Friends Trainer's Notebook.* Order from Chapel Hill Training-Outreach Project, Lincoln Center, Merritt Mill Road, Chapel Hill, NC 27514; $18.00, 270 pp.

The purpose of this notebook is to assist special educators and other disability specialists in conducting workshops to teach teachers, parents, and others the New Friends approach. The extensive activities are intended to (1) facilitate the expression of feelings and concerns about mainstreaming and related topics; (2) help participants make low-cost, life-size dolls with selected disabilities; and (3) prepare participants to use dolls in the classroom. Sample activities include role-playing, values clarification, and simulation exercises.

Higgins, J. (1982). *Guidelines for adapting battery operated toys for the physically handicapped.* Order from California Avenue School, 215 West California Avenue, Vista, CA; $3.50, 28 pp.

This booklet gives step-by-step instructions for constructing a toy inline jack and three switches (touch panel, pillow, and on-off switch). Clear illustrations are provided for each step.

Hogan, P. (1974). *Playgrounds for free.* Order from MIT Press, 28 Carleton Street, Cambridge, MA 02142; $9.95, 93 pp.

This book suggests numerous strategies for developing an adventure playground at minimal cost. Ideas are presented for using recycled materials, such as tires. Illustrations and descriptions are provided for numerous pieces of equipment. Although this is not intended for children with disabilities, many of the ideas could be incorporated into an adaptive playground.

Jeffree, D., McConkey, R., and Hewson, S. (1977). *Let me play.* Order from Souvenir Press (Educational and Academic) Ltd., 43 Great Russell Street, London, England, WCIB 3PA (published in Canada by Methuen Publications, Agincourt, Ontario); £2.5, 252 pp.

This is primarily a "how-to" publication, although some theoretical issues are presented. The book is organized into sections covering six general types of play: exploratory, energetic, skillful, social, imaginative, and puzzle-it-out play. Each section is further divided into booklets, describing additional levels of play, and suggesting specific activities to encourage play and learning at each level. Training activities are presented in sufficient detail to be replicated. Most sections also present yes-no checklists to determine at what level intervention should begin.

Langley, B., and DuBose, R. F. (1976). Functional vision screening for severely handicapped children. *New Outlook for the Blind, 8,*
346–350.

This article presents an overview of literature relative to assessing
vision in children with disabilities. Teacher-oriented checklists for
screening functional vision are provided, including specific assessment procedures and an assessment form. The five areas covered
are presence and nature of the visual response (blink reflex, eye
preference); reaction to visual stimuli (tracking, shifting gaze); distance and size of objects or pictures; integration of visual and cognitive processing (causality, object concept); and integration of
visual and motor processing (performing fine motor tasks).

Lear, R. (1977). *Play helps: Toys and activities for handicapped children.*
Order from Heinemann Health Books, Kingwood, Tadworth, Surrey,
England KT20 6TG; £2.50, or International Ideas, 127 Spruce
Street, Philadelphia, PA 19130; $18.95, 158 pp.

A teacher of handicapped children and a toy library developer
share a wealth of information regarding play for disabled children.
The book is arranged into sections relating to the five senses:
sight, hearing, touch, taste, and smell. Each section includes a rationale; ideas regarding toys, games, and activities for developing
the specific sense; homemade toys to encourage use of the sense;
and brief annotated book lists. Appendices provide basic recipes
(e.g., finger paint) and list additional books, supportive organizations, and toy manufacturers. This book is extremely personalized,
with many examples of applications of the ideas with specific children. A majority of the ideas are directed toward children who are
cognitively at the 5 year level or above.

Lessee, J. (1983). . . . *For all of us: A resource guide especially for people
who work with the differently abled.* Order from Special Needs Service, Tucson Public Library, P.O. Box 27470, Tucson, AZ 85726;
$1.25, 80 pp.

Eight sections in this manual present information on various disabilities: autism, cerebral palsy, epilepsy, hearing impairment,
learning disabilities, mental retardation, physical disabilities, and
visual impairment. Each section includes general information, professional and child-oriented readings, related agencies, and disability simulations appropriate for adults. Although this manual is
intended for use by public librarians, the information will be useful
for any adults working with people who are differently abled.

Let's Play to Grow Kit. (1977). Order from *Let's Play to Grow,* 1701 K
Street, NW, Suite 201, Washington, DC 20006, $5.00.

This kit contains family-oriented materials for use with children
with delayed development or disabled children. A parent-teacher
manual, "I'm a Winner" chart, and 12 play guides are included

(e.g., fun with rhythm, movement and dance, fun in the water, fun with bowling/volleyball/basketball).

Lowe, M., and Costello, A. J. (1976). *The symbolic play test.* Order from NFER-Nelson Publishing Co., Ltd., Darville House, 2 Oxford Road East, Windsor, Berkshire SL4 1DF, England.

This test allows evaluations of a child's spontaneous play with toys that are small replicas of familiar objects (doll, brush, comb, tractor). Four situations are presented in order of increasing difficulty, and the child's free play with the objects is observed. The number of appropriate schemas (e.g., setting the plate on the table) used determines the child's score. The total score can be translated to an age equivalent.

MacDonald, J. D., and Gillette, Y. (1984a–d). *Ecological Communication System (ECO).* Order from ECOLETTER, 2423 Portsmouth Road, Toledo, OH 43613; $25.00.

This set of materials includes several components. The *Ecomaps and Assessment Manual* (46 pp.) presents guidelines for conducting an assessment according to the ECO Model, examining targets, problems, and strategies for the child or significant others. A *Training Glossary* (91 pp.) provides the bases for the assessment and treatment components, as descriptive definitions are presented for each target, problem, and strategy. Two treatment modules are currently available; *Turntaking with Actions* (functional interactive play, 60 pp.) and *Turntaking with Communications* (initial conversation, 83 pp.). The *Conversation Routine Manual* (75 pp.) presents sample training activities for many natural events. Each conversation routine includes goals, a materials list, and sample scripts (do's and dont's). Sample topic areas include object play routines (e.g., working a puzzle); people play routines (e.g., greeting); teaching routines (e.g., book reading); and spontaneous routines (e.g., eating, in the car).

Manolson, A. (1984). *It takes two to talk: A Hanen early language parent guide book.* Order from Hanen Early Language Resource Centre, Room 4-126, 252 Bloor Street West, Toronto, Ontario, Canada M5S 1V6; $15.00 plus postage and handling, 142 pp.

This parent handbook was designed to accompany a Hanen Early Language Parent Program; however, it may also be used alone following a professional evaluation. It is divided into two parts. The first section, "Let Your Child Initiate," focuses on the child's attempts to communicate, with suggestions provided to guide parents and teachers in responding in ways that facilitate interaction. The second part, "You Initiate Opportunities for Language Learning," suggests enjoyable ways in which parents can increase opportunities for communication and learning. This includes activities in the domains of play, music, books-"reading," game-playing, and art. Chapters are accompanied by observation checklists, practice opportunities, sample activities, and evaluation sheets, with numerous illustrations for demonstration purposes.

Manual for the aide in adapted aquatics. (1974). Order from American National Red Cross, Washington, DC 20006 (or purchase from local Red Cross); $1.25, 36 pp.

The role and responsibilities of the aide in an adaptive aquatics program are clearly described in this booklet. Descriptive information and specific teaching suggestions are provided for a variety of handicapping conditions (cerebral palsy, mental retardation, and so forth). Appendices present information such as manual signs, the manual alphabet, and a glossary of disability-related terms.

McConkey, R., and Jeffree, D. (1981). *Making toys for handicapped children: A guide for parents and teachers.* Order from Prentice Hall, Englewood Cliffs, NJ 07632; $17.95 ($7.95, paperback), 208 pp.

Although this is primarily a resource book describing actual toy-making designs, it also offers background information regarding play and sample recording forms for assessing and monitoring play behavior. Detailed instructions are provided for making several basic toys; however, there is considerable room for creativity and modification to meet individual needs. One chapter offers background information, such as tools, materials, and ideas for involving others. Several simple practice projects are presented first (e.g., glove puppet, dominoes). Later projects include materials such as formboards and jigsaws. Each toy section includes general information, time, materials, instructions, illustrations, and suggestions for using the completed toy. Most of the toys require moderate to good fine motor control.

McGill, J. (1984). *Play for play's sake: Cooperative games as a strategy for integration.* Order from National Institute on Mental Retardation, 4700 Keele Street, York University Campus, Downsview, Ontario, Canada, M3J 1P3; $5.00, 45 pp.

As the title suggests, this manual focuses on the use of cooperative — as opposed to competitive — games to enhance integration of disabled and nondisabled people. The first section presents a philosophy of cooperative games both in general and as they relate to integration of people with disabilities. In the second section, a number of cooperative games are described briefly, and appendices provide resources for cooperative sports, games, and equipment. Most of the games included would be appropriate only for children with mental ages above three years, and with good to normal gross motor skills; however, the philosophy and games can be incorporated into adapted cooperative games.

Moran, J. M., and Kalakian, L. H. (1977). *Movement experiences for the mentally retarded or emotionally disturbed child.* Order from Burgess Publishing Co., 7108 Ohms Lane, Minneapolis, MN 55435, $17.95, 455 pp.

This textbook is intended for physical educators. In addition to material on general fitness, it covers activities such as play therapy, specialized gymnastics, music and dance therapy, and swimming. Innovative equipment for the school and playground is described and illustrated.

Movement Education for Preschool Children. (1980). Order from American Alliance Publications, P.O. Box 704, Waldorf, MD 20601; $7.90, 56 pp.

This book, published by the American Alliance of Health, Physical Education, Recreation, and Dance, is divided into four sections. Part One develops a rationale for movement education in young children, and Part Two explores content to be included in a good movement program. In Part Three, strategies for presenting appropriate movement activities to preschoolers are described, and the final part describes settings and equipment. The emphasis is on creative movement, rather than on stereotyped movement.

Musselwhite, C. R. (1985). *Songbook: Signs and symbols for children.* Order from Developmental Equipment, 981 Winnetka Terrace, Lake Zurich, IL 60047; $12.00, 96 pp.

This songbook presents more than 40 beginner-level songs, including 18 songs designed to introduce target phonemes. Songs are based on simple melodies or familiar tunes. Signs from the Signed English system and symbols from the Blissymbolics and Picsyms systems are depicted to represent all key words in the songs. The 25 primary songs include specific goals in the areas of communication, motor skills, and cognitive and social skills, with training activities presented for each song. A review of the literature on music in augmentative communication is provided, with general training strategies for facilitating oral language, signing, or symbol use through singing.

Musselwhite, C. R., and St. Louis, K. W. (1982). *Communication programming for the severely handicapped: Vocal and non-vocal strategies.* Order from College-Hill Press, 4284 41st Street, San Diego, CA 92105; $29.50 ($24.50 softcover), 332 pp.

This sourcebook reviews the decision-making process in augmentative communication and summarizes general issues in communication training, preliminary training, and supportive services. Vocal language programs and issues in vocal language training are presented. Both aided (symbolic) and unaided (gestural) communication systems are described extensively. Appendices include an extensive annotated bibliography; reviews of 25 communication programs; descriptions of 39 organizations; and a descriptive list of assessment procedures and tools.

Newman, J. (1976). *Swimming for children with physical and sensory impairments: Methods and techniques for therapy and recreation.* Order from Charles C Thomas, 2600 South First Street, Springfield, IL 62717; $20.00, 208 pp.

This manual is divided according to disability types (e.g., spina bifida, cerebral palsy, blindness), with specific suggestions provided for each population relative to the various swimming strokes. A major training strategy is swim patterning, in which the child is passively patterned until the muscles take over. The book includes many diagrams of positions and movements.

Oatman, K. (1984). *Breaking through the barriers: Puppet plays with the profoundly handicapped.* Order from The Puppetry Store, P.O. Box 3128, Santa Ana, CA 92703; $8.95, 62 pp.

This book is based on the author's experiences in working with children who are physically and cognitively disabled. It includes suggestions for constructing manipulative puppets appropriate for these populations. Ideas for using play therapy with special needs children are also presented.

Owens, R. E. (1982). *Program for acquisition of language with the severely impaired.* Order from Charles E. Merrill Publishing Company, Test Division, 1300 Alum Creek Drive, Box 508, Columbus, OH 43126; $55.00.

This package of materials includes the following components: Program Manual, Caregiver Interview and Environmental Observation (package of 12), Diagnostic Interaction Survey/Developmental Assessment Tool (package of 12), and Training Level Activities Guide. The program emphasizes the communicative context of client-caregiver interaction for assessment and training. Three modes of training are included: formal training (twice per day, 5 to 10 minute sessions); incidental teaching strategies; and stimulation methods. The program targets presymbolic and early symbolic skills for training.

Porter, P. B., Carter, S., Goolsby, E., Martin, N. J., Reed, M., Stowers, S., and Wurth, B. (1985). *Prerequisites to the use of augmentative communication systems.* Order from Augmentative Communication Team, Biological Sciences Research Center 220-H, University of North Carolina, Chapel Hill, NC 27514; $9.50, 32 pp.

This manual assists trainers in teaching behaviors that are preliminary to the conventional use of augmentative communication systems. Eight prerequisite steps are included, from demonstrating preferences to using a signal to indicate a choice among three or more pictured objects or events. Each step presents introduction, assessment questions, assessment procedure, training procedure, and criteria for moving to the next step.

Principles of playground design (film). (1978). Order from University of South Florida, Film Library, 4202 Fowler Avenue, Tampa, FL 33620; sale $315, rental $15.

This 26 minute color film is based on summary of a 3 year research and demonstration project conducted by Dr. Louis Bowers. It focuses on play learning centers for the handicapped and safety concerns relative to traditional playgrounds. Principles of design resulting from the project are identified as they were implemented in various play centers and material and safety construction standards are considered. The role of the adult play facilitator is defined and children are shown playing on the playgrounds designed for them.

Procedural handbook. Order from Nebraska Diagnostic Resource Center, 1910 Meridian, Cozad, NE 38131, Attention Media/Library; $4.00.

This handbook is a description and explanation of implementation procedures for local ToyBraries — a "how to get started" guide.

Renfro, N. (1984). *Puppetry, language, and the special child: Discovering alternate languages.* Order from Nancy Renfro Studios, 1117 West 9th Street, Austin, TX 78703; $14.95, 152 pp.

This book describes activities to integrate the visual and verbal aspects of puppetry into the curriculum to enhance language and communication. One chapter covers kinetic language, another describes story presentation strategies, and a third presents puppetry activities designed to enhance oral speech. Several demonstration projects using puppetry with special populations are summarized. The book includes numerous photographs, illustrations, and patterns, and an appendix provides annotated resources.

Riddick, B. (1982). *Toys and play for handicapped children.* Order from Croom Helm, 51 Washington Street, Dover, NH, 03820; $21.50, 224 pp.

This book begins with general teaching techniques, then suggests strategies appropriate to various ages, from infancy through preschool. One chapter focuses on children with special needs (physically handicapped, deaf, and visually impaired children). Ideas are also presented for choosing and buying toys. Photographs provide samples of toy use with children who have a variety of disabilities. Numerous tables offer recommendations of specific toys for special needs (two-handed play, physically handicapped children, and so forth).

Rottman, F. (1978). *Easy to make puppets and how to use them: Early childhood.* Order from The Puppetry Store, P.O. Box 3128, Santa Ana, CA 92703; $4.95, 96 pp.

Numerous suggestions are presented for introducing puppetry to children ages 2 to 5. Although emphasis is on use of puppets in settings such as churches, day camps, or clubs, many of the simple puppets will be adaptable to use with some disabled children. Many patterns, illustrations, and activity suggestions are included, making this an excellent resource for the beginning puppeteer.

Sacks, G. K., and Young, E. C. (1982). *Infant scale of communicative intent.* Order from St. Christopher's Hospital for Children, 5th and Lehigh Avenue, Philadelphia, PA 19133, $12.00 for 12 copies.

This nonstandardized, descriptive assessment tool was compiled from published tests, research data, and clinical experience. It includes five comprehension and five expression items at each month level from birth to 18 months. The scale is administered through observation, direct testing, and parental reporting.

Sherrill, C. (Ed.). (1979). *Creative arts for the handicapped,* 2nd Edition. Order from Charles C. Thomas, Publishers, 301–327 East Lawrence Avenue, Springfield, IL; $15.50, 304 pp.

This resource book presents 27 short chapters relating to several art forms (music, visual arts, dance, drama) for people with a variety of disabilities (physical, visual, emotional, cognitive). Examples are generic training strategies, such as drama for children who are deaf or mentally retarded. This book is not logically organized as a how-to sourcebook, but it does provide general ideas and philosophies for initiating creative arts programs.

Singer, D. G., and Singer, J. L. (1977). *Partners in play: A step-by-step guide to imaginative play in children.* Order from Harper and Row, New York; $12.95, 205 pp.

This book presents a rationale for focusing on play and helps adults to recapture their own imagination through specific exercises. A variety of contexts are suggested for helping children develop through imaginative play, beginning with preplay activities and progressing through sensory development and transformations. Ideas for using poetry, music, stories, and sociodramatic play are also recommended. One chapter focuses on selecting toys and materials for optimal imaginative play. Appendices suggest readings for children and adults, as well as a research bibliography.

Sinker, M. (1983). *Lekotek guide to good toys.* Order from USA Toy Lending Library, 5940 West Touhy Avenue, Chicago, IL 60648; $14.45, 91 pp.

This 91 page illustrated book describes toys that wold provide a basic inventory for any type of toy lending library. Several areas of development (e.g., gross motor, language) are described briefly, with information on how toys can enhance growth in each area. Sample toys are then reviewed for each developmental area.

Sullivan, D. (1982). *Pocketful of puppets: Activities for the special child.* Order from Nancy Renfro Studios, 1117 W. 9th Street, Austin, TX 78703; $6.50, 46 pp.

The target populations for this book are children with mental, physical, and multiple disabilities. Learning activities are presented through several general puppet types: buddy puppets (traditional hand puppets that can serve as special friends); puppet bracelets (small, specially designed puppets attached to the wrist); bodi-puppets (puppets attached to the child's body, and activated by large movement patterns); table-top puppets (puppets that are moved around a table-top environment); and other simple puppets (stick puppets, paper-plate puppets). Instructions, drawings, and patterns are included for making samples of each type of puppet.

Swimming for the disabled (film). Order from Town and Country Productions Ltd., 21 Cheyne Row, London SW3 5HP, England.

Three tape-slide programs are included in this set: (1) Position and Balance in Water demonstrates two methods of entry, plus activities for familiarizing the child in the water, and developing head control and body balance; (2) Movement in Water demonstrates forward and lateral rotations; and (3) Group Activities and Formations in Water depict appropriate use of hand, arm, and body assistance to the disabled swimmer.

ten Horn, H. Z. (1981). *Touch toys and how to make them.* Order from Touch Toys, Inc., P.O. Box 2224, Rockville, MD 20852; $3.63, 79 pp.

This how-to book presents toys designed for visually handicapped children. Many of these toys are made from everyday household throw-away materials, and projects are at a low level of difficulty. More than 50 toys are described briefly, with hand-drawn illustrations.

Toys help: A guide to choosing toys for handicapped children. (1981). Canadian Association of Toy Libraries, 1207-50 Quebec Avenue, Toronto, Ontario M6P 484, Canada; $8.00.

This portfolio includes the following components: (1) Introduction and Bibliography, providing rationale, sources of information, and lists of toy distributors; (2) selection criteria; (3) poster of selected toys and related skills in 10 areas (e.g., communication, cognitive, social emotional skills); (4) organization and toy lending system, providing rationale and specific suggestions for starting a toy lending library; and (5) special toys for the physically handicapped child, presenting an introduction to adapting battery-operated toys.

Uzgaris, I., and Hunt, J. (1975). *Assessment in infancy; Ordinal scales of psychological development.* Order from University of Illinois Press, 54 East Gregory Drive, Champaign, IL 61820; $17.50, 274 pp.

These scales are used for Piaget's theory of sensorimotor intelligence. They measure the growth of cognitive competencies in seven domains: visual pursuit and the permanence of objects; means for obtaining desired environmental events (problem solving); development of vocal and gestural imitation; development of operational causality; construction of object relations in space; and development of schemes for relating to objects (play).

Water free (film). (1975). Order from Rehabfilm, 1123 Broadway, Suite 704, New York 10010; $60.00 (rental, nonmembers).

This 35 minute film was produced by the Association of Swimming Therapy to demonstrate the Halliwick method of adaptive swimming. It shows both mildly and severely disabled people swimming independently. Games, exercises, and a few simple devices are shown. The film ends with several Halliwick-trained swimmers braving the English Channel. It is a very inspirational film for use when beginning an adaptive swimming program.

Watkinson, E. J., and Wall, A. E. (1982). *PREP: The PREP play program: Play skill instruction for mentally handicapped children.* Order from Canadian Association for Health, Physical Education, and Recreation, 333 River Road, Ottawa, Ontario K1L 8B9, Canada; $6.00, 108 pp.

This program is designed to encourage the development of play skills in children with cognitive disabilities. PREP play sessions include individualized instruction, small group activity, and encouragement of purposeful play during free play. Specifics are included for assessing motor skills and teaching individualized and group-based skills. Task sequences are presented for locomotion (e.g., ascending or descending stairs, hopping); small play equipment (throwing, kicking); large play equipment (trampoline, slide); and play vehicles (scooter, tricycle).

Webb, J. (1978). *ToyBrary Catalogue.* Order from Media/Library, Nebraska Diagnostic Resource Centre, 1910 Meridian, Cozad, NE 68130; $8.00.

This catalogue includes a full description of toys selected for their usefulness in the education of young handicapped children (toys for developing muscle control, toys that encourage exploring, toys that challenge the mind, toys that appeal to the senses). Also included are ideas for home use and construction of toys, sources for ordering, and additional resource information for parents.

Webb, R. C. (1971). *Manual for AMP Index #1.* Order from Glenwood State School, Glenwood, IA 51534.

This scale allows development of an index for awareness, manipulation, and posture. The Awareness section considers avoidance, approach, and integration of memory with present stimuli. The Manipulation scale targets responses to objects, responses to commands (gestures and words), and expression of intentionality. The Posture index rates static and dynamic behaviors ranging from head control to walking.

Wehman, P., and Schleien, S. (1981). *Leisure programs for handicapped persons: Adaptations, techniques, and curriculum.* Order from Pro Ed, 5341 Industrial Oaks Boulevard, Austin, TX 78735; $15.00, 288 pp.

This resource book begins with a focus on normalization in leisure skills. Assessment and the basics of instructions are summarized, and strategies for adapting leisure skills are suggested. Programs are provided in several areas: hobbies (camping, photography); sports (jogging, softball); games (motor, musical or rhythmical games); and object manipulation (blocks, marbles). Each activity includes instructional objective, materials, verbal cues, task analysis, and activity guidelines or special adaptations.

Wethered, C. E. (1982). *Teacher-made response-contingent materials.* In Greer, J. G., Anderson, R. M., and Odle, J. J. (Eds.), *Strategies for helping severely and multiply handicapped citizens.* Pro Ed, 5341 Industrial Oaks Boulevard, Austin, TX 78735; $19.00, pp. 123–156.

This chapter describes educational strategies for using a variety of switches, such as touch and squeeze switches. It also explores use of output devices such as toys, lights, and tape recorders as reinforcers contingent to specific motor behaviors. Appendices provide information on materials and resource manufacturers and organizations.

Wilcox, M. J. (1984). Developmental language disorders: Preschoolers. In A. Holland, *Language disorders in children* (pp. 101–128). San Diego: College-Hill Press, 4284 41st Street, San Diego, CA 92105; $27.50.

This chapter summarizes the implications of the acquisition of communicative competence for language-disordered children. Wilcox also reviews studies with language disordered children relative to communicative competence. An exemplary treatment model is presented that integrates communicative competence into early language intervention. This treatment protocol is divided into three phases, with specific strategies suggested for each: nonverbal intervention, initial verbal intervention, and the expansion of verbal skills.

Appendix B

SUPPORTIVE ORGANIZATIONS

American Alliance of Health, Physical Education, Recreation, and Dance
1900 Association Drive
Reston, VA 22091

This organization produces materials related to the development of the areas listed in their title. For example, it produces a number of guides for teaching sports activities such as swimming to people with disabilities.

American Art Therapy Association
1980 Isaac Newton Square, South
Reston, VA 22090

This organization includes a subscription to a newsletter and a journal *(Art Therapy)*. A list of speakers includes art therapists knowledgeable in working with various areas of disability (physically disabled, developmentally delayed, and so forth). Publications and films are also available.

American Dance Therapy Association
2000 Century Plaza
Columbia, MD 21044

This organization supports dance therapists working in a variety of treatment settings. The ADTA publishes *The American Journal of Dance Therapy*, monographs, conference proceedings, and a newsletter. A list of registered dance therapists can be obtained from ADTA.

American National Red Cross
National Headquarters
17th and D Streets, NW
Washington, DC 20006
(Note: Local offices can supply materials)

One facet of the work of this well-known organization involves teaching water safety. Its extensive program offers courses for potential instructors and support services for adapted aquatics. Materials available include several manuals, fact sheets, and a film "Focus on Ability," which depicts people with various types of disabilities learning to swim. (Note: Red Cross organizations in other countries, such as Canada and England, also support adaptive swimming programs.)

Association of Swimming Therapy
24 Arnas Road
London, England

As its name implies, this organizations provides support for therapeutic swimming programs, through formation of swimming clubs. The AST teaches the Halliwick method of adaptive swimming via films, lectures, demonstrations, and training courses. Two films, *Water Free* and *Swimming for Disabled People*, were produced by the association (see Appendix A). This association also offers proficiency tests and survival awards and arranges galas with several clubs participating.

Canadian Association for Health,
  Physical Education, and
  Recreation
833 River Road
Ottawa, Ontario K1L 8B9, Canada

This national association is committed to promoting health, physical education, and recreation throughout Canada. It publishes the bimonthly CAHPER Journal, a regular newsletter, and additional materials that relate to fulfilling the association's objectives.

Canadian Association of Toy
  Libraries
50 Quebec Avenue, Suite 1207
Toronto, Ontario M6P 4B4, Canada

This organization supports the concept of toy libraries in Canada by promoting standards, disseminating and circulating materials (newsletter, funding strategies, toy selection ideas, films), and serving as a clearinghouse for information sharing between members.

Educational Technology Center
Box 64
Foster, RI 02825

ETC is a nonprofit rehabilitation engineering center serving people with disabilities. It promotes the use of technology, such as adaptive switches, for advancing educational techniques. All age groups are served by means of technical newsletters and manuals offered to professionals at minimal cost.

The Foundation Center
888 7th Avenue
New York, NY 10009

This organization publishes "a bibliography of state foundation directories," which provides an update of funding sources at the state and regional levels. It can also furnish information on directories serving any United States locality. The National Data Book published by this organization profiles all of the more than 21,000 nonprofit United States organizations currently active in issuing grants.

Handicapped Adventure Playground
  Association
Fulham Palace
Bishops Avenue
London, England SW6 6EA

This organization promotes research and dissemination of information relative to adventure playgrounds for persons with a wide range of disabilities. It sponsors the development of play facilities and publishes information packets, a yearbook, and a newsletter to aid their members.

International Society for
  Augmentative and Alternative
  Communication (ISAAC)
c/o Susan Sansone, Membership
NY State A. R. C., Suffolk Chapter
2900 Veterans Memorial Highway
Bohemia, NY 11716

ISAAC was formed to advance the transdisciplinary field of augmentative and alternative communication techniques and aids. Goals include computer conferencing network; advocacy; conventions and scientific meetings; and publications. Membership includes a subscription to Communication Outlook, a quarterly newsletter that includes information on adaptive play materials, computers, communication devices, and other topics related to nonspeech communication.

Johnson & Johnson Company
Child Development Products
Grandview Road
Skillman, NJ 08558

This organization offers several packages of toys at considerable cost reduction for child development professionals. It also sponsors periodic Round Table Discussions, yielding publications on a variety of topics (e.g., Chance, 1979). Numerous general written materials on child development issues are published, plus play and learning booklets that accompany their child development toys.

Lekotek
613 Dempster
Evanston, IL 60201

Lekotek is a nonprofit resource center providing support to the parents of disabled children through information, materials, and skills for successful intervention in their child's development. In addition to direct parent services, training courses are offered to professionals.

Let's Play to Grow
Joseph P. Kennedy Foundation
1701 K Street, NW
Washington, DC 20006

This organization fosters the development of Let's Play to Grow Clubs, small groups of special families that get together periodically to play, learn, and grow. Play guides are provided (see Appendix A) to suggest activities that can be used at club meetings.

National Association of Music
  Therapy
1133 15th Street, NW
Suite 1000
Washington, DC 20005

The NAMT supports music therapy for all areas of exceptionality. It publishes a journal and provides supportive publications, such as the series edited by Lathom and Eagle (1982b).

National Committee Arts with the
  Handicapped
1825 Connecticut Ave, NW
Suite 418
Washington, DC 20009

This organization is the national coordinating agency for the development and implementation of arts programs for people with disabilities. It supports model sites and special projects and coordinates the Very Special Arts Festival. It also sponsors and disseminates publications on arts for the handicapped.

New Games Foundation
P.O. Box 7901
San Francisco, CA 94120

This organization serves as a re-source for equipment and literature pertaining to games and creative play. It also offers training programs for New Games leaders.

Pediatric Projects
P.O. Box 1880
Santa Monica, CA 90406

This nonprofit organization distributes publications and medical toys to people working with children and families in health care. Its products include books on disability awareness and the Special Friends puppets.

Puppetry in Education
164 27th Street
San Francisco, CA 94110

This resource center and puppet store helps to unite educators using puppetry and to promote idea-sharing. A bimonthly newsletter, *PIE News*, assists in this information exchange.

Puppeteers of America
c/o Gayle C. Schluter
5 Cricklewood Path
Pasadena, CA 91107

This organization publishes a quarterly magazine, *The Puppetry Journal*, and periodic newsletters. It also offers consultant services, an audio-visual library, The Puppetry Store, and national puppetry festivals.

Siblings Understanding Needs
Department of Pediatrics, C-19
University of Texas Medical Branch
Galveston, TX 77550

SUN is an organization for brothers and sisters of children who have disabilities. It produces a newspaper, *The Sun*, which helps to share information among siblings.

Special Needs Service
Tucson Public Library
P.O. Box 27470
Tucson, AZ 85726–7470

This facility serves as a clearinghouse of information relating to people with special needs. A free publication, *People to People*, focuses on information concerning a wide range of disabilities. Topical issues, such as computer use and sibling needs, are addressed.

Special Olympics, Inc.
719 Thirteenth St., NW
Suite 510
Washington, DC 20005
This organization sponsors physical activities for impaired, disabled, and handicapped participants. Events are held locally, with winners going on to regional and national competition.

Telephone Pioneers of America
195 Broadway
New York, NY 10017
This volunteer organization comprises 94 chapters of telephone workers throughout the United States and Canada. Many chapters have developed special devices to aid people with various disabilities. The manual "Helping the Handicapped: A Guide to Aids Developed by the Telephone Pioneers of America" presents specific projects (Howard, 1979). Local chapters often provide support in making adaptive play equipment.

TASH: The Association for Persons
   with Severe Handicaps
7010 Roosevelt Way
Seattle, WA 98119

This organization is a coalition of teachers, parents, therapists, and other concerned people working for quality education for people with severe disabilities. It provides a monthly newsletter and a quarterly journal stressing practical application of instructional procedures. It also publishes a variety of other materials (e.g., Goetz et al., 1982).

Toy Libraries Association
Seabrook House
Potters Bar, Hertfordshire, EN6 2AB,
   England
This group provides extensive support of toy lending libraries, including a frequently updated *Good Toy Guide*. It also provides numerous pamphlets in the Noah's Ark Publications series.

USA Toy Library Association
5940 W. Touhy Avenue
Chicago, IL 60648
This newly formed organization was created to promote better understanding of play and to help provide play experiences and materials to stimulate the growth of each child. The organization provides information (e.g., monthly newsletter) and support (e.g., discounts).

Appendix C

MANUFACTURERS

Able Child
325 West 11th Street
New York, NY 10014

This company distributes a range of educational games and toys for children with various disabilities. Battery-operated toys are available either with or without modifications. The majority of toys are unadapted, commercially produced play materials, but custom modifications are available. A personal shopper service is offered, in which therapists select appropriate toys for a child based on a written parent interview form.

Adaptive Aids
P.O. Box 13178
Tucson, AZ 85732

The products distributed by this company are made by adult developmental disability workers. The company manufactures a variety of adaptive switches, a control unit, and several related devices, all at very competitive prices.

Animal Town Game Company
P.O. Box 2002
Santa Barbara, CA 93120

A family business, this company creates, manufactures, and distributes several board games based on the "new games" concept of cooperation. The games are appropriate for a wide age range and can be used at home or in a classroom setting. A sample game is "Save the Whales."

Brad's Toys
1322 Greenwood Road
Glenview, IL 60025

This company, initiated by the parent of a disabled youth, offers approximately 50 special education aids. This includes a number of toys and pieces of equipment that enhance access to toys. Design assistance can also be obtained for persons with product ideas.

Linda J. Burkhart
8503 Rhode Island Avenue
College Park, MD 20740

Toy adapters, adaptive switches, and switch-making kits are available from this source. For people who have the time, experience, and inclination for adapting toys, two books describe procedures for making simple switches and modifying toys to accept the switches (see Burkhart, 1980, 1982).

Developmental Equipment
981 Winnetka Terrace
Lake Zurich, IL 60047

This company manufactures and distributes a range of equipment related to the field of nonspeech communication. Items include communication devices, computer access equipment, assessment tools, and adaptive switches. Several graphic communication systems and equipment to facilitate their display are also available.

Family Pastimes
R.R. # 4
Perth, Ontario K7H 3C6, Canada

This family business specializes in the creation, manufacture, and marketing of cooperative, noncompetitive games. Games are included for all age groups; included are card games, puzzles, and cooperative action and strategy games. "Harvest Time" is a sample board game appropriate for young children.

Folkways Records and
  Service Corporation
117 W. 46th Street
New York, NY 10036

This company offers numerous records for children, including records
that offer learning opportunities.

Kids Come in Special Flavors
Box 562, Forest Park Station
Dayton, OH 45405

This company develops and distributes materials to enhance community awareness and facilitate mainstreaming, including the Kids Come
in Special Flavors Kits. It also markets the Exceptional Children in the
Regular Classroom Series and other
specific supports to mainstreaming
geared for regular classroom
teachers.

Kids on the Block
1712 Eye Street, NW, Suite 1008
Washington, DC 20006

This group creates, manufactures,
and distributes the Kids on the Block
puppets. It provides numerous support materials, such as films, educational materials, and T-shirts with
the logo. A semi-annual newsletter,
"Keeping Up With the Kids," provides
further support information, and
training workshops are available.

Nancy Renfro Studios
1117 West 9th Street
Austin, TX 78703

This company makes a wide variety
of commercial puppets and props,
including some that are appropriate
for use by children with moderate to
severe disabilities (e.g., puppet
bracelets, speech pillow, wheelchair
stage). Numerous books on puppetry
are also available, as well as the
super-sense kits for disability awareness in disabled and nondisabled
children.

Prentke Romich Company
8769 Township Road 513
Shreve, OH 44676-9421

This company offers a variety of electronic assistive devices and services
to people who are severely physically
disabled. It designs, manufactures,
and distributes environmental control units, expressive communication aids, computer-related products, and a range of interface
switches.

Technical Aids and Systems for the
  Handicapped (TASH)
2075 Bayview Avenue
Toronto, Ontario M4N 3M5, Canada

TASH develops and distributes
switches and systems for communication, written output, and computer access. It offers a number of
simple and sophisticated switches
with a wide price range.

Toys for Special Children
101 Lefurgy Avenue
Hastings-on-Hudson, NY 10706

Commonly available commercial
toys are adapted to meet the needs
of children with disabilities. Sample
toys are battery-operated and wind-
up toys, accessed through a variety
of adaptive switches, also available
through this company (e.g., plate,
sip and puff, wobble switch).

ZYGO Industries, Inc.
P.O. Box 1008
Portland, OR 97207

This company provides a range of
primary devices such as expressive
communication aids, an extensive
range of interface switches, and
adaptive fixtures to mount the devices and switches.

REFERENCES

Active Stimulation Programming: An alternative to "learned helplessness." (1984). *Overview, 12*(5), 1–5.

American Alliance of Health, Physical Education, Recreation, and Dance. (1980). *Movement education for preschool children.* Waldorf, MD: American Alliance Publications.

American National Red Cross. (1974). *Manual for the aide in adapted aquatics.* Washington, DC: Author.

American National Red Cross. (1977). *Adapted aquatics.* Garden City, NY: Doubleday and Company, Inc.

Arroyo, R. (1976). Control and communication devices for the severely disabled. *Bulletin of Prosthetics Research, 10*(25), 25–37.

Atack, S. M. (1982). *Art activities for the handicapped.* Tucson: Communication Skill Builders.

Ausberger, C., Martin, M. J., and Creighton, J. (1982). *Learning to talk is child's play.* Tucson: Communication Skill Builders.

Azarnoff, P. (1984). *Health, illness, and disability: A guide to books for children and young adults.* Santa Monica, CA: Pediatric Projects, Inc.

Bailey, D. B., and Simeonsson, R. J. (1985). A functional model of social competence. *Topics in Early Childhood Special Education, 4*(4), 20–31.

Baker, G. P. (1977). Tactile sensitive behavior in hyperactive and nonhyperactive children. *American Journal of Occupational Therapy, 31,* 447–453.

Bambara, L. M., Spiegel-McGill, P., Shores, R. E., and Fox, J. J. (1984). *Journal of The Association for the Severely Handicapped, 9,* 142–149.

Barnes, K. E. (1971), Preschool play norms: A replication. *Developmental Psychology, 5,* 99–103.

Barrie-Blackley, S. (1978). A teacher's guide to communication games. Unpublished manuscript.

Bates, E. (1976). *Language and context: The acquisition of pragmatics.* New York: Academic Press.

Beesley, M., and Preston, S. (1981). A chart of selected toys and related skills in poster form. In *Toys Help.* Toronto: Canadian Association of Toy Libraries.

Bender, M., Brannan, S. A., and Verhoven, P. J. (1984). *Leisure education for the handicapped: Curriculum goals, activities, and resources.* San Diego: College-Hill Press.

Blissymbolics Communication Institute. (1984). *Picture your Blissymbols.* Toronto: Author.

Bloom, L., and Lahey, M. (1978). *Language development and language disorders.* New York: John Wiley and Sons.

Bowerman, M. (1976). Semantic factors in the acquisition of rules for word use and sentence construction. In D. Morehead and A. Morehead (Eds.), *Normal and deficient child language*. Baltimore: University Park Press.

Bricker, D. D., and Dennison, L. (1978). Training prerequisites to verbal behavior. In M. E. Snell, *Systematic instruction of the moderately and severely handicapped* (pp. 157–178). Columbus, OH: Charles E. Merrill Publishing Company.

Brodsky, W. (1983). *Blissongs: Augmentative singing for the non-verbal multi-handicapped client*. Unpublished manual.

Bronfenbrenner, U. (1979). Forward. In P. Chance, *Learning through play*. New York: Gardner Press, Inc.

Brophy, K., and Stone-Zukowski, D. (1984). Social and play behavior of special needs and non-special needs toddlers. *Early Child Development and Care, 13*, 137–154.

Broughton, B. (1982). *Creative experiences*. Chapel Hill, NC: Chapel Hill Training-Outreach Project.

Brown, L., Nietupski, J., and Hamre-Nietupski, S. (1976). Criterion of ultimate functioning. In M. A. Thomas (Ed.), *Hey, don't forget about me*. Reston, VA: The Council for Exceptional Children.

Bruder, M. B. (1984). Instructional programming for the severely handicapped preschool child. Short course presented at Conference for Early Childhood Special Educators, Roanoke, VA.

Burkhart, L. J. (1980). *Homemade battery powered toys and educational devices for severely handicapped children*. College Park, MD: Author.

Burkhart, L. J. (1982). *More handmade battery devices for severely handicapped children with suggested activities*. College Park, MD: Author.

Campbell, J., King, M., and Robson, M. (1975). *Learning through art*. Allen, TX: DLM/Teaching Resources.

Campbell, P. H., Green, K. M., and Carlson, L. M. (1977). Approximating the norm through environmental and child-centered prosthetics and adaptive equipment. In E. Sontag (Ed.), *Educational programming for the severely and profoundly handicapped* (pp. 300–320). Reston, VA: The Council for Exceptional Children, Division on Mental Retardation.

Canadian Association of Toy Libraries. (1978). *How to start a toy library in your community*. Toronto: Author.

Canadian Association of Toy Libraries. (1981). *Toys help: A guide to choosing toys for handicapped children*. Toronto: Author.

Carlson, F. (1981). A format for selecting vocabulary for the nonspeaking child. *Language, Speech, and Hearing Services in Schools, 12*, 240–245.

Carlson, F. (1982). *Prattle and play*. Omaha: Meyer Children's Rehabilitation Center, Media Resource Center.

Carlson, F. (1983). Gadgets, gismos, and junk for communication. *Working with pre-readers: Practical approaches* (pp. 51–56). Omaha: University of Nebraska Medical Center, Meyer Children's Rehabilitation Institute.

Carlson, F. (1985). *Picsyms categorical dictionary*. Lawrence, KS: Baggeboda Press.

Carter, S. (1982). *Music therapy for handicapped children: Mentally retarded.* Washington, DC: National Association for Music Therapy.

Cashdollar, P., and Martin, J. (1981). *Kids come in special flavors: Understanding handicaps.* Dayton, OH: Kids Come In Special Flavors Company.

Catalog of federal domestic assistance (1979). Washington, DC: Superintendent of Documents, United States Government Printing Office.

Champlin, J., and Champlin, C. (1981). *Books, puppets and the mentally retarded student.* Omaha, NE: Special Literature Press.

Chance, P. (1979). *Learning through play.* New York: Gardner Press.

Chappell, G. E., and Johnson, G. A. (1976). Evaluation of cognitive behavior in the young nonverbal child. *Language, Speech, and Hearing Services in Schools, 7*(1), 17–27.

Charlebois-Marois, C. (1985). *Everybody's technology: A sharing of ideas in augmentative communication.* Montreal: Charlecoms.

Cherry, C. (1976). *Creative play for the developing child: Early lifehood education through play.* Belmont, CA: Fearon Pitman Publishers, Inc.

Constable, C. (1983). Creating communicative context. In H. Winitz (Ed.), *Treating language disorders: For clinicians by clinicians.* Baltimore: University Park Press.

Cratty, B. (1973). *Development through action: The physically handicapped, the retarded child.* Anaheim, CA: Skill Development Equipment Company.

Dahood, K., and Lessee, J. (1982). *Celebration! Arts and the handicapped.* Tucson: Tucson Public Library.

Devony, C., Guralnick, M., and Rubin, H. (1974). Integrating handicapped and nonhandicapped preschool children: Effects on social play. *Childhood Education, 50*(6), 360–364.

Downs, M. (1981). *Hear-Kit System.* Denver, CO: BAM World Publications, Inc.

Duffy, L. (1977). An innovative approach to the development of communication skills for severely speech handicapped cerebral palsied children. Unpublished master's thesis, University of Nevada, Las Vegas.

Dunn, M. (1982). *Pre-sign language motor skills.* Tucson: Communication Skill Builders.

Dunst, C. J. (1978). A cognitive-social approach for assessment of early nonverbal communicative behavior. *Journal of Childhood Communicative Disorders, 2*(2), 111–123.

Dunst, C. J. (1980). *A clinical and educational manual for use with the Uzgaris and Hunt scales of infant psychological development.* Baltimore: University Park Press.

Dunst, C. J. (1981). *Infant learning.* Allen, TX: DLM/Teaching Resources.

Dunst, C. (1983). Emerging trends and advances in early intervention programs. *New Jersey Journal of School Psychology, 2*, 26–40.

Dunst, C. J., and Jenkins, V. (1982). *Family Support Scale.* Unpublished rating scale, Family, Infant, and Preschool Program, Western Carolina Center, Morganton, NC.

Evans, A. (1982). *Arts for the handicapped.* Washington, DC: National Committee Arts with the Handicapped.

Faulk, J. P., (1984, November). Adapting toys to facilitate language development in handicapped preschoolers. Poster session presented at the American Speech-Language-Hearing Association Convention, San Francisco.

Favell, J. E., Favell, J. E., and McGimsey, J. F. (1978). Relative effectiveness and efficiency of group vs. individual training of severely retarded persons. *American Journal of Mental Deficiency, 83,* 104–109.

Fell, A. (1984). *The non-oral Communication Assessment.* Ann Arbor, MI: Alternatives to Speech, Inc.

Fewell, R. R., and Vadasy, P. F. (1983). *Learning through play: A resource manual for teachers and parents, birth to three years.* Allen, TX: DLM/Teaching Resources.

Fieber, N. (1983). Informal assessment of visual skills needed for non-speech development. *Working with pre-readers: Practical approaches* (pp. 149–172). Omaha: University of Nebraska Medical Center, Meyer Children's Rehabilitation Institute.

Fink, W. T., and Sandall, S. R. (1980). A comparison of one-to-one and small group instructional strategies with developmentally disabled preschoolers. *Mental Retardation, 18*(1), 34–35.

Flavell, J. (1973). Reduction of stereotypies by reinforcement of toy play. *Mental Retardation, 11,* 21–23.

Fluegelman, A. (1976). *The new games book.* Garden City, NY: Doubleday.

Fluegelman, A. (1981). *More new games.* Garden City, NY: Doubleday.

Foss, G., and Peterson, S. L. (1981). Social-interpersonal skills relevant to job tenure for mentally retarded adults. *Mental Retardation, 19,* 103–106.

Fothergill, J., Luster-Carpenter, M. J., Vanderheiden, G. C., and Holt, C. S. (1978). Illustrated digest of non-vocal communication and writing aid for severely physically handicapped individuals. In G. C. Vanderheiden, *Non-vocal communication resource book.* Baltimore: University Park Press.

Fredericks, H. D., Anderson, R., Baldwin, V. L., Grove, D., Moore, W., Moore, M., and Beaird, J. (1978). The identification of competencies of teachers of the severely handicapped. Unpublished report.

Fredericks, H. D., Moore, M. G., and Baldwin, V. L. (1982). The long-range effects of early childhood education on a trainable mentally retarded population. In E. Edgar, N. Haring, J. Jenkins, and C. Pions (Eds.), *Mentally handicapped children: Education and training* (pp. 172–199). Baltimore: University Park Press.

Friedlander, B., Kamin, P., and Hesse, G. (1974). Operant therapy for prehension disabilities in moderately and severely retarded young children. *Training School Bulletin, 71,* 101–108.

Fristoe, M., and Lloyd, L. L. (1980). Planning an initial expressive sign lexicon for persons having severe communication impairment. *Journal of Speech and Hearing Disorders, 45,* 170–190.

Gilroy, P. J. (1985). *Kids in motion: An early childhood movement education program.* Tucson: Communication Skill Builders.

Glucksberg, S., Krauss, R.M., and Weisberg, R. (1966). Referential communication in nursery school children: Methods and some preliminary findings. *Journal of Exceptional Child Psychology, 3,* 333–342.

Goetz, L., Utley, B., Gee, K., Baldwin, M., and Sailor, W. (1982). *Auditory assessment and programming for severely handicapped deaf-blind students*. Seattle, WA: The Association of Persons with Severe Handicaps.

Goossens', C. (1982). Implications of research for the selection of non-speech instructional procedures. *Proceedings of the Second International Conference on Non-Speech Communication* (pp. 58–65). Toronto: Blissymbolics Communication Institute.

Goossens', C. (1983). The use of gestural communication systems with nonspeakers. *Working with pre-readers: Practical approaches* (pp. 5–33). Omaha: University of Nebraska Medical Center, Meyer Children's Rehabilitation Institute.

Gozali, J., and Charney, B. (1972). Agenda for the '70's: Full social integration of the retarded. *Mental Retardation, 10,* 20-21.

Granger, C., and Wehman, P. (1979). Sensory stimulation. In P. Wehman (Ed.), *Recreation programming for developmentally disabled persons* (pp. 127–143). Baltimore: University Park Press.

Gresham, G. M. (1981). Social skills training with handicapped children: A review. *Review of Educational Research, 51,* 1.

Guide to Controls. (1983). Stanford, CA: Children's Hospital at Stanford.

Gunter, C. D., and van Kleeck, A. E. (1984, November). The integration of social routines into language evaluation and treatment. Poster session presented at the American Speech-Language-Hearing Association Convention, San Francisco.

Guthrie, S. (1979). Criteria for educational toys for preschool visually impaired children. *Visual Impairment and Blindness, 73,* 144–146.

Halle, J. W., Alpert, C. L., and Anderson, S. R. (1984). Natural environment language assessment and intervention with severely impaired preschoolers. *Topics in Early Childhood Special Education, 4*(2), 35–56.

Handicapped Adventure Playground Association. (1978). *Adventure playgrounds for handicapped children*. London: Author.

Handicapped Adventure Playground Association. (1978). *Starting an adventure playground for handicapped children*. London: Author.

Hanna, R. M., Lippert, E. A., and Harris, A. B. (1982). *Developmental communication curriculum*. Columbus, OH: Charles E. Merrill Publishing Company.

Harris, D. (1982). Communication interaction processes involving nonvocal physically handicapped children. *Topics in Language Disorders, 2,* 21–37.

Harris, S. R. (1978). Neurodevelopmental treatment approach for teaching swimming to cerebral palsied children. *American Journal of Occupational Therapy, 58,* 979–983.

Harvey, A. W. (1980). The therapeutic role of music in special education: Historical perspectives. *The Creative Child and Adult Quarterly, 5,* 196–204.

Heekin, S., and Mengel, T. (1983a). *New Friends manual*. Chapel Hill, NC: Chapel Hill Training-Outreach Project.

Heekin, S., and Mengel, T. (1983b). *New Friends trainer's manual*. Chapel Hill, NC: Chapel Hill Training-Outreach Project.

Higgins, J. (1982). *Guidelines for adapting battery operated toys for the physically handicapped*. Vista, CA: California Avenue School.

Hogan, P. (1974). *Playgrounds for free.* Cambridge: MIT Press.

Holland, A. (1975). Language therapy for children: Some thoughts on context and content. *Journal of Speech and Hearing Disorders, 40,* 514–523.

Holroyd, J. (1978). Questionnaire on resources and stress. Unpublished paper, Neuropsychiatric Institute, University of California at Los Angeles.

Hopper, C., and Wambold, C. (1978). Improving the independent play of severely mentally retarded children. *Education and Training of the Mentally Retarded, 13,* 42–46.

Howard, G. (Ed.). (1979). *Helping the handicapped: A guide to aids developed by the Telephone Pioneers of America.* New York: Telephone Pioneers of America.

Huer, M. (1983). *The nonspeech test.* Lake Zurich, IL: Developmental Equipment.

Jameson, J. (1984). The use of melody in training sign acquisition with cognitively-delayed children. Unpublished master's thesis, Western Carolina University, Cullowhee, NC.

Jeffree, D., McConkey, R., and Hewson, S. (1977). *Let me play.* London: Souvenir Press (Educational and Academic) Ltd.

Jeffrey, G. H. (1981a). Introduction and bibliography. In *Toys Help.* Toronto: Canadian Association of Toy Libraries.

Jeffrey, G. H. (1981b). Selection criteria. In *Toys Help.* Toronto: Canadian Association of Toy Libraries.

Kaczmarek, L. A. (1982). Motor activities: A context for language/communication intervention. *Journal of the Division of Early Childhood, 6,* 21–35.

Kahmi, A. (1981). Nonlinguistic symbolic and conceptual abilities in language-impaired and normally developing children. *Journal of Speech and Hearing Research, 24,* 446–453.

Karlan, G. R., Brenn-White, B., Lentz, A., Hodur, P., Egger, D., and Frankoff, D. (1982). Establishing generalized productive verb-noun phrase usage in a manual language system with moderately handicapped children. *Journal of Speech and Hearing Disorders, 47,* 31–42.

Karnes, M. B., and Lee, R. C. (1979). Mainstreaming in the preschool. In L. Katz (Ed.), *Current topics in early childhood education, 11.* New Jersey: Ablex Publishing Company.

Kazdin, A., and Erickson, B. (1975). Developing responsiveness to instruction in severely and profoundly retarded residents. *Journal of Behavioral Therapy and Experimental Psychiatry, 6,* 17–21.

Kissel, R. C., and Whitman, T. L. (1977). An examination of the direct and generalized effects of a play-training and over-correction procedure upon the self-stimulatory behavior of a profoundly retarded boy. *AAESPH Review, 2,* 131–146.

Knapczyk, D., and Yoppi, J. (1975). Development of cooperative and competition play responses in developmentally disabled children. *American Journal of Mental Deficiencies, 80,* 245–255.

Kohl, F., Wilcox, B., and Karlan, G. (1978). Effects of training conditions on the generalization of manual signs with moderately handicapped students. *Education and Training of the Mentally Retarded, 13,* 327–335.

Lahey, M., and Bloom, L. (1977). Planning a first lexicon: Which words to teach first. *Journal of Speech and Hearing Disorders, 42,* 340–350.

Langley, B., and DuBose, R. F. (1976). Functional vision screening for severely handicapped children. *New Outlook for the Blind, 8,* 346–350.

Lathom, W., and Eagle, C. T. (1982a, April). Music for the severely handicapped. *Music Education Journal,* pp. 30–31.

Lathom, W., and Eagle, C. (Eds.). (1982b). *Music therapy for handicapped children.* Washington, DC: National Association for Music Therapy.

Lear, R. (1977). *Play helps: Toys and activities for handicapped children.* London: Heinemann Health Books.

Leonard, L. (1975). Modeling as a clinical procedure in language training. *Language, Speech, and Hearing Services in Schools, 6,* 72–85.

Lessee, J. (1983). . . . *For all of us!* Tucson: Tucson Public Library, Special Needs Service.

Liberty, K. A., Haring, N. G., and Martin, M. M. (1981). Teaching new skills to the severely handicapped. *The Journal of the Association for the Severely Handicapped, 6,* 5–13.

Liman, E. (1977). *The spacemaker book.* New York: Viking Press.

Lowe, M. (1975). Trends in the development of representational play in infants from one to three years — an observational study. *Journal of Child Psychology and Psychiatry, 16,* 33–47.

Lowe, M., and Costello, A. J. (1976). *The symbolic play test.* Windsor, Great Britain: NFER-Nelson Publishing.

Lucas, E. V. (1980). *Semantic and pragmatic language disorders.* Rockville, MD: Aspen Systems Corporation.

Lyon, S., Baumgart, D., Stoll, A., and Brown, L. (1977). Curricular strategies for teaching basic functional object use skills to severely handicapped students. In L. Brown, J. Nietupski, S. Lyon, S. Hamre-Nietupski, T. Crowner, and L. Grunewald (Eds.), *Curricular strategies for teaching nonverbal communication, functional object use and problem-solving skills to severely handicapped students.* Madison, WI: Department of Specialized Educational Services.

McCormick, L., Cooper, M., and Goldman, R. (1979). Training teachers to maximize instructional time provided to severely and profoundly handicapped children. *AAESPH Review, 4,* 301–310.

MacDonald, J. D., and Gillette, Y. (1984a). *Glossary: For ECO intervention program.* Columbus, OH: The Ohio State University.

MacDonald, J. D., and Gillette, Y. (1984b). *Turntaking with actions.* Columbus, OH: The Ohio State University.

MacDonald, J. D., and Gillette, Y. (1984c). *Turntaking with communications.* Columbus, OH: The Ohio State University.

MacDonald, J. D., and Gillette, Y. (1984d). *Ecomaps: A manual for assessing language through conversation.* Columbus, OH: The Ohio State University.

MacDonald, J. D., Gillette, Y., Bickley, M., and Rodriguez, C. (1984). *Conversation routines.* Columbus, OH: The Ohio State University.

Manolson, A. (1984). *It takes two to talk: A Hanen early language parent guide book.* Toronto: Hanen Early Language Resource Centre.

Martin, J. (1981). *The Halliwick Method.* Physiotherapy, *67,* 288–291.

McConkey, R., and Jeffree, D. (1981). Making toys for handicapped children: A guide for parents and teachers. Englewood Cliffs, NJ: Prentice-Hall.

McDonald, E. T. (1980). *Teaching and using Blissymbolics.* Toronto: Blissymbolics Communication Institute.

McGill, J. (1984). *Play for play's sake: Cooperative games as a strategy for integration.* Toronto: National Institute on Mental Retardation.

McLean, J. E., Snyder-McLean, L., Jacobs, P., and Rowland, C. M. (1981). *Process-oriented educational programs for the severely/profoundly handicapped adolescent.* Parsons: Parsons Research Center, University of Kansas, Bureau of Child Research.

Meeting the playground challenge. (1983). *The Exceptional Parent, 13,* 14–20.

Meyers, L. S., Grows, N. L., Coleman, C. L., and Cook, A. M. (1980). *An assessment battery for assistive device systems recommendations, Part I.* Sacramento: Assistive Device Center, California State University.

Miller, K. S. (1984). Aspects of play schemas in young children with developmental disabilities. *Developmental Disabilities Special Interest Section Newsletter, 7,* 1–3.

Montgomery, J. (Project Director). (1980). *Non oral communication assessment forms.* Fountain Valley, CA: Non Oral Communication Center.

Moran, J. M., and Kalakian, L. H. (1977). *Movement experiences for the mentally retarded or emotionally disturbed child.* Minneapolis: Burgess Publishing Company.

Morris, R., and Dolker, M. (1974). Developing cooperative play in socially withdrawn retarded children. *Mental Retardation, 12*(6), 24–27.

Musselwhite, C. R. (1983). Introducing New Friends. *Communication Outlook, 5*(2), 21–22.

Musselwhite, C. R. (1984). Bartering: Kids' play. *Communicating Together, 2*(2), 12–13.

Musselwhite, C. R. (1985). *Songbook: Signs and symbols for children.* Asheville, NC: Caroline Ramsey Musselwhite.

Musselwhite, C. R. (In press, a). Augmentative communication for nonspeakers with cerebral palsy. In E. T. McDonald (Ed.), *Cerebral palsy: For clinicians by clinicians.* Baltimore: University Park Press.

Musselwhite, C. R. (In press, b). Using signs as gestural cues for language-impaired children.

Musselwhite, C. R., Batchelor, S., Roueche, J., Piercy, A., Morissette, G., and Guice, S. (1984). Adaptive swimming: A team opportunity. *North Carolina Augmentative Communication Association News, 2*(2), 5–6.

Musselwhite, C. R., and Childs, H. (In preparation). Making New Friends: Exchange projects between special needs and nondisabled children.

Musselwhite, C. R., and St. Louis, K. W. (1982). *Communication programming for the severely handicapped: Vocal and non-vocal strategies.* San Diego: College-Hill Press.

Musselwhite, C. R., and Thompson, E. R. (1979). *Functional fine motor skills curriculum.* Unpublished manuscript.

Newcomer, B. L., and Morrison, T. L. (1974). Play therapy with institutionalized mentally retarded children. *American Journal of Mental Deficiency, 78,* 727–733.

Newman, J. (1976). *Swimming for children with physical and sensory impairments: Methods and techniques for therapy and recreation.* Springfield, IL: Charles C Thomas.

Nicolich, L. M. (1977). Beyond sensorimotor intelligence: Assessment of symbolic maturity through analysis of pretend play. *Merrill-Palmer Quarterly, 23,* 89–99.

Niziol, O. M., and DeBlassie, R. R. (1972). Work adjustment and the educable mentally retarded adolescent. *Journal of Employment Counseling, 9,* 158–166.

Nocera, S. D. (1979). *Reaching the special learner through music.* Morristown, NJ: Silver Burdett Company.

Odom, S. L., and McConnell, S. R. (1985). A performance-based conceptualization of social competence of handicapped preschool children: Implications for assessment. *Topics in Early Childhood Special Education, 4*(4), 1–19.

Oliver, P., and Scott, T. (1981). Group versus individual training in establishing generalization of language skills with severely handicapped individuals. *Mental Retardation, 19,* 285–289.

Olswang, L. B., Kriegsmann, E., and Mastergeorge, A. (1982). Facilitating functional requesting in pragmatically impaired children. *Language, Speech, and Hearing Services in Schools, 13,* 202–222.

Overs, R. P., Taylor, S., and Adkins, C. (1977). *Avocational counseling manual.* Washington, DC: Hawkins and Associates.

Owens, R. E. (1982). *Program for the acquisition of language with the severely impaired (PALS).* Columbus, OH: Charles E. Merrill Publishing Company.

Parten, M. (1932). Social play among school children. *Journal of Abnormal Psychology, 28,* 136–147.

Peterson, R., and McIntosh, E. (1973). Teaching tricycle riding. *Mental Retardation, 11,* 32–34.

Piaget, J. (1962). *Play, dreams, and imitation in childhood.* New York: W. W. Norton.

Porter, P., Carter, S., Goolsby, E., Martin, N. J., Reed, M., Stowers, S., and Wurth, B. (1985). *Prerequisites to the use of augmentative communication.* Chapel Hill, NC: Division for Disorders of Development and Learning.

Position statement on nonspeech communication. (1981). ASHA, *23,* 577–581.

Rast, M. M. (1984). The use of play activities in therapy. *Developmental Disabilities Special Interest Section Newsletter, 7*(3), 1–4.

Reichle, J., Williams, W., and Ryan, S. (1981). Selecting signs for the formulation of an augmentative communicative modality. *Journal of the Association of the Severely Handicapped, 6,* 48–56.

Renfro, N. (1984). *Puppetry, language, and the special child: Discovering alternate languages.* Austin, TX: Nancy Renfro Studios.

Renfro, N., Click, J., and Harp, C. R. (1982). *Discovering the super senses through puppetmime: The physically disabled — Zookie and Holly.* Austin, TX: Nancy Renfro Studios.

Riddick, B. (1982). *Toys and play for handicapped children*. Notting-ham, England: Croom Helm.

Robinson, C. C., and Robinson, J. H. (1978). Sensorimotor functions and cognitive development. In M. E. Snell (Ed.), *Systematic instruction of the moderately and severely handicapped*. Columbus, OH: Charles E. Merrill Publishing Company.

Robinson, E. J, and Robinson, W. P. (1976). The young child's under-standing of communication. *Developmental Psychology, 12,* 328–333.

Rottman, F. (1978). *Easy-to-make puppets and how to use them*. Ven-tura, CA: Regal Books.

Sacks, G. K., and Young, E. C. (1982). Infant scales of communicative intent. *Update Pediatrics, 7*(1), 1–6.

Sanford, A. R., and Zelman, J. G. (1981). *Learning accomplishment profile: A guide for individualizing educational programming*. Chapel Hill, NC: Chapel Hill Training-Outreach Project.

Schloss, P. J. (1984). *Social development of handicapped children and adolescents*. Rockville, MD: Aspen Systems.

Scheuerman, N., Baumgart, D., Sipsma, K., and Brown, L. (1976). To-ward the development of a curriculum for teaching nonverbal com-munication skills to severely handicapped students. Teaching ba-sic tracking, scanning and selection skills. In L. Brown, N. Scheuerman, and T. Crowner. (Eds.), *Madison's alternative for zero exclusion: Toward an integrated therapy model for teaching motor, tracking and scanning skills to severely handicapped students, volume VI, part 3*. Madison, WI: Department of Specialized Educational Services.

Schumaker, J. B., and Sherman, J. A. (1978). Parent as intervention agent: From birth onward. In R. Schiefelbusch (Ed.), *Language intervention strategies* (pp. 237–315). Baltimore: University Park Press.

Shane, H. C., and Bashir, A. S. (1980). Election criteria for the adoption of an augmentative communication system: Preliminary consider-ations. *Journal of Speech and Hearing Disorders, 45,* 408–414.

Shane, H. C., Lipschultz, R. W., and Shane, C. L. (1982). Facilitating the communicative interaction of nonspeaking persons in large resi-dential settings. *Topics in Language Disorders, 2,* 73–84.

Shane, H. C., and Wilbur, R. B. (1980). Potential for expressive signing based on motor control. *Sign Language Studies, 29,* 331–340.

Sherrill, C. (Ed.). (1979). *Creative arts for the severely handicapped*, 2nd edition. Springfield, IL: Charles C Thomas.

Silverman, F. (1980). *Communication for the speechless*. Englewood Cliffs, NJ: Prentice-Hall, Inc.

Singer, D. G., and Singer, J. L. (1977). *Partners in play: A step-by-step guide to imaginative play in children*. New York: Harper and Row.

Sinker, M. (1983). *The Lekotek guide to good toys*. Evanston, IL: Lekotek.

Snell, M. E., and Gast, D. L. (1981). Applying time delay procedure to the instruction of the severely handicapped. *Journal of the Association for the Severely Handicapped, 6*(3), 3–14.

Snell, M. E., and Smith, D. D. (1978). Intervention strategies. In M. E. Snell (Ed.), *Systematic instruction of the moderately and severely handicapped.* Columbus, OH: Charles E. Merrill Publishing Company.

Stanfield, J. (1973). Graduation: What happens to the retarded child when he grows up? *Exceptional Children, 6,* 1–11.

Storm, R. H., and Willis, J. H. (1978). Small-group training as an alternative to individual programs for profoundly retarded persons. *American Journal of Mental Deficiency, 83,* 283–288.

Strain, P. S. (1975). Increasing social play of severely retarded preschoolers through socio-dramatic activities. *Mental Retardation, 13,* 7–9.

Strain, P. S. (1985). Social and nonsocial determinants of handicapped preschool children's social competence. *Topics in Early Childhood Education, 4*(4), 47–58.

Strain, P. S., and Kerr, M. M. (1979). Treatment issues in the remediation of handicapped preschool children's social isolation. *Education and Treatment of Children, 2*(3), 197–208.

Striefel, S., Wetherby, B., and Karlan, G. R. (1976). Establishing generalized verb-noun instruction-following skills in retarded children. *Journal of Experimental Child Psychology, 22,* 247–260.

Sullivan, D. (1982). *Pocketful of puppets: Activities for the special child.* Austin, TX: Nancy Renfro Studios.

Swimming for disabled people. (Three tape/slide programs). London: Town and Country Productions Ltd.

ten Horn, H. Z. (1981). *Touch Toys and how to make them.* Rockville, MD: Touch Toys, Inc.

Terrell, B. Y., Schwartz, R. G., Prelock, P. A., and Messick, C. K. (1984). Symbolic play in normal and language-impaired children. *Journal of Speech and Hearing Research, 27,* 424–429.

Thursby, D. D. (1977). Everyone's a star. *Teaching Exceptional Children, 9,* 77–78.

Tilton, J., and Ottinger, D. P. (1964). Comparison of toy play behavior of autistic, retarded, and normal children. *Psychological Reports, 15,* 967–975.

Uzgaris, J. C., and Hunt, J. (1975). *Assessment in infancy: Ordinal scales of psychological development.* Urbana: University of Illinois Press.

van den Pol, R. A., Crow, R. E., Rider, D. P., and Offner, R. B. (1985). Social interaction research in an integrated preschool: Implications and applications. *Topics in Early Childhood Special Education, 4*(4), 59–76.

von Levetzow, J. (1981). Organisation and toy lending system. In *Toys help: A guide to choosing toys for handicapped children.* Toronto: Canadian Association of Toy Libraries.

Wambold, C., and Bailey, R. (1979). Improving the leisure-time behaviors of severely/profoundly mentally retarded children through toy play. *American Association for the Education of the Severely and Profoundly Handicapped Review, 4,* 237–250.

Ward, D. (1979). *Sing a rainbow: Musical activities with mentally handicapped children.* London: Oxford University Press.

Water free (Film). (1975). London: Town and Country Productions, Ltd.

Watkinson, E. J., and Wall, A. E. (1982). *PREP: The PREP play program: Play skill instruction for mentally handicapped children.* Ottawa: Canadian Association for Health, Physical Education, and Recreation.

Webb, J. (1978). *ToyBrary catalogue.* Cozad, NE: Nebraska Diagnostic Resource Center.

Webb, R. C., and staff of The Developmental Therapy Department. (1971). *Manual for AMP Index #1.* Glenwood, IA: Glenwood State School.

Wehman, P. (1976). Selection of play materials for the severely handicapped: A continuing dilemma. *Education and Training of the Mentally Retarded 11*(1), 46–51.

Wehman, P. (1977a). *Helping the mentally retarded acquire play skills: A behavioral approach.* Springfield, IL: Charles C Thomas.

Wehman, P. (1977b). Research on leisure time and the severely developmentally disabled. *Rehabilitation Literature, 38*(4), 98–105.

Wehman, P. (1979a). *Curricular design for the severely and profoundly handicapped.* New York: Human Sciences Press.

Wehman, P. (1979b). Instructional strategies for improving toy play skills of severely handicapped children. *AAESPH Review, 4*(2), 125–135.

Wehman, P. (1979c). Toy play. In P. Wehman (Ed.), *Recreation programming for developmentally disabled persons* (pp. 37–64). Baltimore: University Park Press.

Wehman, P. (1984). Partial participation . . . one way to modify a task. *The severely handicapped community training project, 1*(4), 2.

Wehman, P., and Marchant, J. (1977). Developing gross motor recreational skills in children with severe behavioral handicaps. *Therapeutic Recreational Journal, 11*(2), 48–54.

Wehman, P., and Marchant, J. (1978). Improving free play skills of severely retarded children. *American Journal of Occupational Therapy, 32*(2), 100–104.

Wehman, P., and Schleien, S. (1981). *Leisure programs for handicapped persons: Adaptations, techniques, and curriculum.* Baltimore: University Park Press.

Weiner, B., Ottinger, D., and Tilton, J. (1969). Comparison of the toy play behavior of autistic, retarded, and normal children: A reanalysis. *Psychological Reports, 25,* 223–227.

Weiner, E. A., and Weiner, B. J. (1974). Differentiation of retarded and normal children through toy-play analysis. *Multivariate Behavioral Research, 9,* 245–252.

Weinstein, M., and Goodman, J. (1980). *Playfair: Everybody's guide to noncompetitive play.* San Luis Obispo, CA: Impact Publishers.

Westby, C. E. (1980). Assessment of cognitive and language abilities through play. *Language, Speech, and Hearing Services in Schools, 11,* 154–168.

Wethered, C. E. (1982). Teacher-made response-contingent materials. In J. G. Greer, R. M. Anderson, and J. J. Odle (Eds.), *Strategies for helping severely and multiply handicapped citizens* (pp. 123–156). Baltimore: University Park Press.

Wilcox, M. J. (1984). Developmental language disorders: Preschoolers. In A. Holland (Ed.), *Language Disorders in Children* (pp. 101–128). San Diego: College-Hill Press.

Williams, B., Briggs, N., and Williams, R. (1979). Selecting, adapting, and understanding toys and recreation materials. In P. Wehman (Ed.), *Recreation programming for developmentally disabled persons* (pp. 15–36). Baltimore: University Park Press.

Williams, W., Brown, L., and Certo, N. (1975). Basic components of instructional programs for severely handicapped students. *Theory into practice, 14,* 123–136.

Williams, W., and Fox, T. (Eds.). (1977). *Minimum objective system for pupils with severe handicaps: Working draft number one.* Burlington: University of Vermont, Center for Special Education.

Williams, W., Hamre-Nietupski, S., Pumpian, I., Marks, J. M., and Wheeler, J. (1978). Teaching social skills. In M. E. Snell (Ed.), *Systematic instruction of the moderately and severely handicapped.* Columbus, OH: Charles E. Merrill Publishing Company.

Wing, L., Gould, J., Yeates, S. R., and Brierley, L. M. (1977). Symbolic play in severely mentally retarded and in autistic children. *Journal of Child Psychology and Psychiatry, 18,* 167–178.

Yoder, D., and Kraat, A. (1983). Intervention issues in nonspeech communication. In J. Miller, D. Yoder, and R. Schiefelbusch (Eds.), *Contemporary issues in language intervention* (pp. 27–51). Rockville, MD: The American Speech-Language-Hearing Association.

Zuromski, E. S., Smith, N. F., and Brown, R. (1977). A simple electromechanical response device for multihandicapped infants. Paper presented at American Psychological Association Convention, San Francisco.